To Ed and
Jean
With Love'

WITH EYES
TO SEE

WITH EYES TO SEE

A JOURNEY FROM RELIGION TO SPIRITUALITY

Arthur Melville

STILLPOINT

STILLPOINT PUBLISHING

Building a society that honors The Earth,
Humanity, and The Sacred in all Life.

For a free catalog or ordering information, write
Stillpoint Publishing, Box 640, Walpole, NH 03608 USA

or call
1-800-847-4014 TOLL FREE (Continental US, except NH)
1-603-756-9281 (Foreign and NH)

This book is manufactured in the United States of America
Cover and text design by Karen Savary

Published by Stillpoint Publishing, a division of Stillpoint
International, Box 640, Meetinghouse Road, Walpole, NH 03608

Library of Congress Catalog Card Number: 92-80780

Melville, Arthur
With Eyes To See: A Journey From Religion To Spirituality

ISBN 0-913299-88-X
1 3 5 7 9 8 6 4 2

DEDICATION

To Marsha Utain, my wife, my teacher, my love, my friend. Thank you, Marsha, for your endless energy and unbounded belief in me and in the purposeful unfolding of our lives together. Without your presence, encouragement, and support, this book, as well as my life, would still be a rough draft.

CONTENTS

FOREWORD ix

PREFACE xiii

ACKNOWLEDGEMENTS xvii

1 DEATH 1

2 RACISM 16

3 INJUSTICE 27

4 ANIMALS 40

5 RESPONSIBILITY 56

6 SEX 69

7 POWER 82

8 DEVIL 102

9 WOMEN 113

10 RELATIONSHIPS 128

11 NATURE 144

CONTENTS

12 BIRTH CONTROL   158

13 CELIBACY   168

14 RIGHTS   179

15 DECISION   203

16 DOUBT   221

17 MASKS   240

18 ROOTS   255

19 FREEDOM   271

20 COMPLETION   293

21 AWAKENING   304

22 GUIDANCE   314

23 GRATITUDE   330

    EPILOGUE   351

FOREWORD

Reading *With Eyes to See* reminded me of a story I heard while working as a missionary priest in Africa.

One day Father Tomas was meeting with women from his parish when a beggar came to the door. Tomas greeted the man and went to the kitchen to prepare him a meal. One woman followed, warning that the man might be intending to steal or might even be dangerous. Ignoring the woman's advice, Tomas invited the man to the kitchen. As the beggar entered, his broken shoes left muddy, greasy footprints on the floor. The women were horrified and drew back in protest to the strong body odor that hung in the air after the beggar had passed by. The man sat quietly at the kitchen table and eagerly ate his meal. After refilling his guest's bowl Tomas excused himself to return to his meeting.

Half an hour later Tomas went again to the kitchen to see what further assistance he could offer the beggar. To his and the women's amazement, the man had vanished. No evidence remained of his departure; he could not have climbed through the barred window, and no footprints could be found outside in the ever-wet earth of the rainy season. The only tangible signs verifying the encounter were the man's footprints, still clearly visible on the linoleum floor.

The women decided that his inexplicable disappearance was

a sign from the devil. Tomas, however, fell on his knees, giving thanks for having been visited by God. The vision propelled Father Tomas into a spiritual inquiry that changed his life. The church, having no room for his vision, sent someone to exorcise him. Tomas left his house with a knapsack on his back and a begging bowl in his hands, entering the bush to live with the lepers. Events that began an ordinary day catalyzed one person into a deeper engagement with spirituality.

Different factors motivate different persons to begin questioning their lives, but once begun, there is no turning back from the questioning. Life is lived at a wholly new level, pace, and style. Furthermore, the very moment one begins to listen with the heart to the inner self and to the God within, one begins to die to one's old self. Spiritual growth is both joyful and painful: joyful because the heart is lifted to a new height of vision and action; painful because death to the old self is necessary for rebirth.

With Eyes to See is the story of Arthur Melville's spiritual journey. Like Tomas's story, it is a vision quest rooted in the ordinariness of ministry and life. Stunning in its vibrant capture of the details of place and emotion, Arthur's account of his years as a Maryknoll priest in Guatemala has the ability to transform the heart of the reader. As in the story of Tomas, the vision finds the seeker, for Arthur's quest becomes conscious only when an event from his old, religious frame of reference catapults him to a new level of reality.

In a vision quest, the seeker usually goes into retreat and, with the help of guides, experiences an epiphany from the spiritual world. From his or her vision the seeker gains insights from which to act in implementing the new sense of vocation. But not everyone is able or willing to sequester herself or himself in the service of a mystical experience. Arthur's story in *With Eyes to See* is an alternative model for vision questing. The story provides modern spiritual seekers with a pattern for engaging the sacred in the midst of everyday life. In this pattern one is open to the truth, willing to let go of outmoded beliefs, and willing to own and honor changes chosen during daily routines. Instead of retreating, Arthur jumps with fervor into his new role. Endowed with the ability to listen with openness even when that leads to conflict with his belief system, Arthur hears the question in the challenge: "What is the truth here?" He makes a contract with his heart, asking for eyes to see. His subsequent experiences include a series of awakenings, each of which is a thread in the web of life he is weaving and a holographic image of his emerging spirituality.

Many will find reading *With Eyes to See* a spiritual experience: those who discover that organized religion no longer meets their spiritual needs; those in despair over the use of old, hierarchical power that suppresses the human spirit; those who are at heart deep ecologists and feminists; those seeking the strength to shed what no longer works in their lives. All of these people will find solace in Arthur's story.

Read this book, as I did, as a blessing and as an inspiration for your own vision quest. *Gracias a Dios*.

THE REVEREND SUZANNE FAGEOL
PRIEST OF THE ANGLICAN CHURCH
ST. THOMAS, U.S. VIRGIN ISLANDS
JANUARY 1992

PREFACE

When I began my search for myself I never expected life to take the twists and turns that it did. If at any point in my early years I could have looked into the future, I would have recognized little if anything about myself.

This is my story of change, the story of my quest for meaning, of the search for myself, the process of my transformation into a different person. It is a spiritual and cultural odyssey that at times shook me to the roots of my basic beliefs and values. On many occasions during this journey I trembled before the authoritative representatives of established institutions that demanded the subjugation of individuals and their inner voices, and at other times I saw with amazement that their power over me and my relationship to them disintegrated when confronted with the simple truth. I know that seeking one's spiritual center does not have to include such tribulations as mine; but those of us who choose the rewarding road of participating in the expansion of human consciousness frequently feel unsettled as we doubt the self we have known, question inherited beliefs, risk isolation, and face the fear of change. Yet if we trust our inner voice, and if we recognize that spirituality and Godliness are in union with nature and the earth, we can enter the joyful path back to our Source.

I present the story of my awakening as an invitation to you, the reader, not to follow me or my path but to discover yourself on your own path, knowing that our paths are merging and that we are sharing at a deep spiritual level, each of us supporting the rest, each lending to the whole, each contributing from her or his wealth of experience to the growth of all. None of us is alone. What each of us does today is of great significance. When you awaken in the morning you can be confident of your participation in our joint venture, knowing that many others share the same mission, choosing each day to contribute to the expansion of consciousness through the willing experience of emotions, the loving acceptance of all life forms, the responsible communication of truth.

If you have a sense of missing who you are, and for what purpose you are here, if you have simply accepted the values and beliefs handed down to you, if your behavior is frequently determined by pleasing others, if you have submitted to a structure without examining the motives of its leadership, then you will relate to my story, and you will also find that choosing to follow your own path will lead to the rewarding awareness of your spiritual connection to Life without which it is difficult to recognize your own goodness, beauty, and personal power.

My journey begins in Guatemala, a little country separated from the United States only by Mexico. There I found people who still listen to the voice of nature, people who hold what may be considered secret knowledge and answers to society's needs. Believing I was sent by God, I went to the mountains of Guatemala to teach these people. I now know that, yes, I was sent by God, but sent for the purpose of learning from them.

Although I returned to the United States from Guatemala many years ago, a part of me remains in those mountains, and I carry within me many gifts that only earth people, such as those of Guatemala, could have bestowed, gifts in the form of teachings that continue to furnish new lessons for me and provide further opportunity to believe in myself.

As a devout Catholic youth, I believed that the structures of our society were true and good and God-inspired. I had therefore decided, at nineteen, to study for the missionary priesthood.

I truly thought I would attain spiritual heights by caring for impoverished and uneducated peoples, but I had no idea of the slow, difficult, and complicated personal journey I was undertaking.

Nine years of seminary study, training, and discipline confirmed and deepened behavior patterns and beliefs instilled in me from an unquestioned Catholic and staunchly American upbringing, but my six years in the mountains of Guatemala demanded that I confront the reality of other values and practices and led to difficult decisions that changed my life totally. Questioning my hitherto unquestioned fundamental beliefs opened the way for me out of a restricted religious environment into a gratifying and healing spirituality. The people of Guatemala helped me awaken to my present awareness that I myself create not just my health and sickness, my success and failure, but even the details of my reality, and that ultimately I am responsible for my every thought, feeling, experience, and belief.

In learning to trust myself rather than an imposed religious structure, I frequently doubted myself; at times I felt afraid of the risk; I was often tempted to give up and let others be responsible. But I am gratified that I was guided to persist and to learn the basic lessons of life. I now continue to look for opportunities to expand my consciousness and contribute to my further healing, which includes the healing of our species and of our planet. It is time to tell the story of my initiation into wholeness.

I have waited many years to do so, holding back initially because Guatemalan friends depicted in the material could have suffered reprisals at the hands of their government. I also held back because I needed to go further in my own journey, demonstrating to myself that what I had experienced as powerful at certain points in my life was more than passing fantasy and that I could maintain the lessons, meaning, and import over time. Writing this story has put the long process of growth in perspective.

This book is the culmination of many series of events that began in Guatemala and that led to finding myself. It is my desire that readers will benefit from my search for a more spiritual way of life by realizing that they, too, will find in their daily life experience their journey to wholeness.

LONG BEACH, CALIFORNIA
JANUARY 7, 1992

ACKNOWLEDGEMENTS

I want to thank Lee Colton, Frank Gaspar, Patricia Lauer, Barbara Oliver, Karen Savary, Errol Sowers, Barbara Villa, and Trish Wallace for the availability of their loving support. I cannot say enough about my publisher, Meredith Young-Sowers, an unusual woman, deeply committed to the healing of our species and our world, the midwife of this my literary child and a spiritually-oriented professional with whom I have been blessed and privileged to be in association. A special thanks to Dorothy Seymour, my caring and committed editor; to Catherine Sagan and Marian Pahl for the loving and important role they played in this saga; and to my parents, sisters, and brothers, who although frequently not in agreement have given me unquestioning support.

WITH EYES
TO SEE

1

DEATH

For six years as a priest in the mountains of Guatemala I worked with impoverished peasants who shared with me their closeness to the earth and their true spirituality. Always an outsider, I faced continuously the decision of whether to accept their offer and penetrate the nature-based culture or to observe it from my alien niche and neglect their gift. Openness to new ideas required that I refrain from making my own values and beliefs absolute—a difficult task for one who was the product of a technologically-developed society with nine years of seminary training in philosophy and theology and a tradition that bound me resolutely. Only through choosing a broader outlook could I be accessible to an intuitive sense, an inner guide, the voice of the Spirit that encouraged me to be open to the risk and humiliation of accepting uneducated people as teachers.

As I followed my inner guidance, not easily and not without resistance, I began to trust the teachers of the earth. When faced with an opportunity to explore, expand, or experience differently, my education and background invariably screamed, "No, don't, stay put, be the same!" And although I was accustomed to trust the disciplines and teachings of my tradition, something frequently told me to relax them, permitting me to question the nature of my beliefs—a first step in discovering my true self.

After many pitfalls, I realized that if I did not let my pride,

1

guilt, or fear obstruct my inner vision, I could avail myself of a gracious and generous teaching. I then felt pressed to accept the lessons of the peasants—not to pretend to enter their lives, or to pretend to feel their pain, hunger, sickness, or even to suffer their injustices, but to support them in dealing with their suffering, and to learn. The downtrodden of Guatemala guided me close to the earth, leading me to recognize that education is not intelligence, technology is not growth, philosophy is not wisdom, theology is not spirituality.

My journey began in a cemetery shortly after Anita, my Spanish tutor, introduced me to the spirit world and to a mode of listening with the heart. After absorbing her simple insights, everywhere I've gone I've found teachers and lessons to mark the path for my journey.

THE CASA OF THE PRIESTS was a large, sprawling ranch-style adobe structure that sat beside the old cemetery at the end of a narrow dirt road. I began my life in Guatemala at the *Casa*. I lived there for six months with a small group of newly ordained Maryknoll priests studying Spanish individually with tutors and adjusting to the new culture. After nine grueling years of undergoing the regime of the seminary I was beginning my work as a missionary, the role that would give meaning and purpose to my life.

A seven-foot adobe wall secured the *Casa* property, and twenty paces to the right of its gate was the entrance to the cemetery. From the window in my room I saw processions of woeful mourners pass our gate daily. On their shoulders they carried handcrafted coffins shaped like mummy cases and adorned with freshly cut flowers. Sometimes the coffins were painted white for the innocence of children or black to connote the dignity of the elderly, but usually they were plain wooden boards cut and nailed into a box, narrowed snugly at the head and foot to save on waste, respectable and efficient conveyors of corpses to eternal rest.

My visits to the cemetery resulted from something my Spanish tutor told me. Anita López, a native Guatemalan, wise for her forty-two years, was committed to preparing recently arrived Maryknoll Missionaries for their new life.

"Anita," I asked one day, "is there any one aspect of Guatemalan life that I could concentrate on to deepen my understanding of the people?"

She did not respond immediately but sat quietly looking at me, seeming to know her answer yet unsure whether to share it. When she did speak, she gave a most important lesson, saying slowly, "Only prolonged day-to-day experience gives insight into life and culture. However, you might begin to learn about death."

I don't know what I expected to hear, but her answer took me by surprise. I asked, "Can you explain that a little? I mean about death."

Again she looked at me hesitantly, and then said, "I am sorry. Perhaps I should suggest that you begin by concentrating on learning to bargain in the market." I did not push further, and I did not miss her message. And although there was no way at the time for me to grasp the depth of her words, once I made up my mind to take them to heart, unusual opportunities began presenting themselves.

It was November 1961, in the city of Huehuetenango, capital of the state with the same name. I was halfway through my six-month course and feeling comfortable enough in the language to begin learning about death. I chose a sunny afternoon and shyly joined a procession of mourners on the other side of the wall. I listened with my heart, "the only way to listen," Anita had said, to the laments and wails of the bereaved, and heard sad survival expressed in dismal and discordant hymns and prayers. Touched and moved in a way that books and classes cannot touch a person, I was that day offered an initiation into the soul of Guatemala.

With tiny steps yielding time for grief, our group of thirty or so people passed through the high, arched gate and shuffled down constricted aisles of whitewashed tombs to a site where the surrounding bare ground was bedecked with freshly scattered pine needles. The custom being to entomb the bodies one above the other, the fifth tier of the crude elevated crypt was open to receive the box.

The crying and praying intensified as scarred and calloused hands raised the casket carefully on high, pushing it slowly through the tight opening, straining to inch it back and forth until only the very narrow end was showing. A mason, probably a relative or family friend, stood solemnly by with trowel in hand, mortar and bricks at his side, waiting to complete the job.

A tap at my elbow startled me from my musing, and a voice said, *"Padre,* would you please have a blessing for my daughter?" I turned and looked into the drawn, red eyes of a middle-aged man and felt his deep sadness. I also felt a sense of gratitude that he would include me in the ceremony.

I stepped through the mourners to the roughly made sepulcher and, with right hand raised, made the sign of the cross, ending by resting my fingers on the casket and saying, "Daughter, may you rest in peace," aware that for the first time in my priesthood I was taking on the role of spiritual father speaking to one of his children. I knew also that I would never feel the weight of responsibility or experience the depth of pain that the father at my side felt for the daughter of his flesh and blood.

In Spanish class the next day I discussed the burial and the cemetery with Anita. "Entombing bodies one on top of the other is so different from anything I have ever seen," I said.

She smiled, always eager to explain the simple things of a simple life. "What you saw connotes poverty," she said, holding out empty hands. "That family you were with yesterday apparently owns one burial plot and probably found it difficult to buy even that. They may have one body under ground, but without further expense they may bury six or seven corpses, one on top of the other."

Strengthened by the first experience, that same week I joined another funeral procession and found my role expanded. I blessed the casket, blessed water for sprinkling on the grave and "to take home for emergencies," and chatted with the bereaved.

A few days later, taking a break from my studies and not waiting for a funeral procession, I ventured alone into the cemetery. There I saw sorrowful and lonely people praying at grave sites, busying themselves with such chores as arranging faded imitation flowers and cleaning framed religious pictures left to disintegrate at the graves of loved ones. I roamed through the bleak and dejected setting, recalling the cemetery back home with its vast clipped lawns, fresh flowers, trimmed hedges, and groves of shade trees, a veritable vacationland compared to this stark and crowded, unplanned, and ugly graveyard.

As I walked, I read what was left of hand-painted words on wood and inscriptions chiselled crudely in stone: mementos of love, supplications for peace and mercy. And with each care-taker visitor who looked up and out from secret thoughts and sad feelings, I exchanged a somber and soft *Buenos días*.

An elderly man stopped and greeted me in a warm whisper and, pointing to a new wooden grave marker, said, *"Padre, would you pray for the soul of my departed brother?"* Glad to be of service and eager to learn, I stood with him by the freshly turned mound of dirt and recited the Lord's Prayer. With tears in his eyes and difficulty in clearing his throat, the elderly man stooped with evident pain to pull a few sprouting weeds, then stood cautiously and said with hushed voice, "My brother won't go."

I thought that as a priest I should know what to say in any such situation, but I didn't. Feeling perplexed, I simply repeated his words, "Your brother won't go."

"That's right, he won't leave," the man said, "He just stays here."

"Oh . . . where is he?" I asked, looking around.

"He's right there," the old man answered in hushed voice, pointing. "He's there on top of that next tomb, and he's supposed to leave. Please tell him he's dead and that he has to go."

I folded my hands to hide my nervousness, tried to imagine a soul sitting on the tomb, and said, "Dear brother, your life on earth has ended. Your body has died. You have other things to do now. Go your way in peace, and God be with you."

I looked to the man hopefully. "Thank you, *Padre*," he said.

"Is he gone?" I asked hesitantly.

"Yes, he left as you ended, and it's about time. We buried

him three weeks ago." Not understanding what I was involved in, I changed to something more familiar. "How did your brother die?" I asked.

He lowered his head and paused before saying, "It was my fault. I was driving too fast over a small landslide. The truck bounced, and he fell off the back, hitting his head." I knew that the dirt from landslides did not get removed from the roads but were simply driven over and packed down until they were part of the road.

"How very sad," I said. We stood in silence for a moment. And then, feeling a bit more confident, I ventured on. "And you have been able to see him near the grave?"

He looked at me with questioning eyes. "Not him . . . in body," he said, as if trying to find the right words. "I could see him in spirit. But that is him just the same, now that he's dead; isn't it?"

"Yes, that's him," I said with my mind divided between avoidance of further involvement and eagerness for the chance to learn. After a moment of deliberation and with some embarrassment, I went on. "Pardon me, *Señor*, but I myself don't know how to see souls." That seemed to have little meaning to him. I waited a moment, but with no response forthcoming, I asked hesitantly, "What does a soul look like, *Señor?*"

He cocked his head and turned with squinting eyes, probably a bit surprised that I wouldn't know about such things, shrugged and said, "Why . . . you just see them. They are there, and . . . you see them, and you know they are there. Probably no colors, maybe like a cloud or the air, but when they are there, you just see them, and you know."

I stood silently, knowing I was learning an important lesson, until he again shrugged his shoulders, indicating there was no more to say. I thanked him for his explanation, shook his hand, and went on to read a few more inscriptions before returning to the *Casa.*

In class later that day, after reviewing my homework, I cleared my throat as if that would clear my mind and said: "Pardon me for speaking personally, Anita, but do you . . . believe in ghosts?" Her eyes opened wide in surprise, and then

6

just as quickly she looked down as if embarrassed, her hand covering her mouth in typical Guatemalan fashion. She didn't answer.

I waited, confused by her reaction. "Perhaps I should not ask such a question," I said.

With that she took her hand from her mouth, and looking at me with a frown of concern, avoided my question by asking a question. "*Padre* Arturo, have you been to the *campo santo* again?"

"*Sí*. I am finding the cemetery a wonderful place to learn."

"And did someone there talk to you about spirits?"

"*Sí*. That is what led to my question."

"Did someone happen to say they saw a ghost . . .while you were there?"

"A man saw the soul of his brother," I said, "and I was hoping we could discuss that."

As if needing time to think, she busied herself with some books on the table and then said, "Well, let me put it this way. Many of our people believe in ghosts . . . ," she paused, as if not sure of herself, and then, seeming to change her course of thought, said, "but that may be from lack of education, don't you think?"

Knowing that she was hedging and using a statement she heard often from our priests, I answered, "I don't know. I sometimes think I may have been cheated by education."

She groped for a response and as if asking for understanding said, "My family is very Catholic."

Knowing she felt a need to hold back, I said, "I do not want to intrude, but if you are willing to tell me, I would like to know where your family stands on ghosts."

She took a breath, seemed to settle into her chair, and answered meekly, "Well, I suppose you could say that my family believes in ghosts, but many people would misinterpret that."

"I do understand," I said appreciatively, not wanting to probe further, "and I am also sorry that the Church has made it difficult for you to be open about this. I value your answer."

In the cemetery a few days later, I gave blessings and said prayers and talked with mourners. I asked one couple confidently if the soul of their deceased son had left. "Yes, *Padrecito*," the man offered, using the affectionate term for *father*, "he left while we circled the house three times with the body before coming here to the *campo santo*. It's my father who hasn't left."

I nodded understandingly, and asked, "Is he still here?"

"No, he's in my uncle's house and makes noises in the rafters each night." I tried not to show my surprise. The man went on, "I don't think papa will go until his brother returns the money." I nodded. He leaned against a tomb, and continued.

"Let me tell you the story, *Padrecito*." I crouched down facing him and leaned against a nearby tomb. After a moment of thought, he began. "Well, years ago, unbeknown to my family, my father stole money from a wealthy landowner and, afraid to spend it, hid it under a large rock. On his deathbed he told my mother of the theft and explained where the money was located, asking her to promise to return it to the rightful owner.

"She agreed. But my uncle, his brother, was present and heard my father's message. Before my mother could do anything, he dug up the money and used it for himself. I think my father is angry that his dying request was not granted and has decided to remain in my uncle's house until the matter is settled."

The next day I asked Anita, "Have you ever heard of a ghost making noise?" She avoided looking at me as she opened the text to our next chapter and said, "*Padre* Arturo, I am employed by the Maryknoll Fathers as an instructor of Spanish. Please forgive me, but we have to go on with our work."

Everyone I talked with in the cemetery believed in an afterlife, as I would have expected. What was surprising was the number who communicated with their departed. Some had visits from them. Some simply felt their presence. Many claimed to see them. All believed in ghosts. Almost everyone told stories about spirits, talking about their personal experiences simply as part of life.

I had never believed in ghosts. But then ghosts were never given a chance in my life. From my earliest days I was taught that belief in ghosts was crazy, that it was foolish, superstitious, and not permitted. The souls of the dead, we learned from tradition and ecclesiastical authority, went to heaven, purgatory, or hell, and that was indisputable. I had led a sheltered religious life, never having been exposed to any religious views other than those of traditional Catholicism. But with my present experience, I was beginning to doubt and question.

When Anita gave me the assignment of preparing a discourse on a topic of my choice, I began organizing my thoughts regarding beliefs. That evening I wrote out phrases, sentences, and definitions that would help me through my difficult subject.

"Perhaps I have been misled," I began the next day, hesitant with my words. As was her custom, she remained silent. I looked at my notes as I went on. "I have always accepted the beliefs of the Church as true. But, as a result of my present experience, I am beginning to realize that perhaps a belief is not true, even if it is proclaimed so." My thoughts were scattered and slow, but with frequent pauses I was able to get them out. Anita waited in silence.

"I am not sure, but perhaps I am personally responsible before God for my beliefs," I said. "I am free to choose them or not choose them, but I am obliged to make individual choices and not simply accept the beliefs of others."

After permitting me to go on at length, Anita said, "I'm a bit confused, but I believe I understand. Please tell me just what point you are getting at!"

"I am saying that we only believe that our beliefs are truth. That does not make them true. And they are not. The problem is that once we believe something, we become convinced that we are right and proclaim our belief to be truth."

She was no longer listening. I felt frustrated, having worked hard on my preparation. She looked to the clock. Time was almost up. We both stood. She smiled nervously, corrected me on some grammar as she collected her books, said, "*Hasta mañana*," and left. I sat down again, astounding myself with the fact that a belief could be easily changed, a belief about ghosts and probably about anything else. I was learning that my beliefs were unchangeable only if I believed they were, a conclusion that was to influence my life deeply.

In the ensuing days I felt tormented as I began to understand why Catholicism insisted that its doctrine was the truth and why it neither encouraged nor permitted its followers to question beliefs. Even more sad was the realization that I had been led to the very destructive and traditional conclusion that those who held beliefs other than ours were wrong, were less than us, were against us, were potential enemies.

I had been taught to never face the very basic and important truth that all beliefs, no matter whose, are still beliefs, reenforced ideas, and not truth. I was beginning to find it exciting that for the first time in my life I could hold a belief that was truly mine, not one imposed or inherited from someone else's values or needs.

One day as I was standing in front of the cemetery talking to a young Guatemalan man, Father Jim Curtin, the new director of the *Casa* and language school, entered the *Casa* property. I waved as he looked at me, but he turned away without waving back. I finished my conversation, shook hands with the man, and went to study. As I passed Jim's office on the way to my room, he called me.

As I entered, he leaned back in his chair and, with irritation in his voice, asked, "What are you doing off property during study time?"

Surprised by his question and not knowing of any offense, I said, "I've been talking to people."

He straightened up, saying, "You have four hours of individual class each day, and the remainder of your day, except for meals and recreation, is to be spent in your room in study."

I had never confronted a superior. I heard a tremor in my voice as I said, "Look, Jim, I can be in my room with my books and study or not study, but I cannot be speaking Spanish with a Guatemalan without learning."

"There is no discussion," he answered angrily. "Please go to your room."

I was dumbfounded. "I need to say more, Jim. I have to be able to discuss a difference of views. I think. . . ."

"There is no discussion," he said leaning forward. His face was red; the hand on his desk was a fist.

I knew I had to continue. "I am not going to my room until I can talk to you," I said strongly but with my voice trembling.

He stared at me in silence. "I recently completed nine years in the seminary, living by the rule, disciplining myself and being disciplined constantly." I felt my face flushing. "When I was ordained, I thought the training was over. I expected to be treated more maturely. I am twenty-eight years old. This is my life. Spanish is very important to me, and I am learning it. And I insist on being treated as an adult as I do so."

He sat back in his chair breathing deeply. "Please go to your room. I have nothing else to say."

I stood for a moment in silence, then went to my room. I was angry and could not study. But in a short time I began to relax and felt a sense of pride that for the first time in my life I had confronted repressive authority. I also knew that from then on I would not suppress my own views in the face of apparent manipulations or controlling authoritarianism.

One night I actually got up the courage to visit the cemetery. I took a flashlight but did not need it. The moon was bright. The gate was unlocked. Although I opened it slowly, its hinges creaked, filling the damp evening air with screeches. I entered, walking hesitantly. Conversations with myself always seemed to lighten fear. "What are you afraid of?" I asked myself. And I answered back, "Spirits, ghosts, that's what everyone is afraid of in cemeteries." I considered the answer, then further asked myself, "If that is so, does that mean everyone has an underlying belief in the existence of ghosts? Interesting," I thought, "that those who say they don't believe in ghosts should be so afraid of them." I wondered where I had learned that ghosts were frightening, and I got up the courage to cautiously invite any ghosts present to show themselves. None did. I thought I might have keeled over from fright if one had appeared, and that possibly they stayed hidden out of consideration for me. I knew, however, that I no longer doubted the existence of the spirit world.

Anita usually began our conversation class with *"Buenos días. Como está usted?"* and then introduced the subject to be discussed with such a statement as "I bought an umbrella." Or "A horse threw its rider." Or "The soccer team won." Although I had become accustomed to her approach in discussing local events, one day I was shaken and surprised by her subject. She began with, "Two men slit the throat of a seven-year-old boy."

I looked at her in silence, and then asked incredulously, "Are you joking?"

She saw my stunned look and hesitated before saying, "I'm sorry. Perhaps this is not an appropriate subject for today."

"No, not at all, Anita," I said, raising my hand in protest, "I want to discuss it."

She nodded her head in agreement and said, "I do realize this is strange for you, but do you not have some brutality in your society also?"

I thought for a moment and then answered, "Of course, although I have never been personally exposed to it." I paused again, refusing to consider the violence of my own society, and then said, "But here, in this tranquil environment, or in my idealistic view of it, I never expected such violence."

She smiled slightly, raised her eyebrows, and said, "I understand. But your idealizing our society is not going to help you or us. You must be aware that in Guatemala you will at times be confronting unusual behavior. It stems from the fact that most of our people have no opportunity to get ahead and so are for the most part illiterate, sick, and poverty-stricken. On top of that, they are treated very harshly, even brutally, if they try to change their situation." This was my first insight into the fact that violence is used to suppress the poor, who are then blamed for violence.

I sat silent, thinking of the seven-year-old boy. A few moments passed before I asked, "But a child, why would anyone do such a thing to a child?"

"Astounding as it may seem," she answered, "they did it in order to drain the boy's blood."

"That is incredible," I said, cradling my head in my hands as if to hide from what I was hearing.

"Yes," she went on, "the men are brothers, and their father is suffering from a blood disease. It was their belief that if their father drank a boy's blood, he would heal. This ignorance is the result of. . . ."

I was not listening. I had heard that it was not an act based on passion or vengeance but an act based on belief. I was hearing the consequences of ignorant belief and realizing, possibly for the first time in my life, the danger inherent in belief. I was getting insight into the fact that following one's beliefs could lead anyone, including me, to any form of violence against any person. And because it was based on belief, any behavior would be justified.

I was dealing with this in my mind, when Anita's voice broke through, " . . . but if this violence of the poor surprises you, the violence of the wealthy and educated will shock you."

Not wanting to consider that, nor to imagine anything worse than the death of the boy, I asked, "And what will become of the two men?"

"They murdered the boy yesterday. The judge found them guilty today. They have been sentenced to be shot early tomorrow," she pointed to her left, "on the hill overlooking the *campo santo*." I knew the hill. It was visible from my bedroom window.

I awoke at sunrise, having dreamt of the boy. I thought of the men but chose not to look out the window. With a knot in my stomach I began my meditation, and then I heard the volley of shots. Two more lives gone. Feeling nauseous, I went to the chapel for my Mass.

A few days later I started conversation class by asking, "*Doña* Anita, what were you saying the other day about the violence of wealthy and educated people?"

She smiled, raised an index finger, and said, "That is a delicate subject. You will learn soon enough about our system. But briefly, it is a very old political approach based on protecting the wealthy at any cost. The system does not permit change. If any are so foolish as to attempt deviation, for them everything is at risk. You will find that most people are hesitant even to discuss the possibility of change."

"What kind of change are you talking about, Anita?"

"Perhaps we will discuss that at some other time, *Padre*. Is there another topic you would like to discuss today?"

"Yes, but this is all so new to me, and it interests me, Anita. Tell me what is the Church's response to this."

"Well, I don't know specifically. But everyone, including the bishops, understands and accepts that you either support the political and economic system or keep quiet."

"Why haven't I learned anything about this during my years of seminary preparation?"

She looked at me curiously and said, "Perhaps this is not a subject to be discussed in the United States. Perhaps the people of the United States are not to know that their government supports such policy here. However, if you read our newspapers and talk carefully with people, you will get some information, although you never know how accurate. But you don't have to worry," she said pointing out the window to the surrounding mountains, "political violence has not yet really been experienced here in the highlands. It usually happens in the capital, where there is industry, or in the coastal regions of the large coffee, sugarcane, and cotton plantations."

Exciting news came to the language school. One of our priests, Father Hugo "Tex" Gerbermann, previous Superior of the Maryknoll Fathers in the State of Huehuetenango and presently residing with us at the *Casa de los Padres*, was named by the Vatican to become the first bishop of the State and the first American bishop in Guatemala. His consecration was to take place at the old colonial church in the center of Huehuetenango, which would become his official seat and thus the cathedral.

The big day came. Bishops, nuns, priests, and politicians came from all over the country, and, along with the local laity, filled the cathedral. I assisted in the ceremony as bearer of the pastoral staff, symbol of the bishop's power over his flock. As I stood at the side of Tex and the consecrating bishop, I considered the privilege of being so close to the seat of power. I thought of the opportunity available to me of remaining close to this power and of the benefits it might bring, of the future that could be mine. Someone had to do it, I thought. Why not I?

As I looked out from the sanctuary to the congregation I saw the president of Guatemala, General Miguel Ydígoras Fuentes, former minister of dictator Jorge Ubico, sitting in the first pew with his entourage, surrounded by bishops. Again I sensed the presence of power and felt privileged.

At the official reception back at the *Casa*, I knelt on one knee and kissed Tex's episcopal ring, symbol of his power. As I stood, he shook my hand and said, "Thanks for your support, Art." I felt important. The president of Guatemala stood beside the bishop, surrounded by bodyguards. As I shook hands with him he said, *"Gracias por su colaboración, Padre."* At that moment I recalled that Anita had said I would be shocked by the violence of the educated and wealthy, and wondered, if that were true, how I could ever live in the midst of their power.

2
RACISM

In many parts of this "Land of Eternal Spring," civilization has barely encroached on the indigenous society, and technology is of little interest. Mountain trails are worn deep by centuries of bare feet treading under heavy loads. Stick houses with thatched roofs and dirt floors hold open cook-fires and mats for bedding. Young children carry firewood and water; older children tend animals and work the earth with their fathers. Mothers carry babies on their backs and have not learned shame in nursing them. Hand-woven blouses and skirts are veritable works of art. People gather in open market for a social life of bartering the earth's fruits in the form of food, handcrafted baskets, mats, dipped candles, and rope woven from plant fibers. Many generations together support the elderly and the young.

I still remember the shock at penetrating the surface of Guatemalan society and finding an underlying violent current of racism against these indigenous people. I sat in the mayor's office one day and heard and saw a poor, young, vulnerable Indian brother and sister being degraded by the very authority whose protection they sought. The incident made me want to withdraw from the ugly part of that society and simply focus on a genteel ministry to needy souls. I too was young and vulnerable, unprepared to face the reality of sexual violence and unaccustomed to witnessing such abuse of authority, let alone being expected to act as a party to it.

That day and in the ensuing years, as I witnessed racism against the indigenous Guatemalan people, the heirs to the great Mayan culture, my concern about the cause and perpetuation of such violent discrimination failed to diminish. In time I opened my eyes to the difficult revelation that as a priest, in separating out the saved from the lost I had accepted the belief that Catholics are more favored by God than those outside the fold—a belief that is the basis for every other type of discrimination. I began to realize that if I taught about discrimination and prejudice I would have to criticize the Roman Catholic Church.

Five hundred years ago the Church initiated prejudice in the Americas by declaring the native people to be without souls. Although the Church reversed that decision, it cooperated with the military to subjugate those same inhabitants for the salvation of their souls and the confiscation of their wealth. I began to think that if prejudice and domination were to be dealt with, the children of God would have to choose beliefs and qualities that went beyond the normal limits of religion.

Mateo and Lita, the young Indian brother and sister, poor, uneducated, and dark-skinned, ignorant of the ways of western culture, natural targets of historical racist and sexist opprobrium, quickly became my teachers, shattering my dream world and bringing me face to face with the truth that their suffering and oppression were based in part on the work of the Church.

I FELT RELIEVED that the period of six months' intense language study was winding down. Bishop Tex would soon assign my classmates and me to our first parishes. One of our small class of language students would be chosen to go out alone, filling in for sick or vacationing priests, while the others would receive a normal assignment to assist an established pastor. In my mind I picked the few pastors I would enjoy working under and learning from, hoping I would not be burdened with the responsibility and loneliness of filling in.

When my time came, Bishop Tex summoned me to his isolated second-story office adjacent to the cathedral. I entered, dressed in my normal slacks and sport shirt, trying to hide my anxiety, and said, "Hello, Tex."

Without looking up from the papers on his desk, this private and quiet man said, "Hi, Art, have a seat." I sat in one of the straight-back chairs along the wall with the anxiety of waiting to see a dentist. I looked at the bishop, dressed impeccably in his crimson robes, and saw what looked like a sad, lonely man. As expected, he was smoking a cigar, now locked firmly in his jaw. He usually removed it for speaking, which he did seldom and only briefly, and then held it in strange contrast to the large, dark stone of his episcopal ring. The cigar seemed ever-present except during official or liturgical functions or while eating. During meals the dead butt would sit on an ashtray with the saturated end overhanging and pointing toward him. I was aware that Tex required time before speaking, and that when ready he would suddenly remove the cigar, turn, and begin. It was as if he had to rev up the energy needed to deal on a personal level.

Then he turned, and in one abrupt motion he removed the cigar with the ring hand, raised his silken cassock so as not to wrinkle it in crossing his legs, blew a puff of heavy smoke slightly to the side of me, and, trying to make eye contact over his bifocals, said with studied and staccato words, "I am pleased to say that because you have developed good skills in the language, I am choosing you to work on your own." I sat unmoved. I was flattered and scared. I said nothing. Cigar back in mouth, a forced smile on his face, eyes focused on his nervously rotating well-shined shoe, he was silent. I took a deep breath and let myself relax, my mind telling me it was wonderful that the bishop held me in such esteem. In the silence, I considered the meaning of the challenge before me and began to feel some excitement. "Yes," he said, and after a brief pause went on, "I'm sending you to San Sebastián for three months. I know you'll do well. Just don't make any changes." I smiled and nodded agreement. He mouthed the cigar and turned to his desk.

I waited a few moments in silence, not quite sure if we were finished, and then said, "Thanks, Tex," which came out in a meek and squeaky voice.

He turned to me again as if he had forgotten that I was there, "Oh, yes, sure," he said, as he held the cigar about six inches from his lips and made a slight motion as if to rise from the chair, "God bless, Art," and then settled back, cigar in mouth, and turned to the desk with a sigh. I left the office and ran down the steep steps two at a time, whistling as I walked back to the *Casa* to tell the others of my good fortune.

I gathered and evaluated information about San Sebastián. The population was Indian, as were most of the people of Guatemala, but the town was run by *Ladinos*, people of Spanish and Indian blood. *Ladinos* generally held the positions of influence, maintaining historic control and suppression of the native population. The Indians usually spoke only a native language, of which there are twenty-one in Guatemala, and dressed in traditional attire, which was often very colorful and varied from town to town.

Most of the people of San Sebastián traveled on foot. Those able to get ahead a few cents might take a bus if going into the city, while the better-off owned a horse or mule. Most of the parishes had horses for traveling to outlying areas. I wanted to economize on my time in traveling where roads existed, so I chose the facility offered by a motorcycle. With part of the money I had received as gifts at ordination, I bought a shiny, new black Zundap, a rugged German bike that would serve on the unpaved Panamerican Highway and on trail-like roads into some of the towns.

Arriving in San Sebastián and embarking on my long-awaited missionary career, I got the awakening of my life as I suddenly found myself in the midst of blatant racial oppression. Unsettling as the experience was, it soon led me to the realization that I would have practiced the same inequities if my early environment had been that of Guatemala, just as I practiced the inequities of the environment in which I grew up.

Having been born into Irish Catholicism, I was unconscious of, and unquestioning of, the prejudicial seeds planted at birth, which for many years grew strong and deep. Racist slurs, demeaning references, and belittling jokes found acceptance in my devoutly religious home. Although as children we were programmed basically against Jews and blacks, the obvious and righteous prejudice against any religion other than our own subtly laid the basis for prejudice against anyone who was different. Since I accepted my early teachings and influences as truth, I had no idea how destructive or deeply imbedded they were until I reached San Sebastián and saw others accepting their own blatant form of prejudice as truth and behaving accordingly.

I became aware of a growing, gnawing, painful sensitivity to what was normal, everyday treatment of Indians that helped me bring to the surface the hidden roots of my own ignorance. The unacceptable situation in San Sebastián gave me insight and motivation to begin dealing with my own lifelong prejudices. Developing disgust with my righteous legacy and desiring to root it out was not enough. Dealing with my beliefs called for a tough and continual probing into the depths of my upbringing— something I had never been encouraged to do or had thought to do in the seminary, despite nine years of daily meditation and examination of conscience. With this re-evaluation began an even deeper questioning of the beliefs handed down to me as correct and true.

In San Sebastián, people appeared on the surface to accept their role in the racial status quo, with the Indians considered in every sense inferior. They themselves had learned to make excuses for their alleged inadequacy, saying, "I am only an Indian," while *Ladinos* and foreigners might express their deprecation or blame with a shrug, saying, "What can you expect from an *Indito?*"

Under the surface lay another story. *Don* Benito, the Spanish-speaking Indian sacristan and catechist at San Sebastián, who became my interpreter, companion, and teacher, a man of patience and kindness, told me differently. "I ache. I vomit inside. I hate being treated as if I were less than human. At times I feel like taking my machete and killing. I cannot stand to see my people trampled upon. Yet I will continue to vomit inside all my life."

The *Ladinos* lived in the *pueblo*, running the town hall, the police, the school, and the few shops. The Indians, outnumbering the *Ladinos* many times over, lived in the surrounding villages, some of them three or four hours away on foot or horseback. The *pueblo* was close to the Panamerican Highway and connected to it by road, while the villages connected to the town only by trails and paths.

So this was the environment that introduced me to the life of a missionary priest. Despite the poverty and the racism, I quickly fell in love with the area. It fit my dreams. The beauty of the mountains, the rivers, and the people at times overwhelmed me. Every day seemed new and different. I was like a child caught up in the excitement and amazement of experiencing the unknown and had already begun thinking I could easily spend the rest of my life in San Sebastián.

After some weeks of gaining practice and exposure in my new position, I felt prepared to acquaint myself with the town structure. It was ten in the morning and already very hot the day I got up the courage to go across the plaza to the town hall and present myself to the mayor. I was mentally practicing my introduction, saying in Spanish, "I am the temporary pastor . . . ," as I entered the rustic adobe building and knocked on the partly-open faded blue door where someone had long ago painted the word *Alcalde*.

A short, balding, intense, middle-aged man looked up from a pile of papers and, seeing me, smiled and jumped from his chair, took the big rusty latch of the heavy door in both hands and lifted the door open on its broken hinges. He said *Buenos días* and started to extend his hand when he saw the rust on his palms and laughingly wiped them on his pants. In another environment the mayor would have looked strange in his oversized, double-breasted green suit with large padded shoulders and a dirty-collared shirt buttoned to the neck with no tie, but in San Sebastián he looked quite dignified.

The worn boards of the floor creaked and gave slightly under my feet as I entered. On the desk I recognized the stack of ever present official lined paper with the seal of the quetzal at the top. The quetzal, the beautiful multi-colored bird that lives in the rain forests of Guatemala and cannot survive in captivity, is an ironic national symbol. The mayor acted warmly and cordially in typical *Ladino* style and did not seem to mind leaving the work of the official documents to attend me. Shaking my hand with a big up and downward motion, he said, "My name is Carlos Henrique Machado Figueroa, your servant, mayor of San Sebastián and official representative for the municipality."

When he paused, I came in with, "I am very pleased to meet you, *Don* Carlos. My name is Arturo Melville, and I am the temporary pastor of the parish of San Sebastián, and I likewise am your servant." He smiled approvingly, and I felt good as we continued with the custom of each claiming to be there to serve the other in any way possible with the greatest of pleasure, until he directed me to a well-worn wicker chair, which he pulled close to the scarred desk of a former time. I waited for him to arrive at his chair and then sat down. I was about to begin with typical chatter about the weather when he signalled with a raised finger and said he needed a moment. With that he called in the town secretary, a fat young man who bowed to me graciously and called me *padrecito*. I thought he was slickly amiable, and I had a sense that I should never trust either of these men. *Don* Carlos gave a knowing nod and wink to the secretary as he told him to take the pile of documents from his desk and see that all fees were collected and noted. He then turned his attention to me, apologized for the delay, smiled, and said that all the town was delighted with my presence, and that everyone wanted to make me feel welcome, reiterating that if he could be of any service to me, I was only to ask, because he was my servant.

As we chatted, routine business went on, with *Don* Carlos excusing himself at each interruption. At one point a teenage Indian girl in her colorful native blouse and skirt and her older brother in loose, white shirt and pants, both barefoot, were ushered in. The boy stood to one side, twisting his straw hat in his hands. The girl knelt self-abasingly by the desk, obviously petrified, with tears in her eyes. She was a heavy-set and well developed girl, with unblemished skin, long silky black hair, shining black eyes, and white, even teeth. Her long blue wraparound skirt and red blouse adorned with blue and yellow embroidery were tied tightly with a colorful waistband, all hand-woven and freshly clean.

I found her attractive but was careful not to let my eyes or mind wander, practicing the discipline of the vow of celibacy. But from time to time I found it difficult not to fixate on her, particularly on the protrusion of her breasts when she leaned back on her feet, stretching her body. I could feel my sexual juices stir and was irritated with myself, knowing my vow did not permit such a feeling.

The secretary came in with his pencil and pad of paper and sat down beside me in another well-worn wicker chair. Obviously, I was to witness some serious business. Before beginning the proceedings the mayor again excused himself for taking time from our conversation, acknowledging that I was a person of respect and dignity, and then began.

I realized that there were two sides here, and everyone was being shown which side I was on. I did not like what was happening and felt uncomfortable being one of those who sit in chairs. In accepting privilege, I aligned myself with the successors of the conquistadores. In some not-too-unconscious way the mayor was cementing our relationship and using me to reconfirm on a local level the alliance of Church and State against the indigenous population.

I stood up slowly, stepped to the side of the chair, and leaned against the cool adobe wall. *Don* Carlos cast a surprised glance towards me, leaned back in his creaky chair, lit a cigarette, called the young man by name, Mateo, and told him to begin. It seemed that the mayor already had a sense of what was to follow.

Mateo looked as if he didn't know where to begin and after a moment's hesitation turned to his sister and spoke in dialect. She began sobbing as she looked up pleadingly to the mayor and also spoke in dialect. She obviously knew no Spanish. The mayor interrupted, exasperatedly telling the brother to translate. In his broken Spanish, Mateo began explaining bluntly.

"A man named Federico Delvalle, who lives here in the *pueblo*, came to our village last Friday and forced my sister to lie with him."

"He raped your sister?" the mayor asked as if to clarify, but in a voice that seemed to mock.

I felt myself pull back from such blunt reality and what it represented. My knowledge of rape was what I had read in newspapers. In my seminary course in Moral Theology the instructor had simply and briefly covered the subject as one of the grave sins against the sixth commandment. I was unprepared to be a party to such an explicit meeting as this and didn't know if there was an appropriate way to react. The mayor and the secretary, however, smiled knowingly at each other.

For a moment my mind got caught up in what the experience of rape might be. I wondered what the girl had gone through and imagined the terror. Then I wondered about the man's experience, something I had never before permitted myself to consider. I began to feel a sexual tingling, an automatic signal that brought me back to the situation before me. I felt irritated at my ignorance, frustrated that such questions were handled inadequately in the seminary and merely passed off as sinful. I felt ashamed that I would react sexually to the description of a violent crime.

The girl buried her face in her hands. The brother waited until the mayor told him to go on, then said, "This is the second time that *Don* Federico has done this to my sister," using the title of respect for the accused rapist. The secretary smiled and continued taking notes. I began to feel angry about the proceedings and angry that anyone would abuse this young girl.

The mayor interrupted, "I want to point out that in the first instance of alleged rape, the accused man was summoned to this office, only to explain that he had paid your sister to lie with him, and the case was dismissed." The mayor leaned forward, resting his forearm on the desk and, with what I thought was a sneer, asked, "How much did *Don* Federico pay her this time?"

My body tensed. I was stunned by the way this woman was being treated, the way these Indians were being mistreated, and the way a serious problem was being distorted. I felt like interrupting, but checked myself, realizing I was witnessing an extraordinary event and that if I wanted to remain present I had to remain quiet.

The brother jumped at the mayor's question, and in unexpected frustration, answered, "She has not ever taken money from that. . . ." He quickly calmed himself and, as expected of an Indian, apologized for speaking loudly, then went on slowly. "*Don* Federico waited until my mother had gone for water. The rest of us were in the fields away from the *ranchito*. He entered while my sister was weaving and forced himself on her. She is a very good weaver. My mother heard the screams, but by the time she got to the house, *Don* Federico was walking down the trail, and my sister was lying on the floor, crying."

I had a sense that the rape probably happened the way the brother was saying and that the mayor intended to make it difficult for him to state the case. I wondered how, after so many years of such treatment, the Indians were able to go on presenting cases. I was to learn that most had given up. The hearing ended quickly, with the mayor saying, "Since there were no witnesses to the alleged rape, I am dismissing the case." The secretary stood up and asked the mayor a question about the documents he was working on. The sister stood up and brushed the dirt from her skirt.

As the brother and sister moved to the door, Mateo said, "Thank you, *Señor* Mayor. Please pardon us for disturbing you. With your permission, we will leave." They bowed to each of us and left.

I was incensed. I did not know what to do. I had been warned not to get involved in legal issues. But this was not a legal issue. The legal structure had swallowed the rights of the people; it was an illegal issue. The secretary left the room as if nothing had happened. The mayor turned to me, smiled, and said, "Come, *Padre*, sit down again and let us continue our conversation."

"Thank you, *Don* Carlos," I said, "but it's time for me to go. I have some things to attend to. I appreciate this first visit. It will not be the last." As he shook my hand vigorously, he again told me how happy he and all the townspeople were to have me in their *pueblo*. I repeated my thanks and left. I could not believe he had let me stay in his office during the hearing. I was amazed at the confidence he had that a priest would support the status quo. He expected me to play a role, as both Indians were playing the painful role imposed on their people since the time they were conquered by the European military and suppressed by the Catholic Church. I was observing a people without rights, a people permitted to live only if they submitted. I was aware of the shame I felt, a feeling that I knew I could erase by simply accepting the results of historic process—as might be expected of a priest.

3
INJUSTICE

As I recount the strange and wondrous tale of my personal spiritual journey and the difficult path my life was to follow, I am still filled with the grief and sadness I felt over the situation that unfolded for Lita. It has never been easy for me to watch people in authority take advantage of the innocents of the world. For five hundred years the drama of European man versus earth people has been and still is enacted when outsiders enter an indigenous village for purposes of exploitation. The resulting dominance imposed on a simple and earthy way of life takes among its first victims the young, who have no rights, particularly the Indian girl, who is considered property.

My present awareness of exploitation was gained from my experience in Guatemala. I had gone there unaware of my own inbred prejudices and the resulting blindness to problems like those that women suffer. I believed simply that I was there to save the souls of backward people.

San Sebastián opened my eyes to my blinding beliefs and demonstrated blatantly that the poor and oppressed are subject to the law but not protected by it. Sadly, I learned that in a country where Church and State are closely allied, such a legal and judicial system depends on the willingness of both entities to justify and indulge the wealthy while ignoring the abuse and oppression of the poor. The clergy can remain free of active *involvement by maintaining the role of saving souls through dogma and ritual.*

My religious training failed to prepare me for sociosexual problems, and only belatedly did I realize that a man who is prepared for celibacy by isolation from women cannot be prepared to teach and counsel regarding sexual issues, relationship conflicts, and women's rights.

Outside the mayor's office I shielded my eyes from the bright sun, looked around, and saw Mateo and his sister standing quietly in the shade of a tree. Mateo was peeling an orange. I expected them to appear at least bewildered. They looked indifferent. I was bewildered, realizing the vast difference between the way I experienced life and the way they did. I wondered what they were thinking and feeling. I wondered if I would ever really know them and their people. They appeared unaware of me until I stood beside them, and even then the sister did not raise her eyes.

"Excuse me, Mateo," I said. "Can I ask permission to talk with you and your sister?" He looked at me without expression. I wondered if they knew who I was because I wasn't accustomed to dress as a priest, and we hadn't been introduced. "I am the parish priest," I said. Mateo nodded as he put a piece of orange in his mouth. "Can we go over to the churchyard and talk?" I asked. He shrugged his shoulders. I crossed the dirt road to the churchyard, went in, and sat on a step. It seemed as if they were not going to come. I waited. A few minutes later Mateo poked his head into the entrance. I didn't say anything. He entered slowly, looking with interest at the cement walks, the large circular fountain filled with clean water, and my motorcycle. I invited him to sit on the step beside me, but instead he crouched on his haunches in front of me.

"What happened in the *alcalde*'s office was terrible," I said. He looked briefly in my eyes, his face expressionless. I spoke softly, "I want to help, if I can."

He glanced into my eyes again, and then at the ground.

He took a deep breath, sighed, and then spoke even more softly, "Nothing can be done . . . and *Don* Federico is free to return to our village."

The girl's name had never been mentioned. I asked, "What is your sister's name?"

He hesitated before he answered. "Her name is Lita." He looked at me as if for a response. I didn't have one.

"We have the same mother and father," he said, looking at me again. I waited. "Our father died on the coast." He offered a piece of his orange.

I put it in my mouth and asked, "What was Federico doing in your village?"

He pressed his lips together and shook his head, then slowly explained. "My family and my people are poor. We have no amusement. Our only enjoyment is in each other. We try to save what money we can for the annual fiesta. And on the first day of that, many get drunk and then quickly have no money. *Don* Federico comes to the fiesta on the second and third day and gives money to the drunken men so they can continue drinking. But they have to sign his contracts that force them to go to the coast at harvest time. There they work hard on the farms of the rich. Many get sick, and some die." I was aware of the truckloads of men, sometimes with their families, that were herded like animals to the coast when needed for harvesting the crops of the wealthy. I had been told of the horrible conditions they worked and lived under, of the slave wages, and of the extensive sickness. Now I was learning how the landowners obtained their labor. He went on, "Sometimes the men are sick or can't go to the coast when their contract says. Don Federico comes looking for them. He carries a gun. Everyone is scared of him." Mateo fell silent, his finger drawing aimlessly in the dirt. I waited.

"My sister is not the only girl of the village that this man has forced himself on, but people won't talk. They are afraid of him. Even now I am afraid that he might punish us for reporting to the *alcalde*. I wish I had a gun. But Indians go to jail for having a gun." He stopped, pulled up a piece of grass and put it in his teeth. "The *alcalde* is a friend of *Don* Federico. I knew it was useless to come to talk to him. My mother asked me to do it. But I'll never step foot in the *alcaldía* again." Pushing his fist into the dirt, he said with disgust, "*Ladinos* are free to rape Indian girls," and stood up as if ready to leave.

Apart from whether Mateo was telling the truth or not, it was clear that his people were defenseless. I stood up and faced him. "Mateo, would you be willing to take this case further . . . if I promise to help?"

He paused with eyes cast down, mumbled something to himself in his dialect, and then said, "No." He paused, shook his head, and went on, "No, that would only cause more problems. We don't need more problems." That caught me up short. He was probably right. In trying to help them, I might cause more trouble. I didn't even know how to take a case further. I asked myself if I wanted to do it for them or for me. I thought it was probably both and still concluded that it needed to be done.

"I think it needs to be done, Mateo. Already you think that Federico may punish you. Let us try to stop him by bringing the case to court." He looked afraid, raising his hand repeatedly to his face and looking around. Not knowing what we were up against, I said, "I have never done this before, Mateo. If we take the case to court, it may not work. It will be difficult. It may be dangerous." I paused, then added, "But I think we ought to try." He looked at me and said nothing. I waited. Then thinking he was waiting for me to speak, I asked, "Is there something I'm missing or not understanding, Mateo?" He still looked at me in silence. "What is it, Mateo?"

He started as if embarrassed, "I am not . . . we are not . . . my family is not . . . Catholic." He waited for me to say something. I didn't. He went on slowly, "Our father, the one who died on the coast . . . hated the priests." He lowered his head as if expecting me to be disappointed. I wasn't.

He raised his head. "My father's father was a *chimán*." I had some understanding of the native priests or witch doctors. I nodded for him to go on. "My father told us that the priest had his father put in jail because he would not give up his *chimanería*."

The cook came out to hang up some dishtowels. I waited

until she had left, and then said, "I understand, Mateo. It's fine with me that you are not Catholic. And I am ashamed of what happened to your grandfather." He looked at me in a questioning way. I went on, "I also do not like what happened to Lita in your village, and I do not agree with what took place in the *alcaldía* this morning. I want you to think about bringing a case against Federico Delvalle. I want the *alcalde* to know that he cannot treat you the way he did." I hoped I wasn't just shooting my mouth off. I knew I could do nothing without Mateo's support. I asked, "Are you willing to think about that, Mateo?" He didn't answer. I put my hand on his arm and said, "Even though I have no idea what we can do, I want to do all we can." I saw his expression changing. "Will you think about it?" I asked.

He again glanced in my eyes, and nodded assent, saying, "*Bien*, we do it."

"Do what?" I asked.

"We do it," he said, showing no feeling. "We see if there is a way to trap the rodent."

"Fine," I said, but then began wondering whether Lita would be willing to go through an ordeal. "What do you think about inviting Lita into the yard so we can talk with her?" He shrugged and left.

A few minutes later he returned with Lita following. She entered slowly, eyes cast down, shuffling little steps in her tight ankle-length skirt. I asked Mateo to tell her of our conversation. We stood in a small circle as he spoke in dialect, looking at his sister, then at me, then at the ground. And Lita listened with eyes down, occasionally mumbling a few words in dialect. Mateo finished, paused, and then nodded to me, saying he had covered everything with Lita. He said she was very afraid but had agreed to go ahead with the case because he wanted her to and because she was terrified of *Don* Federico's returning. I stood looking at them. They were so helpless. I did not want to give them hope that might only get dashed to the ground. But what was I to do?

I asked myself if I had the right to risk this. I thought maybe I didn't. I vacillated and began inclining toward backing off. I was aware of a long silence. Neither of them had a problem with silence. Finally Mateo turned to me and said, "We are pleased that someone is willing to do something, even though we think not much can be done."

I smiled and said, "I will go to Huehuetenango and perhaps register a case against the man." We said a simple good-bye without shaking hands, and I watched them start down the trail, silently, gently, mysteriously, single file, Mateo in front. I wondered what had kept Indians going for the past five hundred years.

My schedule that day called for supervising some doctrine classes. I went to the church and sat on the communion steps and listened to *Don* Benito teach. I was present physically but totally distracted. Since my own childhood catechism classes I had never focused well on memorization of the doctrine. Still vivid was the image of myself at age seven, sitting in a church bench with eight or ten other children, scared to death that Sister was going to ask me a question. And when she did, I would stand up, fingernails digging into the back of the bench in front, my foot nervously wandering from floor to kneeler, and try desperately to answer about sins and sacraments, always confused that I had to be recognized as a sinner before I could receive Jesus in the Eucharist.

Looking at *Don* Benito I wondered what these people were going through as they memorized doctrine, at times in a language that was not theirs. The doctrine was said to give them the key to God's Church and eternal happiness. I knew I wanted no part of it, but the permanent pastor had set up his system, and I was supposed to follow it.

What I had on my mind, and what I considered important, was what I had witnessed that morning. I had been in parish work only a very short time, and already I wondered how much of the inequity and contradiction of this environment and structure I was going to be able to accept.

I knew I would be unable to sleep that night if I didn't begin to help Lita and Mateo. I could not put it off. Shortly after noon I cranked up the motorcycle. So anxious was I about what to do next and where to begin that for the first time I failed to enjoy the rugged mountains, the billowing clouds, the river winding along the highway. Arriving in Huehuetenango covered with dust and eager to move on, I searched out and went directly to the office of the judge. I found him alone, presented myself, and received a cordial welcome. The priesthood carried with it the privilege of entry to such important offices, even without an appointment.

I explained the case of the alleged rape and my impression of the difficulty for the Indians presenting it. The judge told me he was familiar with this type of problem, and that at times the mayors were unprepared to handle such cases, but that he would look into it. He asked for the data I had on the girl, her brother, and the accused, and said that I should advise the brother and sister, and anyone else from the village having a complaint against the accused man, to come and give the necessary data to his secretary. He assured me that I would not have to do anything else and that he would get the case handled judicially. I was happy that I had found such a sincere and helpful ally.

I returned to the parish eager to advise Mateo and Lita that they could get on with the case, only to get a lesson in the difficulties of sending a message in rural Guatemala. There were, of course, no telephones. Towns were connected by a telegraph line, but the villages had no communication. *Don* Benito told me I had to wait until someone came to town from their village. I was on edge until a few days later he advised me that someone had arrived. I sent a note addressed to Mateo, hoping he could read or that someone would be available who could.

Four days later Mateo stood at my door. I felt delighted to see him and to hear that he had received my message. He said he would have come earlier but wanted to wait until he had a sack of oranges to sell. A leather strap across his forehead was tied to the large net of oranges on his back. He held his hat in his hand and was covered with sweat from the three-hour walk.

I felt as if I were seeing a friend and, eager to give him news about the case, I reached for the sack, saying, "Let me help put that on the ground, Mateo."

"No," he said taking a step backwards. "I am taking them

to the plaza to sell," giving me an important lesson in values. Oranges came before news and, as I was yet to find out, oranges were more than a monetary issue.

Recovering from my surprise, I asked, "Oh, how much are oranges going for, Mateo?"

"Probably two for three cents, I think."

"Well, how many do you have there?"

"Close to a hundred. I ate one on the trail."

"How about if I buy them from you," I said, thinking of fresh orange juice and still wanting to begin talk about the judge.

He looked at me strangely and said, "All of them?"

"Sure, I can use them."

He hesitated and then said, "But what would I sell in the plaza?" giving me a good laugh at my unawareness.

"Oh, of course," I said. "After you get settled in the plaza, I'll come out to talk with you."

"You can buy what I have left over," he said as he turned to the gate.

I arrived at the plaza to find Mateo sitting cross-legged under a tree with the open net in front of him, eating an orange. I sat down beside him. He didn't offer me a piece. As he savored a slice, I realized he was advertising his product. "So, how is it going, Mateo?"

"*Un poco bien.*"

"Have you sold any oranges?"

"No, not yet," he said, unconcerned.

"I'll have one," I said reaching for change in my pocket.

He looked at me, selected an orange carefully, handed it to me, took my five-cent piece and said he didn't have change. "How many for five cents?" I asked.

He considered that for a moment and then said, "Two or three, and I'll owe you one or two cents." I selected another orange and we sat quietly together as I peeled the first.

"I want to tell you about my trip to the city," I said. He nodded and kept nibbling at the orange slice. I told him about the judge and explained that he had prepared the way for Mateo and his sister, and anyone else who had a complaint against the rapist, to file a case. Mateo held the slice between his thumb and forefinger, looking at it, and said nothing.

"Have you ever been to a law office, Mateo?"

He thought about it, as if he might have been, and then said, "No. My grandfather went once."

As I talked about it, he showed some fear, then some interest, and finally a little enthusiasm. An Indian woman and her daughter, speaking in dialect, stopped to inquire about the oranges. They got two oranges for a penny. A *Ladino* woman came by and bargained hard in Spanish. Mateo was quiet but firm. She got two for three cents. I asked him if the *Ladinos* respected the Indians. He quickly said yes. We talked more about the judge and then sat quietly, watching the other vendors watching us.

He finally spoke. "We are going to Huehuetenango to see the judge." I kept looking at the ground and did not respond. "I am going to speak to my people and gather together anyone willing to make the journey and testify." I looked at him. His head was high and his chest was out. As we talked about the logistics of the trip, he gave me a sense of its difficulty. They would spend a day walking to the city and then have to find a place to stay and to cook their food. They would try to register their complaint early the second day, leaving time to walk back to their village that afternoon in order not to miss more than two days in the fields.

"But who knows if we can do that," he explained, "because in these office places *Ladinos* are taken first. And so, even if we arrive early, we never know." He was right. He could not be assured that they would receive attention and complete their task in two days. When he asked how many trips they might have to make to the judge's office and the court, I began to see the immensity of the problem for the poor in presenting a case.

As it turned out three men and three women with two babies made the journey the following week. For another week I received no word on the result of their visit. Then Mateo came into the *pueblo* to sell some oranges and stopped by the *convento*.

I opened the door. There he stood, eyes down, hat in hand, covered with sweat, a net of oranges on his back. He held out his hand and gave me two cents. I said thanks and took them. The message was clear.

I felt like crying, but I invited him in and helped lower the net to the floor. Downhearted and defeated, he explained, "When we got to see the judge's secretary, he told us to go back outside and wait." With that Mateo stopped talking. I waited several minutes, wondering where his mind was. Then he went on as if he had never paused. "We waited longer than three hours on the sidewalk close to the door. The cement was hot. When the *señor secretario* called us in, we picked up our belongings and followed him and stood right in front of his desk. I explained carefully who we were, and that you had sent us, and that you had told us that if we came to the office, the judge would talk to Federico Delvalle to make him stop molesting Lita and some other women. But the *señor secretario* told us we should not have come to Huehuetenango because the case had been dismissed."

"Did he write anything down?" I asked, amazed.

"He wrote down nothing and refused to talk more to us. I knew there was a terrible wrong going on and pleaded for permission to see the judge. But the *señor secretario* told us it was time to leave." Mateo had his fists clenched as he said, "It did not matter what we said or asked. The bastard told us the case was finished." Mateo was completely discouraged and resigned—common characteristics among the Indians. As I talked about the inequity and the insult, he looked to the sky and said hopelessly, "*Así es, así es.*" That's the way it goes. That's the way it is.

My body was trembling. "You did well, Mateo. I am angry at what has happened." He shook his head. "I will check with the judge's office as soon as possible. I want to see what's going on and what we can do."

"Don't bother yourself," he said. "They will let nothing be done. And my people will do no more about this." He was sad and downcast, and I knew he was right about his people.

I set out to do my parish work of the day but was so furious that I could not get the judge off my mind. Finally, I jumped on my motorcycle and drove anxiously into Huehuetenango. I went directly to the judge's office and was met warmly by his secretary, an older, bespectacled man. On the surface the cordiality appeared sincere. But I was disgusted with this kind of deceit.

In answer to my question, the secretary explained, "Yes, a group of Indians did present themselves with a case against a *Don* Federico Delvalle from San Sebastián. And I am very sorry, *Padre*, that . . . ." He hesitated and looked at me. " . . . I was so burdened with work that . . . I was unable to take their information that day. But I did ask them to return in a few days, and I am still waiting for them."

I knew he was lying. Frustrated, I asked, "May I see the judge?"

"Oh, I am so sorry," he said nervously, "The judge is out of town."

"But I can hear him in his office," I said.

"Oh, no," he said, looking towards the inner door, "That is not the judge's voice. The judge is not here."

I left, thinking that no matter what the truth was the judge would probably have backed the secretary. Angry at myself for having failed to accompany the group and frustrated at the system, I walked out into the late afternoon wondering about my role. Was I going to submit, as the Indians had learned to do? Or was my life going to be one of confrontations? There seemed to be no other option.

I sat down on a bench in the park and gazed absent-mindedly down the main street to the cathedral dominating the center of the small city. It looked beautiful and peaceful. But my reverie was short-lived as a voice said, *"Hola, Padre,"* bringing me back to the present and the problem of Indian injustice. I turned to see an older man waving to me as he walked along one of the cement paths of the small park. It was a lawyer I once met while in language school. I could not remember his name and replied simply, *"Hola, amigo."*

A moment later the thought of consulting with this man struck me. I rose quickly from the bench and glanced around in time to see him enter an office down a side street. I hurried to follow, and as I entered the slat-ventilated swinging doors so common and practical in the warm climate, I saw his shiny brass nameplate: "*Licenciado* Andrés Sánchez." He opened the inner door to my knock, welcomed me with a warm handshake, and invited me in.

He sat not behind his desk but in a cushioned chair beside the one he indicated for me. I began with a customary apology. "I am sorry for walking in on you like this, *Licenciado* Sánchez, and beg your pardon for such an intrusion. . . ."

He interrupted, as is custom, "There is no need to apologize, *Padre*. You are in your house, and I am here only wanting to serve you, and now tell me in what way I can do that."

I continued, "*Licenciado*, I want to know if I can pay you for a small piece of advice."

"I am here as your servant," he said, as he would to anyone of his class, and went on, "and I will not take your money if you don't need much time. What can I do to help?"

I nodded appreciation and began to relate the details of the case, expressing my disturbance about it. He listened with care, and when I was almost finished, he put his hand on my shoulder and leaning close, said softly, "*Padre*, you have to learn: that which speaks in my country is not the person but the payoff." He lowered his voice even more, as if someone might be listening, "What most probably happened in this case, as in so many others, is that the judge's secretary called in the alleged rapist and explained the upcoming charges against him, permitting him the option of paying a certain sum with the assurance that the case would never reach court." He stopped and smiled knowingly. Then as if remembering something important, he again leaned close and said even more cautiously, "The judge never gets involved directly, but of course everyone knows who is running the show."

In my innocence I'm sure I showed some dismay, and again he touched my shoulder and said, "This is common practice, and difficult as it may be, you will have to learn to live with it."

On my way back to San Sebastián I went by the *Casa de los Padres* and talked to several older priests. When I explained what had been happening and what I had been going through, one said rather off-handedly, "There is only one virgin in Guatemala, and that's the Silver Virgin above the altar in Chiantla, and I sometimes have my doubts about her. How do you know that the *Ladino* guy didn't pay the girl? Let it go." I felt some anger but said nothing.

Another said more sympathetically, "I agree with the lawyer. Mind your own business and learn to live with it." I had not resented the advice when it came from the lawyer but found it difficult to accept from a fellow priest.

The other said, "Put your time into teaching doctrine; that's what you're here for. Keep involving yourself in this other stuff and you'll get yourself in trouble." I rejected what he said. I hated the memorization of the doctrine and felt it was foolish to impose it on those who simply wanted to participate in the true religion of God. I knew I would never teach the doctrine. More frustrated than before, I got on my motorcycle and headed back to San Sebastián, not knowing whom to turn to or what to do.

I never learned to live with the system. In the future I would try to get other cases into the judiciary, never succeeding in much more than dashing the hopes of those involved and in frustrating myself. Witnesses forgot. Accused were released without trial. Cases got lost. Except when the wealthy accused the poor: then justice usually came down harshly and effectively. As difficult as it was, I did not lose sight of the fact that I was receiving my true education from day-to-day involvement and could see already that it was going to be a valuable and painful education. I was viewing from the inside a system of inequity.

During my stay at San Sebastián I never heard of Federico Delvalle bothering anyone else. I did not know whether he had learned a lesson or if the people of Mateo's and Lita's village were too frustrated and too afraid to speak up. But each week or so, a few ripe oranges appeared on my doorstep.

4

ANIMALS

Although I was willing to relax my beliefs in order to be open to the ways of the people, it was difficult to consider lowering myself from the position I believed I held as teacher of the word of God. I never thought that an Indian with a second-grade education would be more prepared to speak in the name of God than would the priest he was hired to assist. But as I was to learn, my vision of the word of God was very limited. I found Don Benito more interesting than enlightening when he first said that God speaks to us through ways unknown to the Church. If there was any truth to that, I needed to broaden my outlook beyond what I had studied for nine years as the correct interpretation of God's word as spoken in the Scriptures.

My theology teachers had made clear that the Scriptures must be properly rendered and that the job of presenting them required erudite translators, discriminating interpreters, and authoritarian preservation. But I was beginning to grasp that such an unfeeling approach lacked the simplicity, love, spontaneity, and creativity that our Creator communicates. Perhaps the reasons that the Old Testament, written by men recounting history through myth and teaching through stories, needed official interpretation were to control readers, maintain an organized line of belief, and assure disregard for confusing and un-Godlike passages, such as the conflicting stories of creation, the racism in the belief that a particular people was superior, and the orientation toward violence that condoned ferocious wars.

Thinking of ways Don Benito, my earth teacher, could be an apt interpreter of God's message, I recalled that some of the New Testament authors never heard Christ speak or saw what he did but only put to writing their version of what happened and what He said forty or more years after His death. I also thought about the important role politics played in the formation of the early Church, and that early Church leaders included in the New Testament only those books that followed the party line. When I considered that there were no printed books for fourteen hundred years after Jesus and relatively few for the next several hundred, and that only a small part of the population could read, I wondered why the Master would ever choose the written word as a means of communicating. I permitted myself to think that a loving Creator might have found more creative ways to teach human beings than through the traditionally-believed approach. Perhaps the Master actually chose to leave the story of His words and deeds unrecorded. The written word errs as much as the human mind that interprets it, and as I thought of the wars fought over religion or supported by scriptures or by religious factions I could see a vast capacity for error. I realized that if I could relax my rigid beliefs, I might be able to relate to both God and nature from my heart, an approach that offered possibilities to learn much that my literate Western mode seemed to lack.

Don Benito, a man who listened with his heart, heard God speak in an unusual manner. After many years of practice, I have learned to stop, relax, and listen with my heart, and Benito's teachings are making sense. After two thousand years of righteous confusion, we can perhaps afford to relax a bit in order to listen for the heavenly teaching that comes through nature and to have a marvelous learning experience that the human mind cannot understand, interpret, explain, be right about or make war over.

DON BENITO was much more than the wise and respected sacristan of San Sebastián. To his people he was friend, counselor, and father—perhaps, the "Catholic *chimán*"; to me he was an honest and loving teacher. He was the only Indian of the area whom the *Ladinos* addressed with the title of respect *Don*. Fifty-three years old, five feet tall, broad-shouldered with almost no neck, dark-skinned, black-haired, with shining black eyes, *Don* Benito was slow and gentle in movement but like greased lightning in time of need. I soon found out that with *Don* Benito by my side, I had no need for an experienced pastor to guide me. In fact, no veteran priest could ever have taught me, shared with me, or introduced me to my new work and new culture with the depth and grace of *Don* Benito. He accompanied me to the villages where I would say Mass and administer the sacraments. He made the arrangements for mules, horses, confessions, and visits to the sick. He was altar boy. He was choirmaster. He was guide.

He was also my interpreter. After my sermon in Spanish, Benito would stand before the people and repeat the sermon in the native language. At least, I thought he did, until one day I sat watching the people react to his translation. At times wide-eyed with interest, or chuckling and even laughing, they were obviously not responding to anything I had said.

So I caught on that Benito was an entertaining storyteller who basically made up his own sermons. And the people loved to hear him. At first I was hurt. I was the official teacher, preacher, and representative of God, and it was not my understanding of the teachings of the Church or the word of God that was going out to the people, it was his. I wanted to put a stop to such a practice.

During his next translation I observed carefully. More of the same, and the people not only enjoyed it, they appreciated it. What was I to do? I decided to let it go on for the present, although it was difficult for my ego to accept. After a number of sermons it began to dawn on me that Benito was a real teacher and that I could possibly reach his people if I learned to be his student.

One day during my sermon I glanced over at Benito and saw my very dedicated and hardworking companion asleep. I was distracted and somewhat humiliated. I had become accustomed to seeing such lack of interest among the people: they had no problem reciting their own prayers out loud in their native language during my sermon, or talking among themselves, or nursing the baby, or sleeping, or looking at me with a blank stare. But when, on that day, Benito allegedly translated what I had said without having heard my sermon, I decided it was time to get some answers.

Sitting in the adobe house in which we had just celebrated Mass, being served breakfast of hot freshly-made tortillas and hotly seasoned beans, we were discussing our work. I said, "You know, Benito, I don't think you like my sermons."

He stopped with mouth open, truly surprised. "No, *Padre*," he said sincerely, trying to get the mouthful of food down while feeling the need for an immediate response, "I like your sermons very much. Why do you say such a thing?"

Afraid that he was going to be embarrassed and yet wanting to confront what was going on, I said, "*Don* Benito, what did I preach about today?"

He looked at me for a moment, and then looked down at the tin plate with large rust spots where the enamel paint was chipped. Benito was a truthful man. I knew if I waited, I would learn. I waited. I had another tortilla and waited. He kept eating and said nothing, a deep frown on his brow. The situation began to strike me as humorous. I held back laughter, but as the silence went on, I no longer could. Benito was so relieved that he too began to laugh, and he put both hands to his mouth to keep from spitting out food. "Benito," I said, still laughing, "you don't translate my sermons!"

With that he became serious and began to protest, shaking his head and saying, "No, it's just that . . ." and looked at me still laughing, and knew he was caught. He went on sheepishly, "You're right, *Padre*, I sometimes change the sermon when I think it's important."

"Change it?" I said, still laughing, "You didn't have anything to change today. You slept through the sermon!"

He lowered his head and said, "I know; I was tired."

"You do work hard," I said. "But even when you're awake, you give your own sermon." He did not deny it. Our hostess for the day took away the remaining tortillas, and returned immediately with a piping-hot stack. I reached for a fresh one, rolled a few chiles inside it, and said, "Benito, I want to know what's going on."

He took a long time to finish his tortilla. "Well," he began slowly, "for years I tried to translate the sermons of the *padres* accurately." He hesitated and looked at me to see if it was safe to go on.

I nodded and said again, "I want to know."

"Well, sometimes the people didn't know what I was talking about." He paused to check me out.

"I understand," I said.

"And sometimes they weren't interested," he said, and waited.

"That makes sense to me," I said.

"And sometimes I didn't know what the priest was talking about." I smiled. Then he sat up straight as if gaining courage, and said, "And sometimes the priest didn't know what he was talking about." I nearly choked on my tortilla as I doubled over with laughter. When I had quieted down, he added sincerely and meekly, "And sometimes it didn't interest me."

I was learning. "Thanks, *Don* Benito. It takes some courage to say all that." He used a tortilla to spoon in beans as I thought about his conflict. And then, wondering about my own courage, I asked, "Are my sermons useful to you or interesting to the people?"

He was sipping coffee and seemed to prolong the sips while thinking out an answer. "I'm sorry for what I have done with your sermons, *Padre*." He was beginning to backtrack.

"None of that, *Don* Benito," I interrupted. "Are my sermons of value or interesting?"

More coffee, slowly, and then, "Well, you know my people are very different from you. . . ." He was going to hedge.

I put down my cup and said, "Benito, please tell me. Do you like my sermons?"

"Well, *Padre*," he said, twisting in his chair, "your sermons are very good and interesting, but they don't interest me very much. Not all the time, anyway."

It was my turn to sip coffee slowly. "Is that why you don't translate them?" I asked.

"Oh, I translate them," he said; "I just don't say what you say."

I felt hurt but figured that a priest's ego had to be hurt if he was going to learn from the people he came to teach. I sat wondering, never having expected my education to come in this manner. Yet, knowing there was much more for me to learn and not wanting to miss the opportunity, I asked, "What do you talk about in your translations?"

With that he became enthusiastic. "I talk about the corn, the frijoles, the chile, the sugarcane, but mostly the corn." He saw I approved and continued, "I talk about sickness, worms, pains, constipation, diarrhea, the price of corn, and infections."

I knew I was learning and was willing to let him go on all day. "I talk about work and going to the coast and who you can trust to harvest your corn while you're gone. Sometimes I talk about," he started counting on his fingers, "animals. . . ." He smiled to himself, hesitated as if confused, looked quickly at me, and then looked away somewhat, took a shaky sip of coffee, and went on: "sheep, grazing land, the benefits of shoeing a mule, making tortillas, cutting down a tree, having a baby, drought, and rain." He looked at me as if finished.

"Why did you hesitate when you mentioned the animals?" I asked curiously. He kept eating, only raising his eyes momentarily. He wasn't going to answer. I thought that maybe I was misreading him. I wanted to check it out. I asked again, "Benito, what is it about the animals that you say in your sermons?"

He straightened up his body and surprised me with his somber look. "You may not want to hear about that," he said.

Although I was virtually ignorant of animals and marvelled at the way he could walk up to a loose horse or mule, who would not shy or run as it would with me, I could not imagine anything that he could possibly say about animals that would surprise me. "Benito, you don't have to tell me what it is, but if you are putting it in your sermons, I think I ought to know."

His eyes fixed on mine, so that I almost wanted to look away. I held firm as he said, "You may wish you never asked, and I may wish I never told . . . but, since my people themselves are forgetting. . . ."

My armpits began to sweat. I held to his gaze. There was nothing for me to say. He sat up even higher in his low chair. "There are some truths that have been lost to the Church," he said. I swallowed. I tried to imagine where he was going. I came up with nothing. "I talk to my people about the animals, because God speaks to us through the animals." He paused, never dropping his eyes. "I don't expect you to believe that. You may never understand it. You may not even like it. But that truth is older than the doctrine."

I did not speak. This was strange talk. I wanted to learn more, yet knew this subject was in conflict with one of my fundamental beliefs. "In what way does God speak through the animals?" I finally asked.

Still looking directly at me, he went on, "My people have lost sight of the way God speaks. It is difficult for me to talk to them about this. It is impossible for me to talk to you about it. But perhaps in time, if it is God's will, you will know of what I speak. If what I say is the truth, then few people are hearing the word of God." He relaxed, lowered his eyes, and picked up his half-eaten tortilla. Then, shifting completely, he again raised his eyes, and as if there had been no interruption, added, "And, of course, in my translations I talk about the commandments and sin and the sacraments and the collection. . . ."

I smiled and said, "*Tata* Benito," using for the first time the Indian title of respect and endearment, "I think you are a good sermon-giver. And the people listen. And they laugh. And you teach them." He cast his eyes downward. I went on. "How about if you tell me when I give a good sermon?" He nodded with a slight smile. "And," I added, "you continue to decide whether my sermon deserves a translation or not."

Sometimes after Mass, Benito would say, "Good sermon, *Padre*." That was usually when I talked about the animals, or the corn, or digging a well, or putting a new straw roof on your house. And sometimes after Mass, *Don* Benito would say nothing.

One day I was standing in the plaza watching some boys kick a soccer ball around when Benito approached from the market and introduced me to a spry eighty-two-year-old Indian man named Pablo from the village of Pueblo Viejo. Pablo had a youthful smile and, like a boy, played with rather than leaned on his walking stick. Obviously, Benito cared deeply for Pablo, for he chided jokingly, "You're one of the old holdouts, Pablo. How are you going to get into heaven without the help of the Church?" They laughed together. Then Benito looked at me and added, "Pablo and his woman, and she with her seventy-eight years, do not believe they have to be married in the Church." I shrugged my shoulders.

Pablo laughed and said, "I'm still not sure of her yet. You really can't tell about these women." Benito laughed, turned to me and said, "Pablo wants to talk to you, *Padre*," and left us.

Leaning on his cane, Pablo became serious. "Pardon me for bothering you, *Don Padre*, but I've come to ask you to offer a Mass." With his free hand he reached in his pocket and took out two crumpled *quetzales*, the equivalent of two dollars. "Can you do that for me?"

I felt a little guilty taking his money, but knew I had to learn. "I certainly can. How would it be if I offer Mass tomorrow for your intention?"

"That would be very good, *Padre*. And I want you to do it for rain." I knew it was not yet the rainy season but listened as he went on to explain. "The corn seed has been in the ground too long without water. If we don't get water soon, we could lose the crop."

I found out that an isolated storm was needed well before the season of rain in order to start sprouting the seed. "That's a good idea, *Don* Pablo. I'll offer a Mass tomorrow for rain," I said as I took his two *quetzales*, "and let's see if God hears our prayer." He surprised me by saying, "God always hears our

47

prayers, but sometimes we don't want to hear His answers."

The next morning I offered two Masses. But with many things to remember, I irresponsibly forgot about Pablo's intention. I went about my business of the day until it was time to leave for my visit to the *pueblo* on the mountain, the other *Ladino* center of the parish, San Rafael, for a three o'clock Mass.

Since Benito was afraid to ride on my motorcycle, he strapped the Mass kit on the back, and I set out alone. My Zundap, climbing that mountain, truly proved itself. Over rock, through gullies, around and around and up and up until ragged and happy, I arrived in that proud and desolate little town.

I found *Ladinos* to be very interesting. If they were not involved with Indians, they were in their own way a wonderful people. Although generally astute, sharp, deceptive, street-wise hustlers and tough competitors, in a moment they could become caring, generous, self-sacrificing, loving, and empathic. And as I learned from them and about them, I learned to respect and love them.

I parked my bike in the shade and chatted with a few people in the plaza—really, a pot-holed dirt basketball court. I felt cold chills as I entered the small, dark, damp, dirt-floored church with its ugly statues, dusty paper adornments, and the heavy smell of burning wax. I opened the Mass kit and set up the altar, put on my cassock and slipped the narrow purple stole around my neck, backed into and sat down in the cramped confessional, and listened to people trying to soothe their consciences as they blamed others and made excuses for themselves in their moral gymnastics.

The positive aspect of *Ladino* confessions was that I could understand them, and although confessions were mostly boring, sometimes my ears perked up. Who was being lured into the bushes with whom? Who stole what from whom in order to retaliate for what? Who went to the *chimán* for what? Who fought with whom over what? Confessions covered the spectrum of sin from the extreme of violence on the part of the man who, while in the army, shot seven suspects in the back of the head, to the little boy who peed on the church wall. With the smell in the dank church, I was prepared to give a heavier penance if the child said it was an inside wall. I noticed that I was particularly attentive to the confession of the pretty young married woman who was having many affairs and confessed each eagerly and in some detail. I could rationalize sexual enjoyment from such a confession, for I was administering God's forgiveness.

The confusion about sin and the hypocrisy of confession was not confined to San Rafael. It was universal. I had only to reflect on the seminary, where each day at noon we had examination of conscience. This exercise was to prevent any sin from slipping by and to prevent any pattern of sin from forming. We would carefully search for any dereliction of thought, word, act, or omission that had possibly been committed since the previous noon. Any sins found were to be remembered for the weekly confession. Unless they were mortal sins. Since grievous sins could take one to hell if death should come before confession, and since the reception of any other sacrament was forbidden until they were confessed, mortal sins required immediate attention.

When I first entered the seminary it seemed strange to see people confessing on a daily basis. I wondered what they could be getting into in those hallowed halls, but in time I became aware of the serious sins one can commit in a totally protected and isolated environment. You could, for example, sin by feeling tingling in the genitals while thinking of a woman. Once you got the tingling you could be almost sure that you had consented to an impure thought, had committed a mortal sin, had endangered your soul, and had need of immediate confession. The isolation of the seminary, far from limiting these occasions of sin, perhaps enhances opportunities for them. For tingling comes not necessarily from viewing a female but possibly even more so from her absence; and her absence also intensifies one's attraction to males.

I was surprised to feel the same tingling resulting from conversation with or brushing against one of my prettier male classmates. At first I denied this but then began to see many others behaving as if they were experiencing the same attraction—some of it to me. Since we were taught that any form of sexual response to a person of the same gender was not only a grave sin but also unnatural, this tingling was more difficult to confess. It therefore required wording that would leave the confessor in doubt about the true experience and yet be sufficient for forgiveness. Such hypocrisy never acknowledges that living in an all-male society quickly undermines the theory of the nature of heterosexuality. But those of us who have experienced sexual isolation know that given enough time, social views on gender become irrelevant. My classmate, Josh, who had a very pretty face and body, never lacked company or attention. It was common for students, including myself, and even priests, to place a hand on his shoulder, arm, or knee.

I soon learned that confessions frequently revolved around sexuality or the lack thereof. Wet dreams, a frequent cause for confession, were really a seminarian's blessing, for such an event was the only sexual experience not necessarily considered a mortal sin. If one remained in a dream state until ejaculation began and then awoke, he could have that delightful experience, which by then was beyond control, without offending against God. But if one in any way encouraged it, or in waking up willfully took enjoyment in it, he had committed a mortal sin. Such an involuntary, delightful experience could therefore turn easily into dismay or trauma. In the Catholic Church the precarious line between acceptable enjoyment and destructive sin is so narrow that frequent confession is absolutely necessary to alleviate resulting doubts and guilt. And we who have such daily experiences and doubts, and who by environment and training are inclined not only to homosexuality but to dysfunctional sexuality, are ordained to be the teachers and judges of sexual morality. And I, a product of the same, was sitting uncomfortably in a cramped confessional in San Rafael, trying to deal with my own experience and the result of centuries of sexually dysfunctional teaching.

On that day I celebrated Mass and did my usual sacramental routine without Benito's help and became aware of how much he attended to on such a visit. I did a few baptisms and one sick call, then hung around talking with people and playing a little basketball with the youngsters. It was close to dusk when I said good-bye, climbed on the Zundap, and headed down the mountain.

About a third of the way down I was surprised to see the sky darken suddenly and soon open its floodgates and pour forth rain. It came down in torrents. I was drenched immediately. The road turned quickly to mud, leaving no possibility of a return that day to the *pueblo* of San Rafael. Downhill I could maintain momentum and had to concentrate only on keeping the bike from slipping off what was being transformed from a rough path into a hazardous mountainside. Small mudslides that washed across the remains of the road would on level ground have obstructed passing but were made maneuverable by the steep decline.

As I reached the bottom of the mountain, the downpour let up as quickly as it had started, but night had set in. I was exhausted and relieved when my headlight picked up the flat, level stretch of the Panamerican Highway. I swung onto its slippery, unpaved surface and settled back on the seat, thinking it would be a relatively smooth ride back to the *convento*. I had just shifted into high when the beam of my headlight reflected off of a large mudslide reaching clear across the highway. The rain had brought down soil loosened by earthquakes since the last rainy season. I could not tell how deep it was, nor could I see to the other side of it. I had to make a quick decision. I shifted down to second and poured on the gas.

As I entered the slide, the powerful impact nearly threw me, but the bike stayed upright, and I hung on, keeping the gas on full. With mud splashing everywhere, I managed to shift down again and plowed on for a formidable thirty feet—where the motor died, and the bike came to a halt with mud up to its axles.

I stepped off into the knee-deep slime that held the bike upright and shut off the headlamp to look for any light but saw neither a candle nor a star. I felt helpless in the unusual darkness with even the awesome mountain to my left invisible and the drop to the raging river at my right only a feeling and a sound. I turned the light on and with all my strength tried to pull the bike out of the mud by its front wheel. It would not budge.

The closest help was my distant home-base, San Sebastián. I had two options: I could spend the night with the bike and worry *Don* Benito, or I could take the long walk to the *pueblo* and leave the Mass kit and bike prey to anyone in the area. I chose to walk.

Four hours later, covered with mud and sweat, I turned up the little hill into town. A candle in the *convento* window told me *Don* Benito was waiting up. As he hugged me, he told of his fear of the worst and the frustration of knowing nothing and being unable to do anything. Jaime, the town drunk, had waited up with him and now showed caring delight in seeing me. He was as sober as I had ever seen him. Both offered eagerly to return to free my machine. So, armed with flashlights, we trudged off, arriving at the slide in less than two hours' time. We dragged and carried the bike out of the mud, and the motor kicked over immediately. The two *amigos* told me to go ahead, saying that they did not mind walking back together. My return trip was slippery but uneventful. Totally exhausted, I dropped my muddy clothes in the patio and went to bed.

Almost asleep, I suddenly sat up, recalling old Pablo's Mass intention. I had not remembered to celebrate his Mass for rain. I became upset, not only because I had broken an agreement for which he had paid me but also because I wanted to take some responsibility for ending the drought. I tried to convince myself that I had had a role in ending it, even though I had completely forgotten the Mass, but I went to sleep knowing that if anyone had influenced the ending of the drought, it was Pablo.

When I got up the next day, there sitting on the ground outside my house awaiting me was Pablo. As I opened the door he jumped up and embraced me and in rapid-fire speech said, "Thank you, *Padrecito*, for bringing the rain. God does hear your prayers. Our crops will be good. The corn will grow strong." Dancing around without the use of his walking stick, he proclaimed, "I am ready to enter the Church, marry my woman, and receive the sacraments. I want to be blessed by you. You are a priest of God."

I was laughing and embracing him, believing a little that I deserved the acknowledgement and tempted seriously to keep secret what had happened. But it not only seemed appropriate to tell him the truth, I thought it would add to the joy of the moment.

"*Don* Pablo, please sit down with me." He eagerly sat on the step beside me with his hand on my thigh and looked at me with a bliss seen in the faces of children and in the paintings of the masters. I put my hand on his, and said, "Pablito, I celebrated three Masses yesterday, and in each I forgot your intention for rain."

"That's fine, *Padrecito*, really fine. You know what to do. Our Father has heard your request. You know how to talk to God."

"Pablo, stop," I said strongly. "I want you to hear me. Listen to me." He sat still, a look of dismay on his face. "I did not offer Mass for rain. I forgot your intention. I am going to give you your two *quetzales* back. Do you understand?"

"Yes. Of course. I understand." He stood up and began to move around, stamping his feet like an animal dancer in a native religious ceremony. Smiling broadly he chuckled, "You didn't offer my Mass for rain. That is fine. Our Father heard you anyway. I would never take the money. I am grateful to you and Our Father." He stopped moving and joined his hands and bowed his head as if in prayer. "It was a miracle, *Padrecito*. I know God has blessed us. I want to join the Church."

So Pablo went about telling everyone how I had brought the miracle of rain, and Benito started visiting Pablo's rancho to teach him and his woman the doctrine in preparation for receiving the sacraments. A month later two saddle mules were brought to the *convento* to carry Benito and me to the house of Pablo for the wedding ceremony. Arriving at the *ranchito* I became spectator and victim of the traditional wedding fireworks. My mule, frightened by the exploding skyrockets, jumped and lurched and pulled at the bit as the people who had gathered for the occasion howled with laughter, watching me one moment trying only to stay in the saddle and the next moment trying to get down, as Benito sat calmly on his unmoved mule. Benito, holding back his own laughter, finally stepped down from his mule and took the bridle of my animal in his hand, thus bringing the incident to a happy end and initiating the ceremony. Little girls and young women presented me with handfuls of wild flowers. Each person in turn bowed his or her head, waiting for me to touch it with my hand, a traditional sign of submission as well as a request for a blessing—or maybe both are the same.

Pablo and Jacinta, king and queen for a day, were in their glory. Pablo gave me a warm *abrazo*. Jacinta bowed her head. I put my hand on it, and then took her hand and touched it to my forehead, wanting the blessing of such a wise and good soul. They welcomed me to their home of sticks and mud. It was unusually large—three rooms, now filled with smoke from the cook-fires on which the tamales were being readied for the celebration.

As Benito prepared the makeshift altar set in the open patio surrounded by trees, I heard the sinless first confessions of Pablo and Jacinta. We followed with Mass amid floral and pine branch decorations, the ground covered with fresh pine needles. In my sermon, I told about Pablo's asking me to offer Mass for rain, and about my forgetting to do it. I talked about Pablo's belief in God's goodness and said that God had responded with rain. As I talked I looked at my wise old teacher, Benito, smiling and nodding approvingly.

In the marriage ceremony it seemed ironic to ask this beautiful couple who had married themselves more than a half century before if they would take the marriage vows. If ever anyone was committed 'til death did them part, it was these two. I got a sense of their love, devotion, and commitment and felt shame at the implication that they had lived in sin.

After Mass the marimba played, and we had a magnificent feast with delicious tamales, tortillas, coffee, and orange juice. Children, grandchildren, great grandchildren, and great great grandchildren joined the festivities on one of the happiest days of my life.

A few weeks later Don Pablo was again at the *convento* door. He was leaning heavily on his walking stick and had tears in his eyes. "*Padrecito*, come to my *ranchito*. My Jacinta is dying. She is ready to meet our Father. Please come and give her your final blessing."

We walked along the river bank, speaking very little. Pablo was breathing deeply. We walked slowly. It was a warm morning. We rested several times in the shade of trees. At one point he stopped, lifted his cane in the direction of a green field of corn stalks, and said proudly, "That was a great rain, *Padre*."

Jacinta was lying on a mat on the dirt floor in the smoke-filled room. She had lost her eyesight and was very weak. I knelt beside her. She did not stir. I lifted her hand gently and put it on my forehead. "*Padrecito*," she said. Jacinta died a few days later. Pablo in his loneliness came to visit me often.

5

RESPONSIBILITY

As a presidential advisor might rationalize the benefits of illegal acts in carrying out presidential policy, as an elected politician might support a corrupt system that grants him power for effecting possible good, as a policeman might maintain allegiance to unethical superiors who administer his authority to guard and protect, so did I unquestioningly support a controlling hierarchy that declared me the chosen of God, the guardian of truth and the agent of eternal happiness. It is time for a reevaluation of personal participation in all structures at all levels. The situation of the world and the condition of the human race no longer permits an immature and unprincipled approach of blind obedience and devout submission despite compensation or promised rewards.

Pretend for a moment that you are part of the Church through which you believe God directs His work. And imagine that you among all God's people are chosen for the special and highest purpose of being His priest in this Church, to represent Him, to teach His truths as you are convinced He intends, to bring His Son to earth and make Him available to be consumed by those you deem worthy, to forgive any and all sins or offenses, and to exercise the option of selecting who deserves absolution. Would you not, like the policeman or the soldier, devoutly support the structure that claims to channel such power to you?

And would not unconditional support for ranking personnel and self-serving policy be expected in return for such an exalted position? We have become so susceptible and acquiescent to structures and organizations that it seems normal to forget personal responsibility and to surrender to those who reward us and to those who, by their position, supposedly know better.

Coming from a lifetime of immersion in the structure of the Church, I lacked the realization that while serving the Church as a God-sent teacher, I could never deal realistically with the life problems of God's children. Believing that I was chosen for the priesthood by God and appointed and directed by a Christ-founded structure, I had a mandate to teach and preach God's truth, to decide when and for whom His Son would come to earth, to forgive or not forgive the transgressions of the widow or the rapes, murders and plunders of the warrior, to admit to the fold the souls of infants incapable of sharing in the light of God, to join in matrimony those who otherwise would live in sin, to open heaven's gates to those leaving the earth. I was right. I was important. And I was in charge. But in taking such a lofty position, I only had a longer way to come down—just as in the time of Jesus when the priests' naive and arrogant beliefs led only to pride and wrongful choices. But I would find that, through my experiences with the Guatemalan people, I could create a rebirth of belief that would lead to health, healing, responsible freedom and true spirituality.

BENITO HUNG MY HEAVILY PACKED saddlebags over the rear fender of the bike, taking a long time to buckle them. I appreciated having the few extra minutes before we had to say goodbye. Finished, he stood upright, brushed his hands together as he always did, smiled his beautiful boyish smile, as I knew he would, and looked at me with moist eyes— as I had hoped he wouldn't. Not that I didn't want his affection and appreciation: I just didn't know what to do or how to act when saying goodbye.

We shook hands. In that moment, I realized that I had never

before known what it was to have a home or be close to someone. I had been unaware that in our day-by-day involvement for three months we had built such a strong bond. I had never suspected that in a town completely foreign to me I would find a home, that in an Indian with a second-grade education I would find a friend, and that in an illiterate and poor people with a language I couldn't understand and a culture I could never share I would find love. It was time to move on, and I didn't want to go. "Well, *Tata* Benito," I said, hoping I wouldn't choke up, "these three months have been the most wonderful of my life." I began to choke up and had to force myself to go on, "and you have been my greatest friend and teacher." We were holding our hands clasped together.

Benito found it much easier to speak. "These days have been good, and you have been my *padre*, not my student." We stood together. I could find no more words, and I was afraid to look into his eyes. He sensed my predicament, squeezed my hands slightly, and added, "But I must say, you have learned much in your time here." I hugged him. He wrapped me in his short, powerful arms, nearly picking me off the ground. I knew I had to say goodbye.

"*Adiós, mi tata.*"

"*Adiós, mi padre.*"

Opening up the throttle as I entered the Panamerican Highway, I let the wind blow my tears away. I tried to detach myself by thinking of the note I had received from Bishop Tex a week before, sending me for the next three months to the town of Malacatancito. Tex added that I had done a good job at San Sebastián. I appreciated the words, even though he didn't know if I had done anything more than send him monthly reports on numbers of baptisms, marriages, confessions, and communions, along with twenty-five per cent of the stipend.

I felt reckless, leaning the bike over on the big curves and knowing that a little sand could send it down at any moment, but I needed something frivolous to distract me. Only pure habit kept my eyes focused immediately ahead for trouble spots on the road while my mind kept trying to focus immediately behind. I soon slowed down and pulled off the hard-packed Panamerican onto the soft sand road leading through the barren outskirts of the small *pueblo* of Malacatancito. With the dry, soft grains enveloping the tires, I looked in the distance and viewed, with some anxiety, the church steeple standing watch over the small town.

The *pueblo* was quiet, seemingly abandoned, as I rambled down the narrow picture-postcard lanes between whitewashed adobe houses with one window and one door and built to the edge of the street. As I approached the center of town, women in aprons, having heard the motorcycle engine roaring in first gear, began appearing in doorways. Some looked shy, turning their faces to the side as if to hide, but the more venturesome waved or smiled or mouthed *"Buenos días."* Skinny dogs began to bark away their laziness and chase the bike as the *pueblo* seemed to awake from siesta.

I slowly passed the large, stark colonial church, the glaring sun reflecting off its white exterior, one door of the portico open to the dark interior's inviting coolness. As I swung the bike into the large square patio beside the church, the door of the *convento* opened, and I faced the middle-aged, dark-skinned, dimpled cook with a long black braid down her back, eager to tell me her name (Clarita) along with all else that she considered important about herself and the priests she had attended. When she finally paused, I told her how welcomed I felt, thanked her for the introduction, and excused myself to begin looking around the extensive structures.

The school was not functioning. I was glad it had closed down. Clarita told the unfortunate story of the *padre* having built the school exceptionally large in order to compete with the public school and to accommodate the students his academically superior school would draw. She said that as a result, the public school nearly shut down, with parents choosing to send their children to the more prestigious parochial school. All had been fine until the *padre* raised the nominal tuition, and attendance fell off rapidly. She said that organizing the public school and convincing the children to go back to it again was a problem.

I began to walk around the compound, and if I had not heard his whistle as I turned a corner I would have bumped into Pancho. Big smile, twenty years old, muscular, light-skinned, with curly black hair, Pancho had a sixth-grade education, lived with his mother in the *pueblo*, and was paid five dollars a week for being sacristan and taking care of the church and grounds. Having met the parish staff, I was ready for work.

The next day, Saturday, many people arrived from the villages. Most of them wanted to confess and did so in Spanish. Generally, as with my earlier parishioners, they confessed what seemed like habitual and inconsequential behavior while probably denying anything serious that might be considered a sin— as with a young man who confessed, "I disobeyed my mother"; and in my fervor, wanting to help him clarify and see if an offense was committed, I asked, "In what way did you disobey her?"

"She told me not to sleep with my sister," he answered. As I began to explain that this was a serious offense and not one of simple disobedience, I realized that he already knew that, and he did not want to hear what I had to say. Confession was a way of "fooling God" and fooling oneself in order to make destructive behavior acceptable.

Many people from the outlying areas stood around the patio enjoying their major social event of the week. Talking with them, I had my first opportunity to experience the difference between village *Ladinos* and *pueblo Ladinos*, appreciating the goodness, simplicity and sincerity of the village people as they talked about life.

Jaime, an old man from Agua Caliente, waited some time to talk to me, and then cordially invited me to visit his village. I appreciated the invitation and felt such a trip would be good for me. He agreed to bring a horse for me early Wednesday. When the knock came at the door that morning, I had been up for some time, rushing to prepare my suitcase of personal belongings and leaving time for reading the psalms and prayers of the Holy Office. If done rapidly, this reading that the priest was obliged to do daily under pain of mortal sin took about an hour. As I read the psalms that day, I felt distracted and irritated by the fact that I had to read them or I would be offending God. I knew that the Church prohibited any questioning of the doctrine of sin. I also knew that if I were to try to straighten sin out with the people, I had to first do so with myself. Finished with the Holy Office for that day, I made an unusual decision: I terminated compulsory reading for life. It was a very important decision, yet I surprised myself at the ease with which I made it. I felt no guilt but rather an unusual sense of freedom. In the future I read the psalms only because I chose to, usually finding them rewarding and meaningful, realizing that laws about reading the psalms were designed to control priests and had nothing to do with pleasing or displeasing God.

Interrupting my reveries, old Jaime greeted me reverently, removing his hat and bowing his head, saying, "It is my honor to assist the holy *padre*." He took my suitcase and the satchel of liturgical vestments that Pancho had prepared and put them in a large net, to which he tied both ends of a leather strap. He then helped me onto the horse and handed me a *chicote*, or leather whip. Squatting down in front of the net, he took off his hat with one hand, put the leather strap across his forehead with the other, and stood up carefully, hoisting the netted luggage slowly onto his back. Hat again on head, body bent way forward so that the weight rested on his back, Jaime stretched his neck to look up at me and smile. "Ready?" he asked.

I looked down at the simple and beautiful man, his big smile showing most teeth missing, face wrinkled from sun and age, humbling himself in order to honor the *padre*. I answered, "Ready," wondering how I could ever be ready for such an experience.

We made our way slowly and almost silently up and down gently rolling hills and through cool pine forests, winding around mammoth rock formations, crossing a small swift clear stream with its bed of round stones slipping away under the horse's hoofs. Ahead of us big, puffy, billowing white clouds gradually moved across a deep blue sky. While I thought I could not contain more beauty, we dipped into a green meadow valley, and in that incredible scene I found the origin of the name of the village and my first sight and smell of a sulphur hot spring. I stepped from the horse knowing I was in a special place. Jaime, having backed against a large boulder to free himself of his cargo, danced around as I investigated the hot water bubbling up from the earth. He said in a singsong voice, "Many people come here for all kinds of cures."

"And do they get healed?" I asked

"Many do and many don't," he answered confidently.

"And what gets healed most?" I asked.

"Aches and pains and sores. And sometimes cancer," he said mopping the sweat from his brow and stepping beside me.

"I have nothing to heal at this time, Jaime, but I believe that the hot mineral water would be healing." As I squatted down beside the pool I asked myself how much influence the water would have on healing and how much influence belief in the water would have. I knew healing would be an important part of my life and wondered if there could ever be any healing or any pure experience that was not influenced by belief. I casually put my hand in the water and immediately pulled it back with a howl, trying to shake the water from it, to the snickering of old Jaime. When my hand cooled, I reached in again and quickly pulled out a small stone, dropping it at my feet, and again shook my hand vigorously. I turned to Jaime and said, "Anyone who is willing to put up with the stench and the temperature of this water deserves to be healed."

He laughed. "Generally we scoop the water out, and after it cools we immerse the ill part of the body in it, or we soak cloths in it and, after they cool slightly, apply them to the body."

Later at Mass, my mind still on the experience of the waters, I would ask Jesus, the Healer, that I might contribute to the healing of His people.

Back on the trail, we arrived shortly at the village to find a small group of people waiting. As I got down from the horse the first person to greet me was a rather dignified middle-aged man dressed in particularly clean work clothes and wearing a rosary around his neck. He put his hand out to me. I extended mine, which he took in both his hands. I could feel the sharp, cracked skin as his fingers momentarily massaged mine into a position where we fit comfortably together. This was no ordinary handshake. I looked into his eyes and saw a gleam as he took control of submitting himself and began to lower his head for the act that I knew had to follow. The man kissed my hand reverently.

Unclear about the experience, I accepted the honor even though the closeness was difficult. I certainly could not handle more than a kiss on the hand, and even that I needed to stop, because such a demonstration of that kind of respect was dangerous. It was dangerous for the person elevated, for he might believe himself superior and deserving of others' submission and might in time expect and even require such deprecation, as he came to believe that others were less worthy than he. I knew the custom of hand-kissing had been introduced by the early Spanish missionaries. I wondered what Christ would do in these circumstances. If I could get back to that, I knew I would act appropriately. Then I thought I knew. I lowered my head and raised the man's hand to my mouth and pressed my lips to the rough and scratched skin. This was my brother. I stood erect and looked hesitantly into his eyes. Neither of us spoke. As his eyes became moist, he haltingly said, "*Gracias, Padre*, no one has ever before kissed my hand."

I wasn't sure what to say, so I followed his lead. "Thank you, *Señor*. No one has ever before kissed my hand. You have taught me a lesson."

Back at the parish, the week ground on without much activity. On Sunday I was to celebrate the usual three Masses in the old colonial church, each with confessions, communions, and a sermon, that day preaching on the lessons gained from sickness as well as from healing. By afternoon I had finished two Masses, the baptisms, and the blessings of sacred objects, had given a talk to the catechists, and had chatted with the people who came in from the distant villages. After a late lunch, I was relaxing before the activities of the evening Mass. Walking around the compound, never tiring of examining the beauty of adobe structures, I heard a noise in the parish hall. I opened the door and looked inside, but with the window shutters closed I could not see much. I pushed the door further and felt it bump against something. I stepped in and looked behind the door. My eyes, now somewhat accustomed to the darkness, made out the form of a man. I stooped quickly and touched him on the shoulder. The voice of Pancho, the sacristan, said, *"Hola, Padre."* I knelt down beside him, thinking he must be hurt. But then the familiar odor reached me, and my eyes focused on the bottle.

"Come on, Pancho, get up," I said, standing up myself and stepping back to give him room as he tried to struggle to his knees. "Let me have that," I said as I took the bottle from his hand and set it on the floor. "Come on, get up," I said, putting my hand under his arm to lift him. But he was heavy and incapable of standing on his own. I eased him back to the floor, picked up the bottle, and stepped outside. I didn't know what to do. I poured the *aguardiente* into the dirt and continued my walk.

I had to be up to the situation and show that I was a competent substitute pastor, but I had never before dealt with drunkenness. I felt let down by Pancho and embarrassed by his behavior. It seemed important to show my displeasure and make an example, so I finally concluded that I had to let him go and told him so when, disheveled, he appeared before the evening Mass. He said nothing but simply lowered his head and walked away.

I kept thinking of him during confessions. I was angry. He had disappointed me and had been a poor example to the people. I could not concentrate during the Mass. The next morning he was standing outside my room. He stepped forward as I came out, saying, "Padre, I'm sorry for what I did yesterday."

I hesitated, but decided I had to follow my plan. "I cannot let you work for the Church, Pancho. Your behavior is unacceptable." His jaw fell. He didn't think I would do it. I handed him an envelope. "This is your pay and your severance. I hope you do well, Pancho." Saying nothing, he took the envelope and walked slowly away. I felt cold and lonely.

Clarita the cook, who missed nothing, was of course witness to this. It did not take long for the whole town to hear the news. Everyone I spoke to that day had some comment about Pancho. Most were sympathetic to him. I did not like that. I wanted people to support me and recognize that I as a priest had taken the right action.

That night in my room, writing in my journal, I felt sorry for myself. Most people disapproved of what I had done. There was no one to do Pancho's work. I began realizing I would have a hard time replacing him, finding someone literate and capable, and that even if I did the people would not approve of a replacement's taking the job too soon. I was amazed that they would side with the sacristan rather than the priest.

By the following day my thoughts were changing toward Pancho. That night in my journal I wrote quite differently. I wrote that I had made a mistake, that I had failed to talk to him or inquire about his possible personal problems but had condemned him for something that priests did regularly and were not criticized for as long as it was done privately. I had given a sermon on healing but had never considered Pancho's possible sickness or need to heal.

I had been concerned only with the schedule and the scandal. I had taken his behavior personally. My disciplinary training had come through strong—but a big part of it was that I also wanted to show who was in charge. I had pretended that I was holding up the morality of the Church as I stood on my own pride—something I disliked very much in other priests.

The next day I sent for Pancho. He would not come. He was humiliated and had lost face. I heard later that he left the *pueblo*. I never saw Pancho again, never communicated the irresponsibility of my action, never thanked him for an important lesson. It was difficult to manage without him, but I continued to visit the villages and administer thousands of sacraments until my three months were up.

I read the Bishop's note excitedly: I was to go for six months to Jacaltenango, a parish that would offer another and different challenge. Its large, isolated Indian *pueblo* was the center of an extensive network of people speaking several different languages. Because of its size and the number of its programs, the parish maintained three priests and a number of Maryknoll Sisters—more personnel than any other parish. The latter staffed and ran a parochial school and a hospital. This assignment presented my first opportunity of working with nuns and with other priests.

Maryknoll priests, frequently working in desolate or difficult areas, took pride in referring to themselves as the "shock troops" of the Church. The areas I had been in so far, although fitting the "shock-troop" description, had been less isolated than the place I was going. We young missionaries needed confirmation of our manliness through the experience of the hardships and challenges that veteran "shock troopers" traditionally talked about. "Jacal" had the reputation of testing one's stalwartness.

After a four-hour horseback ride I came over the top of a mountain and could see Jacaltenango way below in a valley of unending straw-roofed huts interspersed with fields of corn and sugarcane and framed partly by the very blue Rio Azul. The large white church and its spacious compound occupied the center of the picture. As I descended into town, people were everywhere; men with hoes and machetes, women with water jugs on their heads, children carrying children, and children carrying firewood. All were Indian. Many bowed their heads as I passed, saying *Buenas tardes* and continuing on their way.

Father Denny, the person primarily responsible for the construction of the hospital and the pastor of Jacaltenango—my first boss—stepped out of the rectory, gave me a warm welcome, and showed me around the physical plant. He also told me I would be making long trips. It was not unusual in Jacaltenango to make a two-week horseback trip, visiting from one to three villages a day.

My chief memory of those visits and of that parish was hearing confessions. The people were trained to confess regularly and often. Being zealous and wanting to conform, I would sit for many hours in the cramped, dark wooden box trying to remain focussed as people mumbled and rambled in several different languages. I had no idea what they were saying or whether they knew what a sin was. And I could not stop wondering about the doctrine on forgiveness of sins and questioning the importance of what I was doing. Several times I fell asleep during a lengthy confession. Once when my snoring jolted me awake, I turned to the penitent, an elderly woman, and said

"*Perdóname.*" She said probably the one word she knew in Spanish, "*Gracias,*" made the sign of the cross, kissed her rosary beads, and left. No penance or absolution was needed.

With person after person I would concentrate on the humming sound of indistinguishable words spoken from rote—something that may have had little to do with the dogma of penance but in the mind of the person had something to do with communicating to God. Many were willing to go on endlessly. So I would wait for a pause, a sign that they might have finished, although I never knew, because if I asked, my question would add to the confusion. Then I would give a penance and absolution, wondering whether I was serving the people.

So I visited village after village and heard confession after confession and gave communion after communion. And as I kept hearing confessions and distributing communion and putting mileage on horses, I kept questioning whether anyone's life was improving. I knew that theologically it was all correct, yet it seemed that I was simply part of the big status quo and that I could go on that way for a lifetime without anything's being changed. And I realized that a priest could be held indefinitely in that situation by the simple acknowledgment of his selfless and godly labors. I gained more insight into the importance of the monthly sacramental report: it gave the bishop his share of the income, but more than that, the numbers gave the priest validation of his own importance.

I consoled myself with the thought that I might soon have my own parish, where I would not simply commit time to the routine administration of the sacraments but would involve myself in projects and programs that would deal with my own perception of the needs of the people. Meanwhile, I felt that I was papering over their needs with prayers and blessings and reinforcing their resignation to a life of poverty, frequent sickness, and early death.

I often observed the Sisters working in the hospital, knowing that in their long hours under difficult conditions they were making a real and needed contribution, and I was jealous. Thousands of sacraments later I was released from the routine of Jacal by the return from vacation of the second priest. I said goodbye to the nuns, the priests, and the many employees of the parish and made my way to the city of Huehuetenango and the office of Bishop Tex for my new assignment.

Sitting in his bishop's robes, chomping on his cigar, Tex leaned back in his chair and told me I had done a great job in Jacaltenango. I appreciated his acknowledgement; I knew I had worked hard and conformed completely. Tex didn't ask for thoughts, ideas, or feedback. He simply said, "Now as regards to your next assignment: I am establishing a new parish in La Democracia." He stopped, puffed on his cigar, spun in his chair so as not to blow the smoke in my face, and remained silent. I jumped with enthusiasm at the thought of starting a completely new parish and of being released from ties with existing programs of doctrine, parish school, repetitious administration of the sacraments, or caring for monuments of previous pastors. Tex spun his chair back to me, cleared his throat of some phlegm, excused himself, and went on in a monotone voice. "So I am sending Father Joe to the new parish, and you will take his place as the permanent pastor of La Libertad."

I would have my own parish. Not a new parish, but at least my own. "Thanks very much, Tex," I said trying to appear calm. Wanting to say something bright and meaningful, I added, "I hope the name Liberty will have some significance for me." Removing the cigar from his mouth he looked at me over his glasses, then turned to his desk and shuffled a few papers. Taking that as a signal that we were finished, I hesitantly stood up, saying, "I guess I'll start getting myself ready. . . ."

"Oh. Yes," he said swinging his chair back to me and extending his large, big-knuckled hand. "Good luck, Art. And listen . . . , I don't think Joe has done anything with that parish. I hope you'll be able to." He winked as if he knew that I understood, then added with a chuckle, "And don't forget to send in your monthly sacramental report."

6
SEX

Although theologians may deny it, any casual observer knows that the fundamental and principal sins in Catholicism revolve around sexuality. In my youthful attempt to live devoutly and avoid sexual contamination, I not only developed a fear of human closeness that threw my life out of balance, I distracted myself from real growth. Confronted with this issue in La Libertad, I began a self-examination that led me to realize that an unconscious motive in my entering the protective cover of the celibate priesthood was fear of closeness, sexuality, and intimacy. I began to think that possibly this motive was common among priests.

Historically, and allegedly on divine mandate, the Church is controlled totally by men, and men who presumably have no sexual experience. Knowing this phenomenon had to relate to the Church's approach to sexuality, I asked myself if men were historically afraid of women and thus of relating to them intimately. If that were so, and we as men were too proud to be truthful, might not some of us choose celibacy and then cover ourselves by proclaiming the enduring danger of sex?

Over the years I have continued to observe fear of intimacy in myself and other men. With today's perspective, I find the issue to be one of attempted dominance. I think that the early impairment of emotional experience in boys by teaching them to be "men" leads us to the need to control our relationships and environment in order to avoid the forbidden and thus unpracticed and threatening feelings of fear as well as other emotions. A deeply ingrained pattern that I call the "male dominance syndrome" causes general and pervasive defensiveness or need to control, manifested principally in the primary relationship, the relationship most apt to provoke feelings. This dominance also manifests itself in the surrounding structure or environment, particularly if a primary relationship is not permitted.

The unfortunate result for all of us is that we train males from an early age to inhibit closeness, suppress sadness and fear, and exclude love. Although we find it difficult to admit, we as men are afraid of women, who generally undergo a different cultural training, and we are afraid of intimacy, which brings up all the forbidden emotions. Because the fear of our own emotions drives us to assert control, we have come to dominate all institutions of society, even those that claim a divine mandate. It makes sense that the male-dominated Church in its drive for control would exclude from the Bible the works of the female scriptural writers and the female disciples of Christ and so today prohibit women priests and members of the hierarchy.

Another sad result of male dominance in Catholicism is a high incidence of pedophilia among priests and of incest among the laity. Because of the Church's propensity to secrecy and cover-up, accurate figures of clerical pedophilia are unavailable. Nuns studying the issue of incest, however, are finding that a high percentage of members of female religious orders are incest victims.

How dangerous it is for individuals and society when those directing our institutions are unable to permit feelings, empathy, and compassion and are ruling out of their self-protective fear! A church of the people would, in contrast, educate its members about the dangers of perpetuating this dominance, which may be our basic human problem. The resolution of the problem will not, however, come from the ecclesiastical structure. If clerics shared honestly and equally with women, they *would not only threaten their position of control and expose themselves to their dreaded natural feelings but would place the institutionalized Church at risk.*

Of course, all this analysis is hindsight, which I can lay out for you from my present role as psychotherapist. In the days when I worked as a priest among Guatemalans, I was just getting an inkling of what it meant to be both a priest and a man.

A RETURN VISIT to the *Casa de los Padres* made a welcome opportunity for relaxation and conversation as well as for the best meal in town. Sítting at dinner with several older priests, I discussed my new assignment and gathered information about La Libertad. Those I talked to considered it a *Ladino* parish, despite large pockets of Indians, in that most people of the area were either of mixed blood or had taken on western dress and spoke Spanish. The town perched on a mountain at the end of a steep, crude road the width of a tractor blade, one that lacked only a bridge across a river to connect to the Panamerican Highway. The message came clearly: my motorcycle had lost its usefulness.

The next day I went to the Huehuetenango Airport for the flight to Guatemala City. The solitary salesman-owner of the country's only Toyota agency convinced me quickly of what I wanted. "This all-terrain vehicle goes virtually anywhere, up steep climbs, over rocks, through mud and water." So with the remaining money given me at ordination, I purchased a sturdy, four-wheel-drive Land Cruiser, tan with a cream roof—the only color available.

With pride and satisfaction I drove through the city testing out the Toyota while picking up supplies. I was enjoying the manicured shrubbery, colorful flowers, exquisite homes and mansions of the city's main avenue, when suddenly everything changed. As if I'd blinked and missed their arrival, I saw soldiers in battle gear jumping from trucks and lining the sidewalks, and armored vehicles taking up positions near a hill. A slow-moving personnel carrier rumbled along, covered with soldiers in uniform, berets on their heads and in their hands automatic rifles pointing clumsily in all directions. Shooting erupted in the distance, but traffic continued to move and business seemed to proceed as usual. I was concerned but didn't know what to do. I followed my instinct and drove close to the hill and parked. I stood alone by the Land Cruiser as a large helicopter circled. A soldier in camouflage coveralls stood with legs spread, leaning out its open doorway, a strap around his waist securing him to the frame. As the dark green chopper tilted slightly to one side, tightening its circle, the soldier began spraying the hilltop with machine gun fire. I pushed my trembling hands into my pockets and felt sick to my stomach. I was so caught up in the action and wondering what was going on that I jumped when someone spoke at my side.

A slim, well-built man in a light brown, three-piece suit stepped close as he pulled open his lapel and flashed a police badge. He was abrupt and stern as he asked what I was doing and, without waiting for a response, peered into the back of the vehicle. He moved fast, reaching into the passenger window, opening the glove compartment and pulling its few articles to the floor. I followed him, and when he turned to me I held out my license, saying, "I am a Catholic priest visiting from Huehuetenango." He smiled and nodded, let out a sigh, and seemed to relax. He handed me my license, leaned an elbow on the roof of the car and, looking up at the helicopter, said, "You're nervous, *Padre*."

"I have never before seen anything like this," I answered, attempting to be nonchalant.

"Then you should see a real battle," he said with a smile. "We call this a cleaning detail."

I tried to smile but couldn't. I wanted to know who these people were that were being cleaned up. Trying to appear calm, I asked, "Who are they?"

"Who, them?" he asked, pointing with his chin towards the hill. "They call themselves revolutionaries. But they are nothing more than dogs, malcontents and criminals." He spat contemptuously to the ground, part of the spit landing on his highly polished shoe.

My stomach was tight. I had trouble breathing. I knew that this was the place for a priest. The knot in my stomach grew as I felt an increasing urge to speak. I tried to hesitate, to stifle words that just kept coming. "Excuse the question, *Señor*," I said, trying to control the tremor in my voice. He shook his head indicating he was listening, but he did not look at me. I went on, "but do you think I could go into the area?"

He kept his eyes on the departing helicopter and said with a slight laugh, "What in God's name would you do in there?"

The knot tightened again as I answered flatly, "Attend to the wounded."

"*Padre*," he said, turning and patting my arm, "we try to leave no wounded. And besides, this work is none of your business." He didn't wait for a response but began walking away.

I leaned on the fender, confused, wondering about the pain and fear of the wounded, curious as to what they were trying to accomplish. I was like a child, unprepared for any kind of conflict. Nothing concerning confrontation or violence had ever been brought up or discussed in the seminary training. I wanted to know about and understand such turmoil, although I didn't want any part of it and didn't like the fear that went with it. I climbed into the jeep with many questions on my mind. Anita's words kept coming back, "The violence of the educated and wealthy will shock you."

The long scenic drive back to Huehuetenango was refreshing, with my mind shifting to the new parish. The Land Cruiser took on the challenge of the rugged Panamerican Highway and easily chewed up the six hours of mostly-unpaved road to the base of the mountain on which my new home sat. I turned slowly down the steep ravine to the broad banks of the river, parked at the water's edge and, hesitant to enter, stepped out of the car. The river was fast. I could not see the bottom and wondered about the depth. I thought of holes, rocks, stumps, and the many hundreds of times I would make the crossing, knowing that the river would remain unpredictable.

Having learned that Someone listens when we talk to nature, I spoke to the river of its beauty and power and said I would always respect it. I added that this first passage was my baptism into a new phase of life, asking it to be gentle with me in crossing. Standing on the wobbly round stones, I stooped and touched the water. It was cold. Scooping up a handful, I swung to the Land Cruiser and splashed the hood and windshield, saying, "I baptize thee in the name of Liberty." Realizing that I was delaying the plunge I knew I had to make, I got into the car, shifted to four-wheel drive, and nosed into the river. I poured on the gas, and the car lunged forward, plowing through the water, which rose quickly, entering under the doors. The steering wheel jerked and snapped from side to side. I felt water seeping into my shoe on the accelerator as I kept the engine roaring in low gear. My wrists ached as we began the climb up the other bank, and only when the front wheels rolled onto dry land did I ease up on the gas.

And then began the climb around and up the mountain, a climb so steep at times that I could see only the clouds and blue sky. I began passing huts of sticks with roofs of hay, one-room adobe houses with roofs of clay baked tile, naked little children playing in the dirt, women carrying water on their heads, men working in fields with crude tools, chickens crossing the road frantically, muddy pigs asleep by the roadside, a skinny burro circling a sugarcane press blindly, and finally the typical United Nations-sponsored school with iron-framed windows and real glass. Then I knew I was close. The *municipalidad* appeared, the town offices with blue-shuttered windows, and the town plaza, consisting of a cement basketball court. And then I saw the structure or, as one of the priests had called it, the hulk: a large, partly-constructed cement and brick shell of a church, hovering over and dominating the tiny *pueblo*. Seeing it for the first time after just passing so many wretched hovels, I thought the church a waste and found it curious that Tex had made no mention of it.

I turned the corner at the church's far end and pulled up to the *convento*, a cold, flat, stuccoed house, built right up to the street, with aluminum-framed windows and weatherstained door. My new home. I had hoped to talk to Father Joe but saw no sign of him. As I wondered how to locate a key to the door, up waddled a young woman, about four feet tall and almost as wide, with no teeth. Giggling, she told me she was *Padre* José's cook. We exchanged names, she being Carmencita, an apparent carrier of news and rumor of news, eager to tell a few tidbits including the news item that the *padre* had left hurriedly the day before, the people thinking he was bored with the parish and the construction. I felt disappointed at the lack of introductions, explanations, or information from Father Joe. Entering the *convento*, I thought I understood why.

The house lacked warmth and was filthy. Cockroaches had taken over the kitchen and dining area. The walls were black with smoke and dirt. I opened a drawer and saw rotting food. Of all the shacks and huts I had visited, I had never seen anything so dirty and disorganized. Carmencita must have seen my look. With hands clasped nervously, she said she had prayed to God that she could continue working for the new *padre*. The word "work" failed to fit the situation, but I wanted to avoid making a hasty decision, as I had done with Pancho. My stomach churned disagreement as I said, "I want you to continue working here, but you will have to clean the kitchen area and do acceptable cooking. Meanwhile, I will take my meals in the open air of the patio."

Fortunately, Father Joe had taken his construction workers with him to begin work on his new house in La Democracia. Thus the church construction came to a halt on its own without my having the unpleasant task of letting the workers go, thus freeing me to focus on the organization of the parish.

After a month, despite my encouragement and discouragement, Carmencita was still limiting me to tortillas, beans, her specialty of hard-boiled eggs, and an occasional leather-like piece of meat. I wondered whom she was trying to get rid of, me or herself. The kitchen showed no improvement except for the elimination of the rotten food. Carmencita was not bright, but the real problem was her unwillingness to learn. I told her several times that if she wanted to stay she would have to clean more as well as learn from women in the *pueblo* how to cook vegetables and use seasoning. And each time she would say, "*Sí, Padre,* I have been thinking of doing that," and nothing would change except that I was getting hungrier. So when I gave the sad Carmencita her last month's pay, I included severance of thirty *quetzales*, one month's pay for each of her three years with *Padre* José, and wished her well.

The next day, as I was cooking for myself, a knock came at the kitchen door. I opened it to find a young woman who said she was Federica, a friend of Carmencita, and that she wanted to cook for me. She said she likewise could not read recipes but could sign her name, something that Carmencita could not do. She was nineteen years old, had been married for three years, and had no children. "Maybe there is something wrong with my husband, but who knows, maybe God just doesn't want me to have babies." She was clean, pleasant, and intelligent, and she got the job immediately. Federica whipped the place into shape and cooked meals that included vegetables and meat stews, using herbs native to the area. She worked well and seemed happy at it.

But I soon had a problem. I began feeling attracted to Federica. She had a beautiful face, although her two top front teeth were missing, causing a lisp that I also found attractive. She was short, with a shapely body. She wore cotton dresses, nothing else. Her bare feet and the tan skin of her lovely legs were stimulating. The day she came to my door I saw that she was pretty, but I didn't want to acknowledge that to myself then. Even when I did, I didn't think I would have a problem.

My celibate life did not exclude attraction to women, but it did require awareness and vigilance. Now I was being attracted to a woman who was actually in my house, alone with me daily, smiling at me, talking to me, liking me, serving me, standing close as she put the food before me, reaching across me with her small round breasts close, the shape of her hips and waist pronounced and obvious as she stood or leaned against the wall and talked to me.

I vowed to myself never to approach her, never to touch her, even though I often just wanted to feel the silkiness of her jet-black hair. Each day I put her out of my mind and refused to permit sexual thoughts. Then I would see her bare feet, or her shapely hips, or her breasts as her dress pulled away from her body, and feel the compulsion to touch her.

With time my desire became stronger, and I thought about her even when she wasn't present. I renewed my vow of chastity more and more frequently. But at times the urge to simply touch her hand was so strong that I got up from a meal and went to my room. I gave up going to the kitchen to talk to her about household matters. The desire to embrace or kiss her seemed at times so enticing that I thought there was no way to avoid it.

What was I to do? I was thirty years old and without sexual experience. I had never even touched myself sexually. My relationships with women were limited to those of my teenage years. The most powerful encounter happened while I was a freshman at Boston College and Arla was a junior at Brighton High. She was bright, pleasant, pretty, and socially mature. We went steady for most of that year, going to parties and dances and snuggling and kissing. I felt good about going with someone so attractive.

Arla was the only child of a divorced Protestant mother. No one in our family ever stated explicitly that Protestants were less than we were, but everyone knew. Any time a new acquaintance was mentioned, it seemed important to indicate whether the person was a Catholic. Mother always proudly described a particular person as an Irish Catholic, because in the "only true Church" we all understood that people came in levels of worth, and it made total sense that the Irish were on top.

Of course, Mom frowned on my keeping steady company with any girl, especially a Protestant, and Dad frowned on whatever Mom frowned on. But for a few years I had been exercising some independence, their first child to do so, and took delight in making sure Mom knew Arla was Protestant. No one in our extended family had ever gone with a non-Catholic.

Although I progressed in my attempt to liberate myself, I felt far from free in my relationship with Arla. Once she invited me to spend a day at her apartment while her mother was at work, saying we could paint the kitchen and have fun. I wanted to go, but the scare of getting that close became too much. Feeling threatened without understanding why, I refused. A few months later Arla told me she felt frustrated. She said she wanted to go further in the relationship, that all her friends were "getting it on," and asked why we weren't. Without responding to her suggestion, I soon started putting distance between us while feeling torn about doing so. I had no idea what to do and lacked someone to talk to about it.

Then one night after a movie, while we were parking at the Chestnut Hill Reservoir, I told her I wanted to break up. I could give no reason. She kept silent but acted as if she understood. I tried to grasp what was happening but couldn't. I had what I wanted, but I couldn't handle it. The only clear thing in my mind was the compulsion to cut off our relationship. I drove her home. At the door she hugged me and cried. Leaving her I stopped again at the reservoir, stood by the car, leaning on the open door, my chin resting on my hands, looking at the sky, sad, alone, not understanding. I never considered that I was afraid to risk being loved.

The rest of that freshman year had its sports events, parties, and excitement, but it only left me feeling empty. Knowing I could not go on that way I repeatedly considered my few alternatives. I ruled out the military and a permanent job. The option that most frequently sprang to mind was the one my older brother Tom had chosen early in life. Of my two sisters and three brothers, he, the next oldest to me, had the strongest influence on me. For as long as I could remember, Tom planned to be a Maryknoll priest—an irrevocable childhood decision that pleased my parents no end and for which he received constant praise and acknowledgement. He had decided after the eighth grade to enter the seminary but accepted counsel to first complete high school. Tom never veered from his early-life decision.

Although only two years' difference in age separated Tom and me, we were not close. Our family system, which was not based on cooperation or support, resulted in frequent blame, competition, and tension. Tom and I generally fought or at best put up with each other. But I also made a strange early decision that I could never understand: no matter what happened, it was my job to take care of Tom as well as my mother. And in my mind I always carried a sense of that burden and felt strangely obliged to stick up for my brother, who was going to be a priest.

As I observed Tom's life of studying for the priesthood, I sometimes felt jealous, for it appeared to offer satisfaction, gratification, and deep meaning. Although I had resisted my mother's wish that I also become a priest, as I weighed the possibility I knew I could enjoy the seminary facilities for sports and companionship and be part of a profession that carried much dignity and respect. I could serve God and mankind, save my own immortal soul in helping others to do the same, and find the meaning I so ardently sought. I could even have the excitement and romance of living in a foreign country. I did not consider that my choice might be the result of a need to avoid love, sexuality, and intimacy. So, after completing my first year of college, I followed my brother's lead and my mother's desire for all her children.

The following nine years of isolation in the seminary prepared me for continued isolation. It was no training ground for being a celibate while in close daily contact with an attractive woman. In no way did my family upbringing or my philosophical and theological training prepare me for having a cook like Federica or for the feelings I was having toward her. I tried to transcend them by prayer and suppress them through work.

I still needed an associate, someone I could work with, someone literate, responsible, interesting, and respected. I needed someone to participate in the liturgy, to work closely with me, to organize, to teach the people and to teach me about the people, as well as to travel to the villages with me.

As I roamed the parish, I watched for the person I could invite to be my assistant and finally found him right in the *pueblo*. I had opened up a room in the *convento* for evening music and table games—the only thing happening in town. I was impressed with a twenty-year-old man named Beto, who showed up regularly. His father had a few head of cattle and a few small plots of land, which Beto cared for. As we talked, I realized that he had all the qualifications of the much-needed helper. I explained what I was doing and the ideas I had, and I invited him to work with me. He accepted the invitation immediately.

Beto was mature, literate, intelligent, and trustworthy, a hard worker. He was searching for personal growth and had the respect of the people. Beto spent six days a week visiting the villages with me or working and studying at the *convento*, never knowing the full extent of his contribution: his presence in the house facilitated a distraction of my attention from Federica. Not that I no longer found her attractive, but I felt in control again. From the time Beto came on board I could go back to viewing her as a good and pretty woman and a fine cook.

The parish consisted of ten villages interspersed in the mountains surrounding the *pueblo*. Beto and I made frequent rounds on muleback. In those visits I based the theme of my sermons and discussions on the teachings of Christ and of *Don* Benito: using the events of daily life to serve God through serving self and neighbor. They thus spoke of cooperation, respect, support, and health. I hoped that this approach would eventually lead to the formation of cooperatives.

After a few months of this work, I was taken by surprise in a village discussion when a man asked "What about sin?" Many heads shook in agreement with a question about a subject I had been purposely neglecting. I had naively thought that the people would enjoy religion with a de-emphasis on sin, only to find out that sin held priority as a deeply ingrained and important belief. I had to answer the man, but I knew that even theologians had difficulty applying the subject of sin in a practical manner. From my own life and that of other priests, as well as from the thousands of confessions I had heard, I knew that the Church handled the doctrine of sin in a less than constructive manner. I wanted in no way to perpetuate erroneous beliefs that would lead to more negativity in the lives of people already poor and deprived.

So I answered, "I don't know about sin, even though I've studied it and thought about it a lot." The man looked at me with open mouth. I went on, "I do know that God's intention is to love us, not to punish us. And I do think we're good people and doing a good job in God's regard. What we need to take a look at is the way we limit ourselves and offend our neighbor. So let me ask you. 'What do you think we can do about sin?' "

The same man, Anastasio, obviously respected by his people, stood up and answered, "Well, maybe if we learn to organize ourselves, we can make a better life, and then there will be less sin." His neighbors smiled approvingly.

It was obvious that in order to lay the basis for our first cooperative venture, I still needed to include a discussion of sin for the people; and Anastasio, a down-to-earth and seat-of-the-pants moral theologian, not only did the job but would later go on to become the treasurer of our first cooperative venture, "The Savings and Loan Cooperative of La Libertad."

7
POWER

The ancestors of the present-day indigenous people of Guate-
mala, converted by force to Catholicism, maintained some of
their ancient beliefs and practices clandestinely. They were ac-
customed to communing with the earth, its flora and animals;
they utilized visualization, mantras, and elaborate rituals; they
practiced natural, herbal based medicine and spiritual healing.
The European priests condemned such traditional practices,
invalidated native beliefs, destroyed ancient wisdom literature,
killed indigenous priests, and superimposed the European cul-
ture and religion. Doing this in the name of Jesus Christ made
this obscenity acceptable and laudable to the rest of the civilized
world. As Christian culture took hold, the native culture either
integrated with the new, disappeared, or went underground. I
wanted to study the remnant, but as a priest I lacked trustworthy
credentials. One attempt to learn about native spirituality with
the local chimán *turned into a reversal, whereby I gleaned more*
about myself and my own spirituality than I had in all my
seminary years.

Today I view all life as made in the image and likeness of
God, with humans sharing in Divine Consciousness to the extent
that we discern, decide, learn, remember, choose, create, ex-
perience, know, feel, intuit; and to the extent that we freely
choose to employ these faculties to communicate truthfully and

act responsibly, we expand our consciousness, entering further into the life of God. As an adjunct, we can develop structures or religions, sacraments or symbols, commandments or codes, but my experience has shown that these are not essential to the expansion of consciousness and can well inhibit spiritual growth. If a group agrees to such a religious motif for its own development, all well and good. But if this is done out of an attempt to control, the members of the group will soon proclaim their structure as God's and their leaders as God-appointed, or attempt to impose their beliefs and values on others, and that which they meant originally to lead to spiritual growth becomes destructive. Structures are not of themselves destructive, but those who seek to gain control of them will definitely employ an apparatus that destroys spirituality.

My religious experience has taught me the importance of distinguishing between religion and spirituality, the former basically believed in or adhered to and the latter primarily experienced. Not to make the distinction can lead to a repetitious, stifled, irresponsible life confused easily with service to God. Many religions with the original intent of leading to spiritual growth or harmony with Divine Consciousness have come to make their structure, ritual, tradition, and authority more important than the people whose consciousness they intended to influence. In doing so, they incite to conformity with a doctrine based on sin and fear of punishment—an unfortunate approach that, once believed, is eradicated only with difficulty. Such negative motivation inhibits creativity and freedom, qualities essential for harmony with the Divine.

My experience with the local chimán gave me an inkling of this insight.

MOST PEOPLE CAME to Sunday Mass because they were obliged to do so under pain of sin and divine punishment—an obligation that not only detracted from their relationship to God but also tended to degrade the sacred act of Mass. After discussions with Beto and a number of devout parishioners, I concluded that it was my responsibility to make a change. I did, my first.

I did away with all obligation to assist at Mass, explaining as best I could that each human being was freely and solely responsible for his or her relationship to God. So it came to pass in La Libertad that it was no longer a sin, ever, not to attend Mass. I had lain awake for several nights before taking the step, but when I did I surprised myself at how easily and guiltlessly I could change Sacred Doctrine. Everyone seemed to react favorably. I felt pleased. But the general acceptance had its downside: it showed that repressed people once again simply submitted to the teachings of the priest, thus demonstrating how easily they could be misled.

The commandment to love, be it love of God, neighbor, or self, gave rise to an immense contradiction in me. I failed to understand how one could be commanded or obliged to do something that, by definition, required free choice, or how such an idea had ever been so universally accepted. I hoped the release from the obligation to assist at Mass would lead to some understanding of free choice and a sense that each person in his or her search for spiritual growth had to be responsible for his or her own choices.

Beto spent many hours studying with me, each of us taking turns being the student. He taught the layout of the parish, the population concentration, the location of water, the various crops and their production and income, the potential for new crops, and the ailments of the people. I got out my books on cooperatives and credit unions and began teaching him the principles that I had learned years before at a summer course in Antigonish, Nova Scotia. He seemed to love the work as much as I.

When we felt ready to present the cooperative idea, we invited everyone interested to a workshop-discussion called Christianity Through Cooperation. A good-sized group, men of all ages along with one woman and one girl, showed up. I answered briefly the almost compulsive questions about the Church and its doctrine, and then Beto introduced a first-stage discussion of cooperativism. He demonstrated the potential of working together and the possibilities available to each in working collectively. Discussions arose as to what people needed and what problems they confronted in order to establish cooperatives in the most effective manner. The group asked many questions and expressed fears and doubts. Most of the people wondered whether the government would ever permit such growth and cooperation. One young man said, "I served in the military. We were taught that all such organizations were against God and the *Patria* and were a front for communism." Beto handled it all well. We scheduled another meeting. Individual villages started their own discussions, now called Christian Cooperative Sessions.

Two months later in a general meeting the people who attended agreed that our first joint venture would be a credit union, a savings and loan cooperative. This idea arose out of revelation that the people lacked access to ethical credit. The downtrodden found the banks closed to them, while the money-lenders loved to deal with them, charging twenty-five per cent a month as the going rate of interest. One man told of borrowing ten dollars to take his wife to the doctor; unable to keep up the payments, he lost his house. Others said their wives had never been to a doctor.

The members elected a board of directors. They drew up by-laws, submitted them to the Federal Government, and got them accepted and approved. The members felt proud of their effort and accomplishment. The group encouraged each associate to save regularly, weekly or monthly, as little as one cent a month. Some who had never saved before felt elated on seeing that it could be done. From the accumulating fund, any member could request a loan from the credit committee, an elected body that met each Sunday to consider and grant loans, encouraging and favoring loans that would produce money. A member could buy seed, a hoe, a piece of hand machinery, an animal, roof materials, and so on. The credit union charged interest of one percent a month, from which it would pay annual dividends. Excitement grew as loans were made and new members entered.

Meanwhile, Beto and I set up a much-needed clinic. We attended to everyone, babies and the elderly, Catholics and non-Catholics, even *Doña* Marta the *bruja*, *Don* Virgilio the *chimán*, and *Don* Alberto the mayor. A frequent question was: "Can I get well?" My answer was always the same: "Yes, you can." Simply hearing that statement made a big difference.

My first experience in medical work had taken place in the seminary, where I once found myself assigned to the post of Infirmarian. I enjoyed the work, which served as an excellent distraction from the uninteresting subjects I had to take. I justified spending much of my study time reading the Merck Manual on illnesses and their treatment. Each morning and evening at the seminary I would go to the infirmary to bandage cuts, give an enema, remove something from an eye, or flush an ear, but, most generally, dole out patent medicines for colds, sore throats, and the many headaches. During that time I became aware that sadder people are sicker people.

My time as Infirmarian served me well, but my most valuable medical training came from work done during my last year as a seminarian. Maryknoll had an agreement with a number of hospitals in major cities to permit seminarians to work in emergency rooms during the summer in preparation for future work in foreign countries. I reported to Boston City Hospital, where I received a white suit and a room in the physicians' quarters, worked regular eight hour shifts, and permitted myself to be referred to as "doctor." As I assisted the overburdened physicians and nurses, they taught me wonderful and delicate skills, and when I was ready they gladly assigned me continuous work from the unending line of patients. I cleaned wounds, gashes, and dog bites. I sutured, gave shots, and put on simple splints and casts. I also observed operations and autopsies and loved the excitement of being attendant on ambulance rides.

In addition to acquiring hospital experience, I wanted to learn to extract teeth. So I spent some time shortly after ordination with a dentist friend in Wellesley. He gave me books to study on the bone structure and nervous system of the mouth, then taught me how and where to inject for the various extractions, which instrument to use on each tooth, and the techniques of using them. He also gave me a complete set of hand tools for extractions, thus bringing me to a good practical level for applying my dental skills in the clinic of La Libertad.

At our mountain clinic, besides abscessed and aching teeth we attended to machete wounds, barbed-wire tears, dog bites, pig bites, snake bites, bat bites, all kinds of pains, infections, burns, bone breaks, and rampant malnutrition. Beto and I, the closest thing to doctor, nurse, and dentist for many miles, took care of everyone as best we could, forever instructing on cleanliness and nutrition and advising that everyone had the power to heal.

Until the day he came to the parish clinic, I had never really said more than *Buenos días* to the feared and revered *Don Virgilio*. Considering a Catholic priest to be a competitor of sorts, the *chimán* had always kept his distance—until the day he could no longer stand the pain. Then one Friday morning, the time reserved for extractions, he appeared. The people had told me of his power, how he could heal and curse or cast a spell through his incantations and sacrifices, and how his father had been a *chimán* before him. I welcomed him, thinking it must have been difficult for one known as a healer to show up at a clinic.

Virgilio was a large man, uncommonly so for a Mayan Indian. His body looked good for its forty-three years: like a wrestler—muscular, with a big belly. Confident in speech and action, he commanded respect. The extraction of his molar was difficult and, despite the injection of Novocain, must have pained him horribly as I rocked, twisted, and pried against roots sunk deep into a firm jaw. Virgilio never blinked or made a sound.

As much as I wanted to stop my clinic work and talk to him that day, I was too busy. But as he was leaving, paying his fifteen cents, I asked if I could come by his *rancho* for a visit. He drew back, momentarily surprised and hesitant, probably recalling traditional ecclesiastical opposition to and vilification of his profession, but then shifted and accepted somewhat reluctantly.

The Church's deplorable history of repressing indigenous religion undoubtedly contributed to the present-day working in secret of indigenous priests. But with my interest in healing and spirituality, I had looked forward to learning from such a one as Virgilio, whose religion predated mine in the hemisphere. I knew that to abide strictly by the Church's view of his profession would hinder rather than help me in participating in the life of his people.

The Church required those converted to Catholicism to leave their native practices, and most did. But when crisis struck or need came, usually in the form of sickness, and no other refuge was found, even the most faithful Catholics turned to their indigenous priest for help, healing, and protection. I felt that to reject or avoid Virgilio would mean missing an insight into the culture or soul of the people. I wanted to learn what I could from my rare opportunity, particularly about healing.

For about a week I reflected on the possible discussion with the *chimán*, and then I went to visit him. He saw me approaching, greeted me cordially, and invited me to sit on the log against the veranda wall that stretched the length of his one-room, dirt-floored, adobe house. A house, because he lived in it. But to the people, it was a sacred place of sorts, almost like a church, housing an altar of sacrifice. And Virgilio was the *chimán*, the native priest, the witch doctor, the man believed to possess the power to communicate a person's needs and bring God's powers to earth in the form of blessing, health, curse, or retribution. In exploring Virgilio's ideas I was dealing with an ancient religion that had adapted to Catholicism in order to survive. And as with the Roman Catholic Church, the people believed in it, gave their power over to it, and thus received its benefits as well as becoming victims of its control.

The earthen tiles of the overhanging roof offered shade from the biting afternoon sun but gave little relief to my burning feet. The trail down from the church had not been easy, dropping rapidly, thrusting my body forward, making my feet dig in to resist a forced run over menacing roots and unforgiving stones. My heavy boots were sometimes rough on my feet, but, not knowing from day to day whether I would be sloshing through mud or walking a gentle trail, I found they were often my best bet and a frequent object of attention in that barefoot and sandaled land. Virgilio's large feet, the toes wide-spread in crude sandals of thongs tied to tire-tread, seemed enviably cool. A closer look showed calluses, scars, broken nails, and cracks in the skin that opened into the flesh itself.

We sat close. Having lived in the mountains of Guatemala for several years, I realized that body smells, a clear indication of different lifestyles, no longer bothered me. Virgilio smelled of animals, burned wood, and old sweat built up from lack of running water. I looked into his eyes and saw them discolored and damaged by the smoke of cook-fires. In his mouth I saw tobacco-stained broken teeth never touched by toothpaste and the gaping space where I had extracted the molar.

Except for the times each of us went into the cornfield to urinate, we sat in discussion for almost two hours, facing a windswept plain with rugged mountains in the background. We relaxed, talking about news from Guatemala City and what was happening in our mountain *pueblo*. In response to his questions I told him about growing up in Newton, Massachusetts, what the people there believed regarding spirituality and healing, how the Indians of the United States had been mistreated by the churches and the government, and what I felt about President Kennedy's assassination.

My interest and questions revolved around his tradition and healing practices, subjects he seemed hesitant to discuss. But we had come together, possibly the first time for a Catholic priest and a native priest to talk and question as equals. Although at times we each became defensive, claiming a special channel to God or some monopoly on truth, we experienced no real tension until we arrived at a theological loggerhead. Virgilio was taking my questioning as an attack. I had not wanted our line of discussion to go that way and would normally have avoided conflict by changing the subject. But this was different.

Virgilio, bending forward with a hand on my knee, fingers squeezing for emphasis, intense black eyes searching deeply into mine, was saying, "Yes, I can heal, and I can call down punishment. In so doing, I am simply serving the cross." He lifted his hand and pointed at the well-weathered wooden cross, about six feet high, standing in the clearing in front of us. I knew that this symbol long outdated the Christian cross and over time had integrated some Christian symbology. I folded my hands in my lap to hide my nervousness.

The Church had intended that our present roles be reversed, with the Catholic priest talking of punishment, retribution, and the Christian cross. The Church had not designed theology courses for an encounter with a *chimán*. Our instructors trained us in philosophical distinctions and moral judgements and the use of the Scriptures to validate our position and teachings. They failed to train us to deal with people who claimed to be empowered by divine energy. In fact, they taught us not to deal with such people but to invalidate them.

Virgilio looked at me. I began to explain my belief regarding the use of the cross, putting the idea in words for the first time. "Look, Virgilio, this is how I see it. Each person is endowed with incredible power." I pointed at his chest with my index finger and at mine with my thumb, both of us noticing my trembling hand. "However, that power is activated or limited by the person's beliefs about him or herself." His nod was unconvincing. "But a symbol or instrument like the cross, although useful and important, can direct no power of itself." His head shaking from side to side in disagreement told me that at least I was getting through.

I went on. "Neither you nor I nor the cross has power over anyone, Virgilio." He squinted his eyes and turned away. Then turned back quickly and tried to speak, but I continued. "Virgilio, what would happen if your cross were cut down?"

He pulled back as if shocked by my question. After a pause, he collected himself and came back in a booming voice, enunciating each word, "Anyone who in any way interferes with the power of the cross is punished by the retribution of the cross." His intensity frightened me. The nerves in his neck were quivering. It took him a few moments to calm down. We sat in silence.

I shrank from pushing too far, but I also knew that this discussion was a rare opportunity for both of us. I felt determined not to stop simply because of fear. He was showing that he could hold his own. I broke the silence, trying to keep my voice gentle. "Virgilio, if you believe in yourself, you can bring goodness and healing to people." He gave a slight smile and then cut it off as I added, "But only to those who believe in it." Gaining confidence from my own words, I said, "Likewise, you can bring no harm or evil to any people unless they themselves believe you can." His face tightened. "And then it is they who, by their own negative beliefs, create the negativity."

He began to squirm, but I persisted, slowly biting out the words. "It is fine to use the cross, but it is only a symbol. Everything that you do, Virgilio, you can do without the cross." I wondered how much of that got through, but I saw his body stiffen and his fists clench nervously. We were both on new terrain, but neither wanted to quit. He took a deep breath, straightened his body to an erect position, faced me squarely, and delivered a challenge.

"*Don* Arturo," he said slowly, obviously avoiding the title *padre*, "are you willing to let me call down the evil on you?"

Shock filled my being. I felt my body stiffen as I tried to remain calm and collected, my heart quickening its beat. My palms became damp, sticking to the log's surface, which was smooth and shiny from years of service. Trying to relax, I leaned back against the adobe wall, feeling the grainy blocks imprint themselves on my back. I gulped, trying not to show fear. I never expected such a turn of events and felt in no way prepared for it. Silence followed. Even if I had words, they would not have come out. He challenged me so powerfully I could hardly think. Perhaps the Church was right in its practice of avoiding involvement when it could not be in control.

Virgilio was smiling. He wanted to test his power. But he was also testing my belief. How strong was my belief? I had never tested a belief directly. Yet I knew that if I didn't consent to his test, I didn't believe. Looking at the cross, I wished I could believe in it as Virgilio did. I wished I saw a way out. I knew how easy it would be for me to revert to the structure of the Church, stand on authority and tradition, and walk away. And yet a part of me realized that if I did so I would never forgive myself. He folded his arms across his chest and relaxed, looking out at the cross. "Well, *Don* Arturo. . . ."

I turned to him and with a weak and trembling voice said, "*Bien*, Virgilio, you are free to call down your evil on me." He opened his eyes wide in a brief look of surprise, then leaned forward, rubbed his big hands together, and smiled. But without hesitation and without any forethought, as if someone else were feeding me the words, I immediately added, "under the condition . . . that you let me cut down the cross."

He drew back, his forehead deeply creased. He did not speak. He looked only at the cross. After a moment, still in silence, he turned and faced me with eyes ablaze. I saw fierceness. I also saw the corner of his mouth twitch. He must have been thinking, as I had, that if he didn't grant my request, then he did not believe in the retribution of the cross. "You do not know what you are saying," he muttered, rubbing his hands on his thighs as if drying them. He sat in silence for a long moment, rolled his shoulders several times, and got to his feet. I thought perhaps he was calling our confrontation to a halt, and realized that might be a wise choice. He stood looking at the cross, and then as he turned from me I noticed the back of his tan shirt wet with perspiration. Without a word, he walked into the house.

I wondered if he wanted me to leave. I waited. I heard no sound. I sat nervously, wishing someone besides the few hapless chickens and the sleeping pig would witness whatever might happen. No sound came from the house. I wondered if he was carrying out a ritual against me. After what seemed like ten or fifteen minutes, he reappeared, carrying a large machete. He stopped just outside the doorway and looked to the cross. I was ready to run in case he made any threatening move. But he turned and came slowly and confidently to stand before me with the machete lying across the palms of both hands, holding it out solemnly to me.

I stood, wondering what I had gotten myself into, and then hesitantly took the three-foot-long knife, cool to the touch, honed to a fine blade. I looked into his eyes. He looked confidently at me and said, "I accept no responsibility for whatever might befall you."

I turned away. I felt no confidence, and I walked to the cross thinking that I could still make some excuse and back out graciously. Virgilio might also have been willing to do the same.

I glanced at him. He was expressionless and without movement. I looked at the cross. I wondered what I really believed.

The cross seemed larger as I stood before it. Scattered on the ground around it were chicken bones and feathers, stubs of candles, charcoal remnants, and blackened stones. I reached out and touched the cross, almost afraid it might respond. It was buried solidly in the ground. I glanced back at Virgilio, sitting on the log staring at me, now showing some fear, probably wondering if I would be struck dead at the first cut of the blade. He had put his beliefs, too, at stake.

I knew that if I gave much more thought to what I was doing I would not do it. Feeling the hot sun on the back of my neck, I spread my feet and extended the machete to measure the distance. With both hands I raised the giant knife high above my head and without hesitation brought the sharp blade down, closing my eyes as the blow struck. My hands stung from the impact, and the blade stuck. Working it out, I looked at Virgilio. His jaw was clenched and his brow furrowed.

I raised the machete again and brought it down strongly, beginning to feel confidence. I ripped the blade free and in a flowing movement raised it to full height and again brought it to the base; and then again, the blows growing stronger; and then rapidly, chips flying wildly. My hands no longer stung, and the blade no longer stuck. I was letting loose, letting go of fear, aware that I had to deal only with the power of our mutual beliefs.

With the beam almost cut through, I stopped and raised my foot high and pushed against the upright. It cracked and broke and fell slowly with a thud, raising a small cloud of dust. I stuck the point of the machete into the ground and lifted the cross, twisting it to break the last strands of wood, and dripping with sweat, carried it to Virgilio. I stood before him, noting that he too was perspiring. Short of breath, I put down the cross and spoke softly. "Virgilio . . . does the cross still have power?"

Looking dejected, he cleared his throat. His voice also was soft. "I believe it to still have power," he said. I could deal with my own beliefs, but clearly I had no power to change those of another. Fatigued, I stepped onto the dirt veranda and sat down on the log, wondering what would unfold next. I did not wonder long. He slowly turned to me and said, "You do not know what you have done. But now it is my turn."

I felt the fear again. After a momentary loss for words, I asked, "How much time do you need to call down your evil on me?" And, hearing my own words, I felt a shiver go up my spine.

Without hesitation, as if there were a prescribed formula, he said, "I will need one month" and held up his right index finger before my face. I wished the time could be shorter but nodded agreement. We both stood. Nothing else was said. Like opponents in a sport with pre-arranged rules, we shook hands.

I headed up the trail to the *convento*. With the sun dropping behind the mountains, the air had cooled. I greeted people along the trail, but without a sense of joy. I wanted to be alone with my thoughts and wished the knot in my stomach would leave. Much more than Virgilio's pride lay at stake. I knew he would try as hard as he had ever tried to bring down evil, and I had heard many stories of his successes. I wondered how many candles would be burned, how many chickens sacrificed, how many incantations, invocations, and rituals would be performed against me.

I also knew that I had been very clearly challenged. Challenged to stay well for thirty days. I could not get sick, could not have an accident or mishap. And as I had tried to explain to Virgilio, I could not emphasize this too much, or I myself would create just what I was afraid of. I had to do something that the Church had never taught. I truly had to believe in myself.

Wanting support, I talked with Beto, telling him I was permitting Virgilio to call down the evil on me for thirty days. I said it was an important experiment. His face lost its color as he drew back. He said nothing. I decided not to tell him about the cross. I wanted to relate to the *chimán*, not humiliate him.

Well aware of each day's passing, I went about my work as usual, always cautious and at times apprehensive. It was important that nothing happen to me, not just for my own welfare but as a confirmation of my new approach to life, and so that I could share a basic and essential truth about beliefs. I had begun to make the distinction between religion and spirituality, realizing that true spirituality was based on experience, while religion was based on beliefs.

At one point about half way through the month, my mule, Luna Llena, bogged down on a deep, muddy trail and in desperation tried to leap for a flat, slanted rock. Her wet hooves and iron shoes failed to hold, and she started to slip and fall backward. As I kicked my feet from the stirrups and jumped for safety, I saw in my mind an image of Virgilio pointing at me and shouting, "The retribution of the cross."

On the morning of the thirtieth day Beto put his hand out to me. As I took it, he breathed deeply and said, "The *chimán's* time is up. I have prayed much for you this month. Please don't ever make such an agreement again."

I was more than happy, for I had not so much as gotten the sniffles. "There is no need to do it again, Beto," I said, noticing that only then did I truly begin to relax. "I have learned what I needed to learn."

The following Sunday at the first Mass, I looked up from reading the Gospel, and there was the *chimán*. I was startled. He had never come to Mass before. But there he was, not inconspicuously in the rear, not hiding from anyone's view, but clearly visible, with his unusual size, kneeling in the midst of the congregation that huddled together for lack of benches. I felt a vibration run through my body. I stopped reading the Gospel. He had his hand to his chin and appeared peaceful. Our eyes made contact. He nodded his head and smiled slightly. Tears blurred my eyes. I did not understand what was happening, but smiled, nodded my head to him, and mouthed "*Gracias.*"

Returning to the altar, a mounting charge in my body distracted me, and I had to move by rote through the remainder of the liturgy. I knew I had opened up a hidden part of myself, possibly my very soul. I had broken away from the lack of belief in myself.

But I still missed grasping the meaning of the lesson of two men coming together, each of whom people considered a priest of God, representing oppressor and oppressed in the five-hundred-year saga of socio-religious inequity. At the time I did not consider that possibly the *chimán* was offering me an invitation to further explore our traditions and allow us the opportunity to create a unifying and harmonious spirituality. Aware of the humiliation he risked in coming to Mass, I knew his presence, like our month-long experiment, involved the work of the Spirit. Because I had risked so much, the *chimán* accepted the truth that symbols have power only to those who believe in their power. The experience would serve me well in finding my freedom, and in preserving my health, and in teaching others to do the same. Unfortunately, I convinced myself that the issue with the *chimán* was closed. But it wasn't and isn't. Five hundred years of festering wounds still await healing. Meanwhile, I remain grateful to my brother, the *chimán*, my teacher, a man willing to risk going beyond his beliefs.

By this time the credit union was meeting with small but regular successes. Its members decided that our next step would be the formation of an agricultural cooperative. Meetings, study groups, by-laws, petitions to the government, and elections resulted in *"Cooperativa Agrícola La Libertad, S.A."*

Potatoes had for a long time been raised in the area. A visiting United Nations agronomist gave a workshop in which the co-op potato growers learned about hybrid seed and chemical fertilizers. These members pooled and borrowed enough money for an experiment and, with the help of a United Nations program, bought three types of seeds. The plants grew hearty, with beautiful flowers in three different colors. As harvest time came close, the crops had to be guarded at night. Hungry people look for food where they can get it, and those potato fields had food in abundance. In the first meeting after the harvest, the potato team announced excitedly up to a thousand per cent increase in production. With this encouragement, most members eagerly desired to experiment on another project crop that had the potential of touching all their lives, the sacred *maiz*.

Although corn was the staple of the people, the steep sides of the eroded mountains of La Libertad could no longer produce as they had in the past. We knew that corn grew abundantly on the level and fertile terrain of the hot coastal plains, but such land was distant and owned by the wealthy. We began gathering data and in time planned a venture that would previously have been unthinkable but was feasible collectively.

The *Cooperativa Agrícola* leased fifty acres of land on the Pacific Coast, then selected the first group of *campesinos* to begin the project. After the Sunday liturgy, seven anxious and laughing men crowded into my Land Cruiser with machetes, hoes, bedrolls, a few pots, and many tortillas and beans. We sang and chatted the long trip away, and once in the coastal region we followed a map to our land. The men could hardly believe their eyes on seeing the amount of fertile and flat terrain left unproductive. Ours had lain fallow for about five years—something only the wealthy can permit. That meant much work for us.

We arrived at ten, the heat already unbearable. We divided into groups and started immediately. I worked on the cleaning crew. We took machetes to the heavy shrub, large thorny bushes, and small trees. We cut roots, dug out small stumps, and pulled everything into piles for burning. The housing crew set aside dried sticks for firewood, stripped tree trunks of branches to make posts and poles to frame a shelter, and tied on leaves and straw for protection against sun and rain.

After an hour we retired from the sweltering sun to the shade of our upstart shelter. My clothes were soaked through. The men ate cold tortillas and frijoles. Having no desire for food, I lay down to one side, with the bugs seemingly attracted to my repellent. At three we went back to work. The roof people completed their task skillfully and joined us in the cleaning. Everyone took off his shirt—except me. Knowing how I would burn in that tropical sun, I wore my perspiration-drenched shirt, resting every fifteen minutes. Others rested about once an hour. The strongest worked without rest. I wore work gloves; blisters appeared anyway. One of the men told me it would help to piss on the blisters. I discarded the hot gloves.

We worked until seven. Everyone was tired. Few of us felt like talking as we heated up and ate tortillas and frijoles and drank coffee. We retired early, but I lay awake on my plastic sheet set on leaves and grass, watching and listening to the bats, knowing they would not bother us, there being enough cattle in the area.

Listening to the snoring, too exhausted to sleep, I became restless and slipped into a state of questioning my motivation. I concluded that I was doing this punishing field work for myself, for my priesthood. I wanted the priesthood for me, and to me priesthood meant being with the people, so I needed such opportunities as this. I also wanted to learn all I could about their lives. I had thought that anything that contributed to their lives contributed to mine, but now I had doubts. Sleeping only intermittently because of pains in my back and side, I wondered if I was going too far in being with the people. Once I thought of the tourist motels along the Pacific beach and wished I were there. Instead, I dreamed I was working in a mattress factory. Then someone was up making a fire, and everyone stirred and arose in good spirits. We ate breakfast quietly and were on the job at five-thirty.

The second day I learned that a field of fifty acres was endless. I wondered if we would ever get through it. With my hands raw and swollen and my body aching and weak, I rested every ten minutes and went into the shade at least once an hour. We quit in late morning for siesta. I slept, ate a little, and when the crew went back to work at three I stayed in the shelter. I cut firewood, cleaned a few pots, and read a book. The others worked until seven. I slept better that night. At five-thirty we were back in the field. I rested less often and worked part of the afternoon.

Friday showed us a large clearing. Men sang in the field. I was beginning to swing the machete methodically, not sweating so much, and taking my shirt off for half an hour at a time. My hands were getting hard.

The only available water in the area was from a slow-moving stream, the same that local field workers used. Unfortunately, the landowner's cattle also drank from it. Luckily, only one man got sick. When I found out a month later that he had malaria, I felt irresponsible and guilty. I realized I could have transported water from town and began to see that a part of me wanted to be the heroic missionary adapting to local methods and customs.

The men worked on the coast not for the experiment alone; the co-op was paying them seventy-five cents a day. If they found work in their villages, they would earn from thirty to fifty cents a day. On Friday the group worked feverishly, covering more ground than any other day. I felt strong and happy. As evening came on, we packed up for the journey home. Leaving the project, the men stopped and looked back at the work and spoke of it proudly. We had cleared a major section of the land. But more than that, the clearing was their venture. And they knew that their beginning would lead to further development by others. We left with cheers and smiles. Not long on the road, most were leaning anywhere they could find support, fast asleep.

I had agreed to be back in the parish each Saturday and Sunday for the clinic, marriages, baptisms, and Masses. We arrived in the wee hours of Saturday morning. Beto was waiting up with news of the week and ardent to hear about our work. The men were so eager to talk with him that they forgot their tiredness. Wanting to get to bed, I reminded them that they still had to walk the trail to their homes, and we got them on their way. I never knew a mattress could feel so good.

During the weekend Beto got the second group ready to go, and we left at five o'clock on Monday morning. The team differed in that the one woman of the co-op was present. Amalia, a plump and determined forty-eight-year-old widow, wanted to participate in the project and to accompany her son David. She spoke softly and had a good sense of humor, a deep sense of cooperativism, and a powerful presence that seemed to make the journey more pleasant. I watched the men behave responsibly and respectfully, listening attentively to this bright woman, never engaging in any teasing. I am happy to say that the men of the villages rarely showed chauvinism or machismo.

We pushed hard on clearing. Amalia was always busy, gathering firewood, cooking, mending, and in her spare time going into the field with a machete. The men appreciated her and helped with the kitchen work when they could. The third week, another group arrived, and finally we had cleared the entire fifty-acre tract.

The fourth group immediately began to plant the corn. I

learned this task quickly and soon became adept at it. A few weeks later, with the stalks about one hand high, another group arrived, carrying hoes to clean out weeds capable of sapping nourishment from the soil and cutting off the sun's rays from the young, bright green rows. The plot needed only one cleaning because the normally incredibly-fast-growing weeds would then remain dwarfed in the shadow of the leafy stalks. Except for the small southwest corner, which flooded with rain that rotted the seed, the plot produced a good crop. When growth was complete, the workers permitted the ears to dry on the withering stalks, because fresh ears cannot be shucked or degrained, and what we wanted was the dry grain, to be stored for tortillas.

A group arrived for harvesting and degraining. And in that rewarding phase of the work, although the twisting and pulling of the dried ears from the stalks left the tender skin between my fingers scratched and cut, I felt as if I had been farming for a long time. Once we had husked the corn, I watched adept hands peel the golden grains from the cob—a skill I could not develop. And after many hours of many days of hard labor we were delighted to contract a truck to ship the hundred-pound sacks to the river at the base of the mountain. Beto and I used the Land Cruiser to haul eight sacks at a time through the river and up to the *pueblo* to be stored until a shortage occurred, and then to be sold to the co-op members.

I felt happy that the project was over. We had all learned numerous lessons, and we treasured the human interactions. The greatest reward came from understanding the depth of spirituality that is achievable in working and resolving problems together. Financially, we lost; the rental of the land had made the difference between profiting and losing. The basic problem of the poor became clear to me. They had to have land, in a country where two percent of the population owned more than eighty percent of the land.

En route to the parish from one coastal trip, I had swung by Huehuetenango to pick up supplies and happened to meet Father Rudy, a dedicated missioner and advisor to the Father Superior. He said he had passed by my parish on a Holy Day and was surprised not to find me. As on Sundays, participation at Mass is obligatory on Holy Days of Obligation, under pain of mortal sin. I explained about the co-op experiment and that I had been on the coast. Father Rudy said that I had still missed Mass and that the people had been deprived. I dared not tell him that the people were no longer under obligation to attend. As for myself, I had the wonderful yet frightening realization that I was no longer under the traditional obligation to what I considered an uncaring and unfeeling hierarchical structure.

8
DEVIL

Belief in the devil is a belief, a reinforced idea, and as with any other belief, one can choose to believe in it or not. Children and uninformed adults, not realizing that they have a choice, remain stuck with the beliefs handed down to them, such as the belief in the devil. The devil is a useful tool in controlling such people, locking them into a structure that purportedly protects them. I had no reason to think that my grandmother was manipulating me when she told me that the bogeyman would get me if I wasn't a good boy—that is, do what she wanted. As the belief took hold, however, I became afraid to go into the attic and cellar and any dark place, continuously reenforcing my belief until the bogeyman became for me an undeniable reality. The experience served as a good preparation for the Church-induced fear of the devil, and the Church did not have to work hard to get me to conform and to mold my beliefs.

Many people are angry when they learn that the concept of the devil is used as a tool to induce conformity. In my case I felt deprived of responsibility for my thoughts, feelings, decisions, behavior, and all that I created in my life. It was not the devil that was tempting me, it was my own habits, desires and fears induced by my environment, behavior, and thoughts. When I disobeyed grandmother, it was not the devil that made me do it; it was my desire and need to rebel, to take a stand, to have some independence.

I feel sorry for sincere but immature priests who add stress to their lives by their need to be vigilant for the ever-lurking Satan. And I am angry at them when they mislead simple-minded souls into attributing negative behavior to the work of the devil. It is clear to me that people who are "possessed" have suffered severe and traumatic abuse and need to be treated accordingly. The Church has not taken the responsibility of researching this, and will not do so, for to lose Satan would undermine the basis of Christian doctrine. Religion needs a devil; spirituality needs personal responsibility.

A client of mine, who was dealing with her anger at the Church, recently asked, "Since the devil used to lure us to sin by tempting us to eat meat on Friday, did the souls that had gone to hell for that sin get a reprieve when the Church changed the doctrine on Friday abstinence?" She needed no answer. She went on, "And what about all the work Satan had put in while tempting us to eat meat? Does he get cheated out of recognition for that?"

As I dealt with the doctrine of sin in La Libertad, I had to deal with the devil, the alleged creator of sin. In the process I observed those few who had the courage to examine and alter such manipulating beliefs experience the rewarding and needed sense of liberation and empowerment.

FATHER DAN, a friend of mine from seminary days and pastor of a distant parish on the other side of the mountains, was throwing a party. I was delighted to receive an invitation, since I knew most of the younger priests would be there, including my brother Tom, whom I had not seen in a long time. Tom was one of the few Maryknoll priests assigned outside the State of Huehuetenango. I had several times visited his parish in *Cabricán* in the State of Quetzaltenango and was interested in the successful credit union and outstanding cooperative of lime-mining and marketing he had helped to form. I was proud of him and respected him for his concern for the people and his willingness to experiment in improving their lives.

I drove the five hours to Santa Eulalia, and there amidst a gathering of happy priests I made a decision I had long considered. The host had mixed a batch of Manhattans and was passing them around. I decided it was time. Taking one, I smelled it and slowly sipped. I got a rush, a feeling of exhilaration. After twelve years of abstinence, except for Mass wine, my nervous system did a double take on the high-proof alcohol. I had drunk beer in my latter high school years and my one year of college. But when I entered the seminary I gave up beer as well as every other form of alcohol, in the belief that in so doing I could make reparation for sins of intemperance committed by others and gain indulgences for souls in purgatory. As I gained clarity on the doctrine of sin, indulgences no longer made sense to me, and I no longer needed to boost my ego by pretending to make reparation for the alleged sins of others. I considered my new decision another step in personal liberation.

But, as experience has taught me, one seldom swings from an extreme position to moderation, and I didn't. I got high that day, and many times afterward, with moderation put on hold, while risking a disease common to priests, alcoholism. I began to learn an important lesson regarding the use of alcohol by priests in dealing with, or rather not dealing with, loneliness and frustration. I felt the momentary relief that a drink can bring and realized that, at times, alcohol would appear to be all that a priest could turn to. It began to make sense that there should be so many alcoholic priests, the vow of celibacy leading more to alcoholism than to holiness.

On my return to La Libertad I realized I was tired of looking at the unfinished hulk of the church. Joe's starting it had been an unfortunate mistake, but now the building was an unfinished horror, an ominous cloud that overshadowed the *pueblo*. Many people who had contributed labor wanted to see the work finished, while some of the old timers said it was a shame to have lost their old church. I tried to imagine the simple little adobe structure that had stood before and also wished it had not been torn down. Reluctantly, I decided to go on with the construction, but for that I needed money, and the best place to collect it was back home.

Having completed three years in Guatemala, I was entitled to a three-month vacation in the States. I wanted the vacation and looked forward to going home. Dad and Mom met me at the airport. It felt good to hug Mom. Dad put out his hand. I grabbed him and hugged him for the first time in my life.

I found the vacation profitable in many ways, including raising money for the construction of the church, a monument to the ignorance of a foreign priesthood. I also raised enough money to replace my well-worn car. I enjoyed being with my family and friends, but I truly missed the Guatemalan people and my accustomed involvement in the mountains of Huehuetenango. And so, I returned early, cutting short the vacation by one month.

Awaiting me in La Libertad were teeth to extract, sickness to attend, and problems to discuss. I wanted Beto to spend some time catching me up on the news, but he insisted that I first see a husband and wife who had been coming by for the last three days asking if I had returned. He said that he told them each time that I would not be back for a month, but that they persisted in saying that I was due back. I stepped outside. They were sitting on the cobblestones, leaning against the *convento* wall, apparently dozing. Their clothes were old and worn; both in their thirties, they looked fifty. Tired and victims of malnutrition, living at the level of survival, they were poor even among the poor. When I said their names, both jumped up and, without a smile or the usual *buenos días*, the man began anxiously, "Thank God you are here, *Padrecito*. Our only son, Roberto, has been sick for two months and now does not speak or eat." He was wringing his callused hands. His wife was crying, clenching the corner of her shawl in her teeth, tears streaming down her face. Their son used to visit me occasionally, walking up the mountain from their home of sticks and straw just off the road by the first curve above the highway. He was twelve years old, slim but muscular from hard work, with black hair and eyes, very white teeth, and a great smile.

I took medicines and the holy oils and got in the Land Cruiser with them. As we bumped along, the heartbroken father could not stop talking about his son. The mother held on tight, as does one who has never been in a motorized vehicle before, and continued to cry. As I pulled the car into the brush near their home, their eight-year-old daughter stepped from the hut, unsmiling and now looking sick herself, exhausted from long hours of keeping watch.

We entered. Inside it was cool and quiet. The one-room stick house, about eight feet by ten feet, had no furnishings. A few pots and jugs hung on the wall near the fire stones. The well-worn dirt floor showed marks of recent sweeping. I knelt by the motionless body, so thin I hardly recognized Roberto. His open eyes stared straight up. I touched his hot forehead and called on healing energy. A slight smile came over the child's face. I gave him the last rites and several injections.

The next day I visited again but saw no change. Roberto lay on the mat, motionless, soundless, staring. The family looked on helplessly. Kneeling beside him, I felt something unusually holy in the closeness, the simplicity, the uncomplicated experience. I wanted Roberto to heal. I called on God's healing energy and gave several more injections into the almost lifeless body. Unwilling to give up, I spoke to the parents, and with their permission I carried the boy's dried-out body to the car and took him to the Maryknoll Sisters' Hospital in San Pedro Necta. The Sísters received Roberto lovingly, but after three days of close attention and care they sent a telegram advising me to take him home. As I carried the limp body to the Land Cruiser, tears ran down my face. I felt like a father letting go of a son.

In a few days the parents appeared again at the *convento* door. They said Roberto was still alive and now speaking. I was amazed at both pieces of information. They went on that he was speaking as if in a trance, talking about the heavens opening and seeing lightning and strange beings. I stood in silence. But the father interrupted my thought by touching my arm softly and saying, "Although we ourselves doubt it, *Padre*, could he . . . be possessed . . . possibly . . . by the devil?"

Not prepared to answer that question, I was taken aback. I had given much thought to belief in a devil. I had prayed, meditated, and talked about the problems and the confusion resulting from such a destructive belief. I knew that truth and responsibilty called for choosing my beliefs independent of any controlling structure. And I was doing that and was willing to take responsibilty for my choices. But now these people were calling on me to consider whether I could go along with a traditionally taught and commonly accepted belief, a belief that I now considered to be taught and encouraged irresponsibly by the Church. My first reaction was to say, "No, I don't believe in the devil. That is simply an effective tool for controlling people." I held back. I needed to think. I reflected on my experience with Virgilio, the *chimán*, and knew that we were all free to employ energy as we chose. While anyone could bring about negativity in his or her own life and call the effects the work of the devil, possession, or anything else, no outside power could force good or evil upon anyone.

I didn't like being rushed into giving an answer, but for the sake of the two distraught parents, I had to get some clarity. Feeling frustrated, I answered the father, saying, "Look. I am sorry. I don't know how to explain this, and wish I was better prepared, but I do not believe in a devil or possession." The couple stood expressionless. I went on, "Maybe some day the Church will open its eyes regarding this, although I doubt it."

The woman was not paying any attention. The sad man simply looked at me, not hearing anything I said. I couldn't expect them to grasp such theological confusion. I looked at the couple, and my heart poured out to them. Who was I to disqualify something they deeply believed in as truth? My job was not to change the beliefs of others but to support people in their growth. *"Bien,"* I said, wondering if my job could encompass perpetuating destructive beliefs, "I am willing to do an exorcism." The father's face lit up. The mother stepped closer, looking to her husband, thinking they had some hope.

I got out an old ritual and my sick-call set, and we all piled into the car once again. At the house, the parents hesitated. They had been taught that a cast-out devil can take up residence in a person nearby. I said they could wait outside.

The child was motionless. He seemed to look at me through slightly opened eyelids. I knelt beside him and touched his hot forehead. I could find no pulse. I set out the candles and holy water and opened the book, and then began remembering from my studies that only a holy person should attempt to cast out Satan and that this person must be chosen by the bishop. I began to doubt myself, certainly not considering myself to be holy. To me that meant conformity, repetitious recital of prayers, and multiplication of pious practices. I wanted spirituality, a reverence for life, and an appreciation for people. No one would consider me holy. Yet here I was about to cast out Satan. I wondered. The old beliefs and teachings still had a hold. I felt the fear I had felt with Virgilio and again asked myself, "What if I am wrong?" This only led to other questions. "What if there is sin? What if there is a devil? Should I go through with this?" My answer was that I had to go on with it. I had to know. I began the readings of exorcism, and as I did, stories came back to me, stories of terror and violence, and my fear increased. "What if possession was a reality? What if Satan entered into me? Should I go on?"

I knew I had to continue with the exorcism, and as I did the realization came to me that I was again testing the beliefs I had tested with Virgilio the *chimán*, beliefs in myself and in a loving God. I knew that I was capable of creating destructiveness and negativity in my life, and that if I were unwilling to recognize myself as the source, I could take the traditional approach and blame a devil—and refuse to acknowledge that I had created that devil. I went on with the prayers, blessings, and invocations, commanding Satan to abandon the body and soul of the boy and to immediately leave the surroundings, knowing I would never have to do this ritual again. I was beginning to get clear that the origin of belief in a devil arose from the unwillingness to acknowledge the creative power that God shares with humans.

I heard a noise. A vehicle stopped on the road by the *ranchito*. I jumped as I heard the voice of the Father Superior, Jim Curtin. He had spotted my car and stopped. He asked the parents if I was there. He had never visited my parish before; now of all times he was coming to see me. He came to the doorway, looked in, and in a hushed voice said, "Hi, Art, what's happening?"

I could not believe my own words. I tried to say them without apology. They came out softly. "Hi, Jim. I'm doing an exorcism."

His mouth dropped and for a moment he was speechless. Then, "Oh, yah. Well, I'll go up to the *convento* and wait for you there." He left hurriedly. I finished the ritual, now probably more nervous about the Father Superior than I had been about Satan.

I spoke slowly. "You are a good person, Roberto. God loves you very much. Your visit to earth has been important. I am sad that I am unable to help you heal physically. Your time here is almost finished. You will soon be with Jesus and Mary." Tears came to my eyes as his eyes strained to communicate with me. "I am privileged to know you, Roberto. The voices you hear and the images you see are your preparation for heaven. You have nothing to fear." His eyes moved slightly and relaxed. I blew out the candles and called to the parents. The father stood beside me. The Mother knelt on the mat across from me. I said to them, "God has blessed you with a fine son who was willing to teach us an important lesson. Roberto is preparing to go to heaven. He is not possessed. He will always love you and be grateful to you." They both cried. I touched his eyelids and they closed. I knew I would have a companion on the other side. "*Adiós*, Roberto," I whispered. "*Que te vaya bien.*" The parents each gave me an *abrazo* and spoke words of thanks through their sobs. They looked relieved.

As I drove up the mountain I reminded myself that I could not interfere positively or negatively with another person's development; I could influence, but not determine; that no matter how much I wanted Roberto to heal, his beliefs and choices would determine the outcome. I also had to reflect on the fact that death was not negative and could certainly be healing.

Arriving at the *convento*, I tried to look relaxed despite the fear of a flare-up with the Father Superior. Fortunately, he had found my Scotch and was sitting with a drink and a cigarette. He made no move to get up or to shake hands but asked warmly. "What's the condition of the boy?"

"Well," I said, starting to sit down, "He's been sick. . . ."

"Do you have the bishop's permission to exorcise?" he interrupted.

I felt embarrassed. I hesitated. "No, I don't, Jim," I said softly, trying to keep eye contact so as to not be intimidated.

He sat pensively, making no comment, probably thinking of the devil leaving an exorcised person and entering into the priest. He picked up his drink and finished it in one gulp, stood and very uncomfortably said, "I have a few more stops to make." With no other words he left, and so ended the only visit I ever got from the Father Superior. I was sorry to see him go. No other mention of the exorcism was ever made. Roberto died the next day.

A few months later the bishop sent for me, the first time since my assignment to La Libertad. As I sat down in his office, he congratulated me and said he wanted to move me to a bigger parish. As the system goes, this was an acknowledgement of my work. I had ambivalent feelings. I had sunk roots and got close to people in La Libertad, but I also felt excited about moving on.

Tex told me he was going to assign me to San Antonio Huista. I jumped at the name. San Antonio was special. I never thought I would have a chance to work there. I had passed through the town a number of times and liked the area and was impressed by the people. If I could have chosen a parish, it would have been that one. I had a big smile on my face and was sitting on the edge of my chair as I thanked Tex and gladly accepted. San Antonio was to me a very special place.

He smiled back, saying, "I know you will do a good job." He paused, looked at some papers, then went on. "San Antonio now has two Maryknoll Sisters." I felt uneasy. I had never worked with women. Tex went on, "Father Ed is incapable of getting along with them. I want you to go there and work with the Sisters and not against them." I made no response. "I want you to work with Ed for a month to get to know the parish, and then I'll transfer him. You have until the beginning of next week to finish at La Libertad."

"Thank you, Tex," I said, bubbling over inside, "and who is replacing me?"

"I'm bringing in your old pastor from Jacaltenango," he said. I felt sad, knowing how differently Denny and I worked and believed. Then realizing that I was making me and my way right, I shifted my thoughts, thanked Tex, and left. I returned to La Libertad to put things in order and to pack. I called Beto and Federica together, and with sadness told them the news. Federica burst into tears, raising her soiled apron to her face. Beto gave me a long *abrazo*. I had come to love both of them very much. We had been through so much together. So many lessons.

I prepared my files for Denny, requested a final session of the cooperative, and made the formal announcement at Mass the following Sunday. That evening the people held a small farewell gathering in the town hall. I exchanged the *abrazo* with young and old. Goodbyes had always been sad for me. As I hugged person after person, tears streamed down my face.

Returning to the *convento* for the last night, I thought of my time in La Libertad, knowing I had grown much and feeling grateful for the experience. Unable to sleep, I arose about one o'clock and walked the only two streets in town, then continued down the road to the first plateau, where we had a small field. Beto had fenced it with barbed wire and made a pasture for Luna Llena, my faithful and beautiful mule. I went into the pasture and found her in a corner munching away. I stroked her, talking about the trips we had taken together. I told her I would miss her, and I acknowledged her for her courage, her strength, her gentleness, and her patience. I asked her to treat Father Denny well and hoped he would do the same for her. I thanked her, hugged her around the neck, and said goodbye. I walked back to the *convento* and slept.

In the morning I was up before the sun. Beto had the Land Cruiser all packed. We gave a tight *abrazo*. "Goodbye, my brother," I said, my eyes avoiding his. He said the same, *"Adiós, mi hermano."* As I drove out of the sad little town, two boys chased the car. I waved as they faded in the dust and said out loud, "Thank you, Liberty."

9

WOMEN

Having lived and trained all my life under controlling men and controlled women in male-dominated institutions, I wondered how, if ever given the chance, I would react to a situation in which I was free to share with women. When such an opportunity did present itself in San Antonio Huista, I felt bewildered and unprepared. Trying to adjust and lacking the tools to do so, I often felt threatened and fell back on my lifelong training of suppressing feelings and exerting dominance. But, fortunately for me, the persistent warmth and openness of the nuns of San Antonio permitted me eventually to recognize my ongoing denial of fear as well as my denial of the personal power of women.

Years later, a veteran of many internal and external conflicts, living and working as part of the healing profession of psychotherapy, I continue to learn from women willing to be with their personal power in the experience of their emotions. Today the contrast between a person with power and one lacking it is usually most obvious to me when I deal with a married couple. I often regretfully see myself reflected in the man: in charge, in control, reasonable, rational, with little or no experience of his emotions, resulting in powerlessness and the need to exert control. His fear of the woman and her power is so suppressed that he actually believes he is telling the truth as he portrays her faults and weaknesses. When the couple present a sexual problem, the man often describes the wife's coldness and inability to share his love, unaware that his need to control sexually often stems from his repressed fear of sexuality and intimacy and other undesirable emotions that might surface.

Women seeking to resolve problems resulting from inequality may look for opportunities in the male structures of church, military, and business, but the results are frequently discouraging. Women often seem compelled to sell out to the system or to fight an endless, unsuccessful battle against it. Structure, although theoretically practical, connotes control, or "power," and controlling power corrupts all of us, including women and those who claim to represent God. As we open our eyes to history, we see that once a structure is established and imposed, its representatives rationalize the resulting injustice, deceit, and violence, and its adherents accept those results.

Structures do not of themselves submit to change, and attempts to alter them, or replace them directly, only strengthen them. Those who want to shift an historically accepted and complicated structural condition must be committed to the truth. An appropriate place to initiate change would be in examining the truth about maleness, or, at "the beginning," taking responsibility for the one-sided litany we have perpetuated about our Ultimate Source. The truth is that God is neither male nor female. If I, out of my own needs, want to conceive of God as having a gender, I might be closer to the truth by consigning the Creator of life to the only gender that has ever brought forth life. And the same applies to man. If out of my own needs I want to pretend that man is the only source of life on earth, I will have to lie. For no man, even Adam, has ever given life. But if the objective is to rob women of their power, the story of man begetting woman certainly serves. Such long-standing beliefs turn God against Nature in order to justify and give credence to male dominance.

If the male of a couple I am counseling is not to undermine the possibility of a mutually-nurturing relationship, and if male-dominated institutions are not to take earthly life over the brink of extinction, we must all reject those teachings that laid the foundation for male control. I choose to reject such distor-

tions and invite others to do the same, committing ourselves to the attainment of true personal power rather than to control, with the possibility of regaining our individual identities and intimate relationships through the responsible experience and appropriate communication of our emotions.

My work with powerful women began with my experience of cooperation with the Maryknoll nuns in Guatemala. That experience laid the groundwork for my later understanding of the power of women.

A N HOUR AFTER ARRIVING at the Toyota Agency in the capital, I was driving away the proud owner of a new, grey, six cylinder, four-wheel drive, long-bed pick-up truck, leaving behind my Land Cruiser, now loose and scarred from a life on unpaved mountain roads. About a hundred and fifty kilometers out of the city, appreciating the powerful engine pulling ahead on steep climbs and the strong shock absorbers smoothing out holes, bumps, and washboards, I came across a barefoot Indian family laboring up a long hill and offered a ride. They were at first hesitant. But after a few moments of consideration the two children, the mother, the baby, and the chicken climbed awkwardly into the cab, each move monitored by the father's inept directions. He, with his big sack and the little pig, along with the firewood that the children had been carrying, got in the back. Only the father knew any Spanish, and very little of that, so we did not talk much in the cab. The girl and boy sat tensely until their curiosity overcame their shyness and they knelt up on the seat to see out the windows. Together we pointed at things and made sounds, and after a while they were laughing and enjoying my demonstration of the horn, the windshield wipers, and the various blinking lights. They watched as I pushed in the lighter and were amazed when it popped out and astounded when I lit a cigarette with it. That was too much even for the mother, who had been sitting stiffly pokerfaced. She looked at me and smiled her first smile. I held out the package of cigarettes, but she waved her hand indicating the package out, shaking it so several cigarettes popped up. She took three. I held out the lighter. She again waved her hand indicating "no" and dropped the cigarettes somewhere into her clothing.

When it started to rain, we squeezed the father and the pig into the cab. The pig was smaller than the baby but made more noise. The wife held out a cigarette to the husband and put another in her mouth. Without saying a word, he took out matches and lit his. She sat with the unlit one in her mouth. At a bend in the road, high in the clouds, the father signalled me to stop, and everyone got out into the downpour. The woman swung the infant onto her back, then with the wet unlit cigarette in her mouth came to the driver's window and bowed her head as she wrapped herself in a sheet of blue plastic. The man kept repeating *"Gracias."* The children wore big smiles and said something happy in their language. As I pulled away, they waved goodbye with their characteristic upside-down wave. No house or village could be seen, and no path, so they slipped over the edge into what looked like nowhere.

Several hours later, close to the Mexican border, I pulled off the Panamerican Highway onto a deeply rutted access road. After a bumpy hour I could see its abrupt end, and there, awaiting me, were the horse and horseboy I had telegraphed for to take me the rest of the journey over the rocky mountainous trails. I parked the truck in a small clearing and approached the boy and the untethered horse, standing motionless, side by side. I spoke to the boy, who was very shy. His name was Gabriel. He spoke so softly, I had to ask his name three times. I inquired how long he had been waiting. In his gentle and hushed voice that pulled me closer as I tried to hear, he said, "Maybe a few hours."

Gabriel was an illiterate fourteen-year-old with an unending smile and big wide-open eyes. The horse stood easily by him, turning when told, and motionless as Gabriel tightened the cinch and adjusted the stirrups. Noting that he was not tall enough to put the bridle over the horse's ears, I approached to help. But to my surprise the horse accepted the bit in its mouth without resistance, then lowered its head to receive the bridle.

We set out, Gabriel on foot leading the way. As I rode behind in a leisurely way, I pulled a peanut-butter-and-jelly sandwich from my shoulder bag and offered him half. He accepted, took a bite, but had trouble swallowing. I asked, "Gabriel, do you not like the sandwich?"

"I like it," he said with the bite still in his mouth, "but the taste makes it difficult." He walked on, carrying the half sandwich in his hand, not wanting to throw it away. With his other hand, he took an orange from his shoulder bag and held it out. "Would the *padrecito* like to share?" he asked.

"No, *gracias*," I said. "But why not give me the sandwich back? And you eat your orange." That worked. He also had several small bananas. I accepted half of one.

We spoke of various subjects, but mostly of his job, horses. During the conversation, I realized I had an opportunity to bring up a subject that usually got no response. I began with, "Do you ever talk to the animals, Gabriel?"

"When I need them to do something and when I'm brushing them, I do. And when I have to graze them and spend all day alone with them." I had to keep the horse close and lean forward on its neck in order to hear.

"And do they talk to you?" I asked, trying to seem detached. He looked back at me, hunched his shoulders and looked away. He did not speak. I waited, left hanging once again. But I persisted. "I wonder if the horses talk to you sometimes, Gabriel."

He took off the well-worn straw hat, scratched his head, turned, and with an embarrassed laugh said, "Well, sometimes, if I'm listening, they might."

I was delighted. I had found a person who still listened. At least, a person who was willing to admit it. "And I wonder, why do you laugh, Gabriel, when you tell me that you listen?"

He laughed again, removed the hat, and said, "Because you will think I am foolish if I say the animals talk to me."

I reined the horse to the side of the trail to let pass two men with large sacks of corn on their backs, then pulled up close to him again and said, "Well, I don't think you are foolish; in fact, I wish I knew how to listen to the animals."

We traveled a few minutes before he turned his head and

said, "It is not so difficult." I kept silence. Another minute passed before he asked, "But why would you want to listen?"

I nudged the horse closer and said, "Because God speaks through the animals." He nodded his head. Of that he seemed to have no doubt. "But," I went on, "where I come from, people have forgotten how to listen."

"And that is sad," he said.

After a few moments, he asked, "Could that be why you are living among us? To learn again to listen?"

I needed a moment to check that out in my own mind, then answered, "I had not thought of it that way, Gabriel, but, yes, that is why I am here."

We went on in silence. His hat, too big for him, kept bouncing from side to side. His shrunken pants, with patches that were wearing out, hung high above his ankles. I watched his bare feet scarcely touching the dirt, the rocks, the roots. At the crest of a small ridge, he stopped and turned to me, the horse halting as he did. "You will pardon me, *Padrecito.* . . ." He looked briefly at the horse. I thought he might be looking in its eyes. Then he looked at me. I waited. He looked at the horse again.

"Gabriel . . . I'm listening," I said.

"Well," he said, looking from the horse to me, now as if exploring in my eyes, "Well . . . I really don't know how to explain." He took off his hat and spoke slowly and softly. Missing a few words, I leaned closer. " . . . but I think . . . if you would graze the animals all day long, perhaps during the season of the rain, and follow them . . . instead of leading them," he said while shaking his finger into the air, "and talk to them . . . like you were singing softly, . . . and listen for the wind . . . and your own footsteps . . . perhaps you will also begin to listen to the animals." I nodded my head. He did the same and turned back to the trail. I was awed by the brilliance of his simplicity.

"*Gracias*, Gabriel. That is important information that I will never forget." He turned and smiled proudly. I watched the bare feet in the dirt and then took out my pencil and notebook.

Two hours of mountain trails brought us to the *pueblo* of San Antonio Huista. I was tired but sat tall in the saddle, proud that I was now part of this *pueblo*. Women waved from doorways, men looked up from their fields, some children ran alongside. "The *Padre* Eduardo will not be present for your arrival," Gabriel told me.

"Where will he be?" I asked.

"He has said that he knows where to find the best horses and has gone to that place to see if there is not one that pleases him. However . . . there will be a surprise awaiting you that I have been advised I cannot tell you about," he added with a big smile, making me laugh.

The surprise was not long in coming. Skyrockets went off as I turned into the church grounds, and the two Sisters and a small group of people gave me a warm welcome. Sister Regina, a native of the Bronx, heavy-set and with an air of confidence, twenty years my senior and a veteran missionary, now Superior of this small community of Sisters, stepped up to the horse and extended her hand. *"Bienvenido, Padrecito,"* she said with a big smile. I felt nervous but tried not to show it.

Her companion, Sister Mary Leo, from Ohio, twenty-eight years old, had arrived recently in Guatemala. Green eyes, soft features, tall, slim, and attractive in the tailored grey habit and black veil, she stepped forward, smiled, and held the bridle for me to dismount from the now-jittery horse. I stepped down beside her. "Hi, Father, welcome to San Antonio," she said, putting out her hand. Our eyes connected and held for a moment, giving me a warm feeling.

I tried to think of something interesting or funny to say, but nothing came. So, I shook her hand and said, "Glad to meet you, Sister."

After I had been introduced to the other members of the welcoming committee, the Sisters invited me to their *convento*, where we chatted over coffee and cake. "I didn't know cake like this was available in the parishes," I said.

Sister Regina answered, "We spend time training our cook. It pays off."

"What about the cook at the priest's *convento*?" I asked.

"Her name is Isabela," Sister Regina said. I noticed that Sister Mary Leo wanted to answer, but just as she got the words ready, Sister Regina said, "She is a wonderful woman, in her forties; cooks okay, but no cake." We laughed.

They had heard the news that I would be taking over as pastor and did not hide their delight, nor, surprisingly, did they hide their dislike for Father Ed. His reported behavior and their openness about it flabbergasted me as they told stories of his impatience and intolerance in dealing with them and the local people. I believed them, but I also thought how difficult it must be for a man untrained in management and unaccustomed to working with women to run such an organization. I wondered if I would do any better.

They showed me through their *convento*, located beautifully on the edge of a stream, and then through the parish school on the edge of a large lot across the dirt street. Recently constructed, the school was complete except for windows and landscaping and was scheduled to open in a few months. My stomach tightened as I again thought of taking over a plan and project that I considered a waste. Sister Regina probably noticed my lack of enthusiasm. With a deep frown, she asked, "How do you feel about the school, Father Art?" I already admired her willingness to express her feelings and state what she liked and disliked, and I had a strong sense that I would like to do the same; now she was inviting me to practice. I hesitated, then decided that for my own good and for that of the work, I must be willing to follow her example and risk speaking my views openly—something I had done only rarely. I would not be protective, as I had always thought it necessary to be, especially with women, and that day I began practicing awkwardly.

"I don't want to be offensive, but I am not in favor of parochial schools," I said, aware that my thinking on education had been much influenced by the writings of Ivan Illich. They nodded their heads. I thought they didn't understand, but they did; and despite their preparation for a school, they were willing to hear an adverse opinion. Gaining confidence as I learned an important lesson, I went on, "I don't like using a school as a bargaining chip. I think our objective is true education, which leads to free choice and spirituality, not submission and religion." I expected them to interrupt; they didn't. "In the long run, I think religious schools will divide the people even more than they are divided today." They were listening.

I felt good and decided to go further. "But it's not just parochial schools. There is much I don't agree with as regards to the teachings of the Church." I paused, breathing deeply. They were waiting. "Primarily, I can't accept the sacraments being used as a means of control." This was a thought I was having daily. They looked at each other with a little surprise, but they apparently had no serious problem with the idea. "I also think the reciprocity that exists between Church and State is abusive." Sister Regina nodded her head in agreement. I went on, "It's simply an outgrowth of the conquest of these people by the collaboration of Church and State." They looked at each other and raised their eyebrows but kept on listening. "I think our role is to contribute through whatever structures are viable, the public education system in particular, and not to divide the people with Church programs."

Regina, obviously in charge, nudged Mary Leo and with a laugh bellowed, "Yea, yea." Mary Leo nodded her head in agreement. I laughed in amazement at these two women.

Back at their *convento*, we sat down again in the dining room. Regina said, "It's about time we grasped that only example teaches. Not proclamations or the memorization of the catechism." I knew then that I was going to learn from the Sísters and that I was going to love being with them. "But go on with what you were saying," she said.

"Well . . . I'm not sure what to add. I have no experience being pastor of a parish with nuns. . . ."

"*No tenga pena, Padre* Arturo," Regina interrupted. She was regularly interjecting into the conversation beautifully-enunciated Spanish. When I commented on the quality of her Spanish, she said, "Thanks. And that's one of the problems I have with Eddie Boy. I don't think the guy ever studied the language."

"Anyway," she said, looking to Mary Leo for agreement, "you don't have to worry about never having been with nuns.

We feel as if we have been here without a priest. I wish you could have listened in on some of our attempted conversations with Eddie Boy."

"Father Ed doesn't want to hear ideas from us," Mary Leo ventured, flushing as she spoke.

"He doesn't want to hear any ideas that don't originate from his bald head," Regina said. "However, he has done a great job at bringing in agronomists for teaching agricultural classes."

"And he has worked hard on the building of the school," Mary Leo added.

"Sure," Regina agreed. "I sometimes feel sorry for the guy, and even now I kind of hate to think of letting him down. He has his heart set on having a traditional parochial school." I was again amazed. She was already talking of not going through with the school. "I for my part have spent my life in church schools," Regina continued, "and hoped I would get a change. But until now it looked as if Eddie's plan was not going to let me off."

We chatted for a bit more, agreeing that our time together was going to be meaningful and acknowledging that our first conversation had gone beyond any of our expectations. I felt eager to look over my new home and get settled in. I thanked what I knew would be real friends and left, feeling great as I walked across the narrow stone bridge, up the cobblestone hill to the plaza, and into the adobe *convento*, my new home. The cramped second floor was set up for a guest—a hot and constricted space under the eaves, but at that moment I could have lived anywhere.

Father Ed returned in a few days. I felt some apprehension as we sat down to talk. He knew that I was arriving as his assistant but was surprised and uncomfortable at learning that I would be taking over as pastor. That Tex had not advised him amazed me. I felt upset with Tex that the nuns had been informed but Ed hadn't, although he had been told that he might soon be transferred.

Ed was clear with me in regards to our relationship. "As long as I am pastor, I will run the show and make the decisions. I am glad to have you here, but remember who is in charge."

And in every sense he was. I noticed that neither the nuns nor the people ever questioned or challenged him. He talked about the difficulty of working with the nuns. He referred to them as "the bitch" and "baby bitch" and said he didn't know if they were worth the trouble.

A few days later Ed assigned me my first wedding in the parish. I stood at the altar with the young couple. It was not unusual to see the bride in a white gown. But this was the first time I saw the groom in a tuxedo. Obviously, these poor people were spending much money on the wedding. The Mass and ceremony finished, I stood by the altar rail watching the couple walk arm-in-arm down the aisle. Outside the main entrance I could see the marimba players with sticks in hand, waiting eagerly to start the music. The newlyweds were halfway to the door when the marimba began to play, signaling the beginning of the celebration. Almost immediately Father Ed, dressed in cassock and collar, rushed out of the sacristy and ran down the aisle, brushing past the couple and out the door. Hearing him yelling, I rushed down the aisle but stopped short as I saw Ed flailing about and pushing the marimba over onto the ground. The confused *marimbistas* were trying to get out of the way of the raging priest while at the same time attempting to protect their prized instrument. The confused couple stood to one side. The bride, with her hands to her face, began crying. Ed yelled to the startled group, half in Spanish, half in English, that they should keep their goddamn marimba away from the church or they would be sorry, and stomped off.

I was as shocked as anyone. I helped stand the marimba upright, wanting to curse Ed, but said nothing. I went to the sacristy, removed my vestments, and entered the *convento*. Ed sat in his dark and damp office-bedroom, breathing deeply and smoking a cigarette. I stood in the doorway.

"What's your gripe?" he asked.

I took a few steps into his room. "I don't like what just happened," I said with fear in my voice.

"That's tough," he said. "When you understand these people and how difficult it is to teach them, you'll change your tune."

"Your behavior was totally uncalled for," I said. "Those people were doing no harm. But you have insulted them and done irreparable damage."

"Don't you tell me how to run this place," he said standing up and taking a step toward me while removing his glasses. His eyes bulged: I was afraid he might hit me. "I am the goddamn pastor of this parish, and no greenhorn is going to tell me how to run it. You're as bad as the goddamn Sisters, always wanting to baby these people. I know what is best for them and what is right." He was waving his finger at me. "And don't forget that as long as I am here, I am the pastor."

"I won't forget," I said. He relaxed a little. I then added, "But I can't wait until you're gone." He clenched his fists and jaw, but said no more. I was to learn that Father Ed was "right" about everything and that whatever he had or did was "the best."

At dinner the next day Ed told me about the fantastic deal he made buying a horse on the coast. "You have to be willing to travel the distance if you are going to get quality," he said. "There is nothing around here worth riding. I had to look at many horses, but the one I finally found has got to be among the best." He went on to say that his ability to evaluate horses was really coming in handy. He said I would see for myself when the horse arrived. He had hired a man to walk the horse the six days to the parish.

It was understood clearly that Ed had bought a male horse. In Spanish only the male is *caballo*. The female or mare is always *yegua*. To mistake this would be like calling a girl a boy. Even when speaking English we were accustomed to distinguish by using the Spanish word *yegua*.

A few days later, Máximo, the houseboy and Ed's righthand man, came in and said, "*Padre* Eduardo, your *yegua* has arrived." Ed answered by saying, "What *yegua*? I didn't buy a *yegua*."

Máximo, thirty years old, five feet tall and robust, had taken on Ed's authoritarian and righteous attitude toward the people. But despite that and despite continuous criticism from Ed, he kept his sense of humor. Máximo laughed nervously at Ed's reply and with a shrug of his shoulders said, "The man who walked your *yegua* from the coast is here and wants to get paid."

In his own Spanish-English, Ed said, "Goddamit, Máximo, can't you get anything straight?" He got up from his chair and stomped angrily out to the patio. I followed. Ed bent down under one side of the "horse." I looked under the other. His jaw dropped. I was delighted. He said nothing. Walking around aimlessly for a few moments, he finally paid the man and went into the house. Máximo, who did not have to look under an animal to know its sex, stood to the side trying to keep a straight face.

Ed did not come to supper that night. At breakfast the next morning he told me of the fine qualities of the mare and how it was his intention to breed her. He then advised me that we were going on our first trip together, that he wanted me to get a sense of how to deal with the village people. He went on to say that he did not have a horse for me, since the Sisters would be using two, another had a sore hoof, he would be using the fourth, and the *yegua* needed to rest. He offered no suggestion as to finding a horse. I asked Máximo what to do, and he volunteered to rent one.

Máximo brought the horse, probably a fine mount in its day but now years past its prime and relegated to the job of town taxi. It had blotches where hair no longer grew, its spine sagged, and its eyelids remained about three-quarters closed. The animal plodded along, however, and we had an easy trip.

Ed and I spent the day at the village fiesta and enjoyed ourselves. On the return trip Ed resumed his usual nonstop talk, saying at one point, "This horse I am riding is probably the fastest horse in the State." Although Ed was riding a beautiful horse, it would have been silly to argue such a point, even though one of the large landholders had several race horses. But this claim, like so many others he made, irritated me.

More out of exasperation than ever thinking of a challenge, I said, "Go on, Ed, I could beat you with this old rental job."

He turned and glared at me as if I had said the most insulting thing possible. He had taken me seriously and went livid as he shouted, "Goddamit, Melville, you'll eat those words. I'll race you back to the church."

With that he brought his whip down angrily on the rump of his horse, and it leapt forward. It seemed foolish to even think of racing on this steep, rocky trail and on this horse. But I chose the one way of acting that the male of the human species reserves for challenges to his manliness: foolishly.

I rolled the pointed wheels of my spurs across the old horse's belly, loosened the reins, and squeezed with my legs, and I got the surprise of my life as the horse took off. It was as if he had been waiting ten years for the chance to prove himself. I pulled off my cowboy hat, waving it overhead, and let out a "Yahoo!" at the surge of power and speed. Ed looked around and knew he was into a race.

In the first few seconds he had opened up the distance to the point that I doubted it was possible to close the gap. But the old horse bred and weaned on these very trails knew just how to put its hooves down around the rocks and roots without hesitation, and we were giving it a go. As we came to the top of the hill and entered onto the main street of town, it was clear that my horse and I had gained some.

Ed and I both knew that galloping down the cobblestone street of a *pueblo* was no more accepted or permitted than speeding a car through a residential district, and yet racing to the church meant we would gallop the whole length of the town. But Ed's reputation and that of his horse were at stake, and his pride had been hurt. Fed up with him and his alleged perfection, I was determined to try to show him up.

The clanking of the iron horseshoes drew much attention. People stopped their work to look. Astounded faces popped out of doorways. The road was clear, and the race went on. My old horse, his head high and his strides long, gained slightly. With a quarter of a mile to go, the old guy hung right in there. Except for the start, I hadn't used the spurs. I just gave him free rein, and he did the rest. As we started to ease alongside, Ed turned and yelled, "You son of a bitch, Melville, you'll get us killed." I felt like a winner, my face down over the old horse's mane, looking out between his ears. I never answered Ed. My horse never glanced at his horse or for a moment lost sight of the race; he just kept pumping like a champion. Coming up the last incline with the church in sight, Ed whipped his horse furiously. But we crossed by the wall of the church with the old guy out in front by at least a length. I was amazed at his strength and had to push the stirrups forward and stand in them to rein in; the old horse didn't want to stop!

In the patio, as we undid the cinches and took the saddles off the panting horses, I was beaming and Ed was fuming. A couple of teenagers who had been standing in the plaza and saw the last leg of the race came into the patio and laughingly proclaimed me the winner. Ed stormed into the house and didn't speak for the rest of the day. I walked the old horse until he cooled down. He held his head high, his chest out, his eyes open, and snorted breath of fire from his nostrils. He knew he had done a good job and was proud of himself. When I told the Sisters, they had already heard the story and were roguishly delighted.

About a week later Ed called me to his bedroom-office. Tex had sent him official word of his transfer. I said nothing. I could not have been happier. There was only one thing about Ed that I was going to miss: his dog. Ed had a four-month-old German Shepherd puppy named Champ that I had fallen in love with and who followed me everywhere.

On the last day the only thing Ed said to me regarding his leaving was "I want you to have Champ." I was surprised and touched, and for that gift I am forever grateful to Ed. He told me he was taking his two best horses and the *yegua*. That night in the adobe-walled, dirt-floored town hall, I sat beside Ed as the townspeople put on a farewell, with kids reciting poetry and elders giving speeches in grateful acknowledgement for the years he spent with them. Ed left.

10

RELATIONSHIPS

Seminary life allowed no close relationships. Abiding by that rule, I never permitted myself to become really close to any of my fellow seminarians, many of whom I considered friends. Long accustomed to sharing only superficially, I was in San Antonio looking not for a comrade or mentor but rather for a helper or an assistant. And out of that search came a young man with whom I unwittingly developed my first close male relationship. Límbano was of a different age group, culture, and race. His background was poverty, and he had little education. But something precious grew up between Límbano and me as we worked together and came to know, trust, accept, and respect each other. In time I would realize that seminary admonitions against closeness, based to a great extent on fear of homosexuality, had led many of us to deprive ourselves of beautiful, special, and nurturing relationships.

In the seminary I had also learned the dangers of a close relationship with women. Although the story of Eve tempting Adam and so being the source of the downfall and suffering of the human race never declared directly that women were evil, it communicated the subtle implication of the snares women supposedly set for men.

Little did I think that in San Antonio I would develop my first close friendship with women, nuns—dedicated, truthful, and loving human beings. We shared warmth, closeness and trust, resulting in the most rewarding relationships I had ever had.

These wonderful friends, Cathy, Regina, Límbano, and later, Marian, were a rich source of social and spiritual growth. The way our friendship unfolded still amazes me. One example will suffice. Cathy, Regina, and Límbano each confessed one time to me as their priest. I distinctly remember feeling humiliated by their goodness and simplicity and their willingness to follow Church doctrine in requesting the sacrament of penance. Those confessions held nothing that even the most scrupulous of priests could have contrived to consider a sin. Looking for more clarity regarding what I considered the destructive consequences of the doctrine of sin, I asked each about their motive for confessing. The ensuing conversations led to further mutual awareness and to friendship rather than the chauvinistic priest-penitent relationship, permitting me to take a step down from my clerical pedestal.

At times in my psychotherapy practice, when I encounter good, ordinary people, perhaps negative towards themselves and others, seeking relief and support, I think of religious confessions and compare them with the confidences of my troubled clients. These relief-seekers, however, differ from those seeking sacramental forgiveness in that they learn to process the symptoms, causes, and effects of their behavior and to take full responsibility for the same—an essential step in their personal, social, physical, and spiritual healing and growth. Forgiveness, although laudatory, fails to lead to healing or change of behavior; rather, it frequently leads to abatement of guilt, neglect of responsibility, suppression of pain, minimization or denial of trauma, and perpetuation of undesirable behavior. Although it is comforting for anyone to confess a dereliction to a supportive person, those who never question sacramental forgiveness of alleged offenses against the Source of our free will may unfortunately confuse the relief they find in confession with personal responsibility and so neglect to resolve the problem that made them feel guilty.

In San Antonio my view of confession and the other sac-

raments evolved to a new stage, along with my understanding of friendship.

PEOPLE WHO HAD BEEN treated impatiently and harshly by Máximo during Father Ed's time now shunned him, some openly resenting him, and I was finding him difficult to relate to. Regina referred to Máximo as Little Eddie. I needed to get the parish team together and doubted if he could play an important role. To make space for someone new, I cut him to half time.

Walking around the *pueblo*, meeting people, talking to workers, evaluating them and my situation, I concluded that I needed someone like Beto in La Libertad, someone to travel with me and to learn cooperativism. Someone who would be committed to the people. Among the many I talked to was a young man named Límbano, eighteen years old, strong, athletic, sharp, grammar school graduate, mature, and friendly. From the start he treated me like an old friend. His father, an alcoholic, had died recently, and Límbano, the oldest child, now supported his mother, brother, and sister on twenty-five cents a day as a stonemason's helper. I thought I had found my man. After talking to him several times, I consulted with the Sisters, telling them the qualities I perceived. They agreed.

I went to speak to Límbano and found him sitting on the ground, legs crossed, shaving a large piece of sandstone with the universal tool, a machete. When he saw me coming, he smiled and waved the machete. I asked about his work, and after he had explained in detail the method of preparing stone used for steps and walls, I said, "Límbano, I want to discuss something." His eyes lit up, and he nodded his head as if he knew what I was about to say. "I am looking for someone to work with me and wondered if you would consider the job."

He stood up, looked at me seriously, and said, "*Claro que sí.*"

I explained. "I'm just getting a feel for the work here, and you could learn with me." His head was erect as he looked me in the eye. "The hours would be long and irregular. The job will include working with people and animals and the sacraments. You would spend time in the *convento*, the office, and the church." He rested the tip of the machete on the ground in front of him and leaned on it like a cane. "You would study and learn and travel with me." He showed a big smile. "I want the work to be serious and fun." I paused. He was smiling his agreement.

From our first encounter, I had felt that the job was his and that it would be a wonderful opportunity for him. I did not know that it would be the same for me, or that Límbano and I would form a deep spiritual relationship. It would be months before he would say, "I knew before I met you that you would be coming here. I didn't know when and didn't know your name, but I knew."

Límbano never ceased to amaze me. It was he who taught me to listen to the fire. "The fire gives important messages," he told me, "like, when a visitor is coming." For anyone living in a remote area of Guatemala, the coming of a visitor is important. When Límbano first said, "Do you hear the wind?" I thought he was talking about the sound of the wind.

"And how did you know I would be coming here?" I would ask, half in humor.

"I used to have the same dream over and over," he said; "a dream about a tall foreigner with blue eyes and blond hair who would come to my house. My parents told me not to go with him, but I did. Together we swam swift rivers and climbed high mountains. He taught me much, yet it was I who guided him." He paused as if embarrassed. "When you came to our *pueblo*, as soon as I saw you I knew it was you of the dream." Such dreams were new to me and not yet important, but I thought it was a great story.

"When do I start?" he asked.

"Tomorrow," I said.

Stabbing his machete into the air, he let out a cry of "Ayaa!"

"How about a dollar a day?" I asked.

"*Tremendo!*" he said with gusto.

And so Límbano and I began the most meaningful relationship either of us had ever known. From the beginning it was built on caring, respect, and support. Without fail, Límbano was always there for me. And I believe I can say the same of myself. I don't think he ever lied to me, and as far as I can remember I never lied to him.

Gabriel was of course part of the team, although I rarely saw him, since he spent his time with the animals. He always called me *padrecito*—unusual for a boy. I didn't know whether this use of the diminutive came from caring and closeness, as when an adult used the form, or from fear and trying to placate, as when the people used it with many priests. I wanted Gabriel to deal with any fear of me and knew that would require my spending some time with him. One day while he was bathing the horses outside the gate, I went out and asked how he was doing. He said, "I am fine, *Padrecito*, but the range is not."

"What is the trouble with the range?" I asked.

"Well, you have to see how the grass is disappearing. Without much rain, and with so many animals out there now, we sometimes have to go great distances to find a good grazing place that will keep the animals together."

Knowing this was my opportunity, I said, "How about showing me the range, Gabriel?" He looked at me questioningly. "Let's go," I said. And so we saddled up two horses and rode out.

"I have never ridden with a *padrecito*," he said, sitting high and proud in the saddle. I remembered when I first met him how he had walked while I rode, and knew that from now on we would both walk or both ride. He said, "When the range dries up, as it is starting to do, everyone's animals get thin, except the *padre's*."

"Because the priest has money to buy grain?" I asked.

"It is that," Gabriel answered, "but more," and left it at that, apparently not intending to tell what else.

I waited a few moments and then asked, "For what other reason do the horses of the *padre* not get thin, Gabriel?"

He looked at me, his brow furrowed in surprise and said, "Oh, you do not know? If you want, I will show you when we return to the *pueblo*." We rode the dry range for an hour, with Gabriel pointing out the few feeding spots. On the way back we were silent until he pulled up in front of a stone wall enclosing a lush plot not far from the center of town. "This is the corral of the *padre*," he said. I was amazed. Ed had spoken to me of the corral that the *pueblo* had ceded long ago to the Church. It was valuable land: level, walled, and fenced. I stepped down from my horse, entered the gate, and walked around, noting that the corral was divided into six areas, each irrigated and growing high grass and each having a trough with piped water. It was beautiful. But it was also sad. I could see that in a sense the horses lived better than the people. Most of the houses in town had no running water, and none of the houses in the villages did. I was also seeing that I had in my charge more land than anyone else in the *pueblo*.

"This is why the padre's horses do not get thin," Gabriel said as I saddled up. We rode to the *convento* in silence.

Another team member, the thirty-five-year-old grounds-keeper, Chilo, was responsible for the upkeep of the corral as well as the grounds around the school, my *convento*, the church, and the Sisters' *convento*. He and his wife had a new baby, their fifth. I went to his house to meet his wife and see the baby. The one-room *casita* was ten feet by ten feet, made of sticks, with a straw roof. It had one bed, also made of sticks, thirty inches wide, where he and his wife slept. The children were filthy and almost naked.

Chilo was illiterate, insecure, always with a forced smile on top of sadness. When speaking to me he used the word *padre* in every phrase. He looked malnourished and got sick regularly. Chilo lived as if in the old Mission. His life was dependent on the Church; he saw no possibility of ever freeing himself from it, nor did he ever consider such a possibility. To him the *padre* was more than in charge, he was like a god. One never challenged the *padre*, for he was always right. One constantly tried to please the *padre* and win his affection. And Chilo knew that the *padre*'s ego needed all of this and more.

Julio, a fourteen-year-old altar boy, was not only literate, he was finishing up the sixth grade at the head of his class. Father Ed had told Julio that when he finished grammar school he would be enrolled to study for the priesthood.

Many of the priests were sending their most talented and even some of their less talented boys to the seminary. The number of seminarians a priest sent had become an important part of the numbers game. I had sent none and had encouraged none. But now I had a boy on my hands who had been promised he would be sent, and both he and his family looked forward to the day. If nothing else, they knew it would give the boy an education otherwise impossible. The day after his graduation, Julio was at my door to talk. We sat down. "Well, first of all," I said, "let me ask you why you want to be a priest."

With a big smile, he gave the pat answer that children everywhere have learned, "To serve God and my people."

"And how by being a priest will you do that?"

"By celebrating Mass and giving the sacraments."

"And what will that do for God and your people?" I asked.

He thought for a moment and then said, "I don't know, but that is what priests do."

"Do you know of any other way of serving God and your people?"

He thought again and then answered, "No, I don't."

"Well, if there is another way of serving God and your people, and your people become healthier and happier as a result, would you want to investigate it?"

He beamed and said, "Of course."

"*Bien*," I said. "Just think for a moment, Julio. What do your people need more than anything else?"

He did not hesitate, "Money, food, animals, medicines, land."

"But you didn't mention the Mass or the sacraments," I said. We both began laughing.

"Julio, I want you to work with me for one year," I said. He looked surprised. "You will get a sense of the life of a priest as you share in the work." He was smiling and moved to the edge of his chair. "If, at the end of the year, you want to go to the seminary, I will do everything necessary for you to do that. If after a year of seminary, you think you can better serve God and your people by studying agriculture and animals, I will help you do that."

Julio came to work for me and was a genuine pleasure to be with. He was truthful, imaginative, questioning, and cooperative. No one in San Antonio ever stood up to me as Julio did. He continually wanted to know why, and always out of candor and honesty.

Isabela had been cooking at the *convento* for sixteen years. Thin, greying, with a tough outward appearance, she had a heart of gold. She was unmarried and—something unusual—she also had no children. Isabela was no gourmet cook, but her meals were hearty. She was clean, efficient, and smart. She was also literate, so I gave her a bread recipe and asked her to try it. She did, and after that we frequently joked about her having invented a substitute for adobe.

The Sisters, or *Madres*, as they were called in Spanish, were the nucleus of our team, their open approach providing the source for much wonderful development. In one of our many discussions they suggested that they were ready to drop the ancient formality of title. And so I began to call them Regina and Cathy, their original names, and I became Art. That change contributed to making our relationship more real and probably helped weaken our roles of "mother and father." But I was in charge, and after having been suppressed all my life I found that out-ranking them took getting used to. At first, not knowing how to use the authority, I sometimes misused it. Once Regina advised me that she would be going to Guatemala City to visit a friend. Since we were coordinating several projects and she hadn't checked out her trip with me, I told her I did not want her to go. Although I felt something wrong in my gut, I did not realize that I was being dominant and controlling, my ego having been hurt when I was not consulted. By asserting my power I was blaming her for my low self-esteem and insufficiency and punishing her for choosing what was totally appropriate. Later I felt bad for what I had done, told her so, and suggested she take the trip. She refused. I thought possibly she liked as much as I did the idea of my taking the reins.

Regarding the school, we agreed that the people who had donated time to its construction had to be considered. We decided not to open a typical parochial school but would initiate provisionally an ungraded school for children from the villages who could board with families in town. We would encourage those who lived in town to stay in the public school. The school's emphasis, instead of doctrine, would be making life work. The Sisters would invite young women volunteers from Guatemala City to help, and all would also teach in the public school. Through this cooperation, we built great rapport with the town officials and the public school teachers.

I always enjoyed the trips when the Sisters went along to the villages. They, Límbano, and I would set out in the early morning. A man from the village to be visited would come in with a mule to carry the Mass kit, bed rolls, cots, a small generator, and a sixteen-millimeter movie projector. Traveling time would be from two to seven hours each way. The scenery, the conversation, stopping for a picnic or a river swim, talking to people along the way, at times racing our horses, was all wonderful. The villagers would turn out in great numbers for the Mass and Sacraments, music, singing, and socializing, along with movies on such subjects as farming, hygiene, sanitation, and family care, and also for co-op sessions. The people would take turns putting us up, the Sisters in one house, Límbano and I in another, but all of us eating together.

After one such visit, riding across a beautiful plain on our way back home, Límbano was out in front and I was last, enjoying the sights ahead of me, particularly that of the Sisters in their full habits, their veils trailing in the breeze. I wore jeans, sport shirt, and cowboy hat. All of us wore riding boots. We were having a gala time when suddenly Regina seemed to lose her balance, screamed, and fell to the ground. I pulled up at her side and jumped to the ground. She looked unconscious. I touched her forehead and spoke to her. Cathy tried to make her comfortable and straightened out her habit and her headpiece. Regina opened her eyes, gave a painful smile, and said to Cathy, "Thanks, pal." She was bruised and badly shaken but suffered no broken bones. We knelt by her, encouraging rest, while Límbano reported that her cinch had broken, causing the saddle to slip. He did a provisional repair job using his machete, his teeth, and some string, and said he would use the mended cinch on his horse. When Regina felt sufficiently strong, we helped her up and gently onto her horse, and we wended our way slowly and carefully. The next day, although limping, she was back at work.

We set up at my house a clinic that the Sisters ran, and in another room I extracted teeth. The more involved we got with such work, the more we recognized that much of the tradition of the Church was not serving the people. The Sisters said that one tradition that was not serving either them or the people was their nun's habit. Permitting only their hands and face to be seen, the habit allegedly offered some kind of protection and inspired respect. The Sisters had heard talk in the Church of nuns changing their dress, and Regina and Cathy decided that for them it was time. They began wearing grey skirts, white blouses, and black veils. As we were to learn, when long-suppressed freedom appears it signals the beginning of an unpredictable process. Soon the veils were not black but a variety of colors, depending on taste. Then the white blouses gave way to colors, and the grey skirts did the same. Then flowers and patterns appeared, and at times there was no veil at all. The Sisters seemed to be freer as they lost their shield and mystery, and the people seemed to be closer as they lost their awe. No one lost respect.

We frequently discussed the subject of sin and confession. The habituated confession was not making sense. The Sisters decided that they no longer needed the weekly confession called for in their "rule." It was becoming clear that getting forgiveness by saying "I am sorry" to a priest leads to irresponsibility, perpetuates negative behavior, and inhibits change. Confessions diminished as we discussed this with the people; and as a transition from the traditional approach, those who wanted to confess would gather in the church or chapel and, instead of confessing to the priest, would acknowledge to themselves that in their own view of things they had brought destructiveness into their relationships, or lessened themselves as human beings. They would then forgive themselves and each other and look for a responsible and effective way to repair harm done.

Prayers of the Mass that may have had significance at one time but had become irrelevant to us and lacked significance for the people were dropped. We wrote prayers based on the lives of the people. The sermons were generally given by me, but the Sisters or any of the people were free to volunteer to give them, with questions and comments encouraged during the sermon. We requested offerings rather than money: a few ears of corn, a handful of wheat, a couple of pieces of sugar cane, an egg or two, a handful of coffee beans placed on the altar were later given to the needy.

While I was back in the States a friend had donated a beautiful oak pump organ, which I had shipped down. I invited anyone interested to practice whenever the church was not in use. Farmers took time off from their fields, and mothers with small children, some walking long distances, came to try their hand at playing it or to let a child have that thrill, and many others would simply stop by to check out their talent. The outcome was not the greatest music, but the liturgy was becoming the people's. We took a further step that delighted everyone and made total sense: we invited marimba players to play their instrument in the church.

One Sunday a man made an unusual offering. He approached the altar leading a sheep. Handing me the rope tied around its neck, the man lowered his head and said, "I want to offer this my sheep, at whose birth I assisted and whose life I have nurtured, in grateful thanks to almighty God for the good health bestowed on my family and my animals." The scene seemed biblical, as I, vested in the beautiful garments of Mass, led the sheep across the sanctuary. For lack of a better place, I tied it to the leg of the old organ. The sheep stood there quietly until the organist began to play his next piece. Then it began to "ba-a-a" along with the music. And at the consecration it finally decided it had enough: straining at the rope, it began to walk across the sanctuary, pulling the organ behind it. The amazed organist, trying not to miss a note, hopped along on one foot while attempting to pump the bellows with the other. This scene had the congregation in an uproar until Límbano could convince the harried sheep to retire to the side again. Out of this donation, a poor family received its first animal, possibly a musically-inclined sheep.

We continued offering Father Ed's courses in agriculture and nutrition, adding a course in health and child care. And Regina began training teachers; she selected one literate person from each village to become an instructor of reading and writing to his or her people. Cathy began training six "nurses" who lived in strategic locations to run medical clinics in their homes, making common remedies affordable and accessible to the whole parish.

Meanwhile, I taught Límbano and Julio the basics of cooperativism. We in turn began teaching the same things to large groups, and out of this grew the credit union, called *La Cooperativa de Ahorro y Crédito de San Antonio.*

Then we had our first setback. Regina began having dizzy spells and took off for Guatemala City for a check-up. To our surprise and sadness we received a telegram saying she had been found to have a heart condition and would not be returning to the mountains. I wept. She had been a friend from whom I had learned much. The whole parish missed her smile, her energy, her ideas, and her labor.

Until another Sister could be permanently assigned in her place, a Sister Gertrude was provisionally sent from Guatemala City to be Cathy's companion. Sister Gertrude was an older nun, pious and devout, set in her ways and suspicious of change. I found it difficult now to work with someone so strict in her interpretation of life and religion. She needed the full traditional habit and accepted no relationship on a first-name basis. I felt threatened by her approach, thinking it might compromise or weaken the direction we had taken. Neither of us worked happily with the other.

One day after Mass Sister Gertrude approached me in the sacristy to talk about the teaching of doctrine. She was simply trying to build rapport, but I lost my temper. It was seven in the morning; I had consumed a cruet of Mass wine; I had a number of things on my mind; I thought she was interfering. I was upset that my understanding and loving friend Regina had gone and resented Gertrude's presence there. I brought my fist down on the vesting case and said, "Son of a bitch." She walked out. She looked for no further discussion, and I never apologized. I had done what I so disliked in Ed.

In Sister Gertrude, Cathy had company but lacked the quality companionship and the partnership she enjoyed with Regina. She never let up or complained, however, as she continued with the work that she and Regina had started. This gave her much more responsibility, and as she accepted and handled it, I watched her grow as a person. She became more confident, more outspoken, more deliberate in her actions. Her self-esteem rose, and she became more attractive to me.

A good part of the work that Cathy and Regina did centered around my house. As a result, Cathy and I now spent more time alone in each other's company. I had never permitted myself to feel so appreciative and warm towards a woman. While carrying out projects, we laughed and chatted constantly. Officially, we were not supposed to develop such a mutual attraction, yet neither of us fought it, and I knew it was contributing greatly to my growth. As time went on we discussed our feelings. I was learning that I could be close to a woman and even feel sexual towards her without diminishing my desire for spiritual growth.

One day she came to me while I was working in the dental clinic. She stood nearby until I finished an extraction, then came forward and said, "Can I interrupt you, Father Dentist?"

I laughed and answered, "I'd be delighted."

Cathy pointed to her mouth and said, "What can you do about my lower teeth?" She opened her mouth and pulled her lip down and muttered, "They are crowded, and several are beginning to twist."

"Let me see," I said, taking her lip in my fingers and gently pulling it down. I hesitated for a moment, then made my decision, and with the index finger of my other hand touched her teeth and gums, feeling the warm saliva. I was slow in the process, prolonging the experience, willingly participating in what I had once believed to be mortally sinful, letting myself feel the tingling in my genitals, delighting in the opportunity to touch her, and asking myself why this type of experience was prohibited. Cathy had her eyes closed. "Possibly something can be done," I said, wondering if she was having the same feeling. "Just hang around until I do these last few extractions." Working on my last "patients" gave me a break from the intensity of the moment and also time to reflect on what I was doing.

Finished, I washed my hands and asked her to get into the dental chair, a large white enamel barber's chair with a green leather seat that I had brought back from the States. I tilted the chair back and lowered her lip. Again I rubbed my finger along her teeth and gums. I thought of how my forearm would at times brush inadvertently against the chest of a person and was tempted to let that happen with Cathy but did not dare. "If you want, we can take one from each side," I said, handing her the mirror and pointing. "The spaces will probably fill in nicely," I added, demonstrating with my wet fingers. I wished I could tell her how wonderful it felt to be touching her. I actually thought of kissing her, an urge that grew so strong that I excused myself and again washed my hands.

"Well, let's get on with it," she said with a big smile. "Can you do both today?" I thought of the benefit of doing them separately, being able to have this warm personal experience with her twice, but said, "Sure we can, but you know my price is fifteen cents each."

I was nervous as I began preparations. This would be not only my first case of cosmetic dentistry but my first extraction performed on a colleague. I had to inject two shots of Novocain, a lower block on each side. "Okay, here we go. Open wide," I said, and kept a monologue going, just as I did with the local people, explaining each step of the way. We chatted until her lower jaw was numb. Then I pried the gum away from the base of the first tooth, applied the appropriate forceps, gave several gentle twisting motions to loosen the roots, and then held the pearly white tusk in front of her eyes. The second tooth also came out easily. She asked for the mirror. "Not a bad job at all, Doctor," she said, her green eyes glistening.

To stop bleeding and help congealing, I would normally put gauze on the hole left by the extraction and have the person close his or her jaw on it. But I gave Cathy special treatment. I inserted the two pieces of gauze and applied pressure with my two index fingers. She had felt no pain and now sat quietly with her eyes closed. I was aware of brushing lightly against her body. When she playfully closed her teeth on my fingers, I moved away, knowing I was in dangerous territory.

After about ten minutes of conversation, she got up from the chair and asked, "Do you want me to help clean the instruments?"

I said, "No, don't bother about anything. Just go home and rest for a while." After she had gone I sat wondering about the Church's teaching regarding such relationships; I also wondered if one who had such a pleasurable experience would forever preserve his vow of chastity.

One day Cathy entered the patio very excited. "Something very unusual is happening to me," she said.

With thoughts of Regina, I felt a tremor in my body as I asked, "What's going on?"

"Oh, don't get shook up," she said, "It's something very positive." I relaxed a bit, and she went on proudly, "I have begun having my menstrual period again."

I was taken aback. No woman had ever talked to me about her period, and seminary training did not include the workings of the female body. In fact, we were left in whatever ignorance we had, something that led to my present embarrassment of not knowing what to say, so I just asked, "What do you mean, it has begun again?"

"I had it normally as a girl," she said, "but it stopped shortly after I entered the convent, ten years ago. At the time, I thought there was something wrong, so I went to the Mother Superior. She told me not to worry, saying that it was a natural and common occurrence among nuns. So I stopped being concerned about it. But yesterday I felt it, and today I have it, and now I feel whole again." She was beaming. I thought she was courageous in sharing with me. I tried to imagine what it would be like for me not to feel like a man, wondering if I would have the courage to discuss such a subject. I knew that she was taking back her power and feeling like a woman.

Cathy sometimes brought me cake or cookies she had baked—something no one had ever done before. She also organized a birthday party for me—something I had never had before. She was teaching my cook to be creative. Cathy made a valuable contribution to our work and endeared herself to the people, particularly in treating the sick. She displayed limitless patience and attended one and all with gentleness, love, and respect. It was never too late, never raining too hard, she was never too tired, there was nothing too difficult. She studied the literature of the medicines and was at ease taking care of wounds, pains, sores, and infections. She was relaxed and calm even in emergencies. The people had great confidence in her. I did, too.

11

NATURE

The belief that only humans are made in the image and likeness of God, deliberately excluding of the rest of life and God's creation, can be arrogant and chauvinistic. While my background and education left me unaware of this, the people of the earth were willing to teach me without ever putting the lesson into words. The message was there when I proved willing to hear it. Today that lesson comes out like a prayer: an atom, a molecule, a cell, an amoeba; a dandelion, a fern, a rose, an oak; a minnow, a salmon, a dolphin, a whale; a bee, a sparrow, a dove, a condor; an ant, a cat, a deer, a dinosaur; a child, an adult, an idiot, a genius—all participate in the Original Consciousness. The Church's teaching that all of creation and all of life exists for the service and benefit of "man" has contributed greatly to the misuse of minerals, the eradication of species, the pollution of air and water, and the erosion and infertility of soil. Such damage may lead to the demise of life on earth. It is time for any structure that proclaims a divine connection and mandate to re-evaluate the consequences of its destructive views of life.

I am sad to say that the Christian faith never encouraged me to respect nature. Fortunately, the peasants of Guatemala saved me from the uncurbed and arrogant belief that I was free to take the life of a tree or any other organic life form only to enhance my own comfort. I am grateful to those who taught me to expand my consciousness, my godliness, through respecting and communicating with other forms of life, other forms of consciousness and godliness. They taught me to see and to hear. And today if my life is richer and if I am closer to God, it is to a great extent as a result of peasants teaching me to see God in all creation and to hear the Creator speak through all of nature.

A woman who respected all of life, a native healer, illiterate and living in poverty, excluded from the sacraments for her practice of the natural arts, became my teacher. María believed in Jesus; she believed in her own power and ability; she believed in the power of each individual person; and she did what any one of us is capable of doing. María demonstrated the power and depth of her love in a miraculous healing. Today I pass on her teachings to my clients, encouraging them to take back their personal power and to never again let any person or institution usurp it. And I continuously renew my belief in myself as well as in them and in our power to heal.

O N A W A R M S A T U R D A Y morning the new co-op study group met in the church. Its thick adobe walls and high roof kept the old building consistently cool. Daniel, a thirty-five-year-old father of four, stood at the edge of the sanctuary, rising nervously on his toes to see farther into the audience. The co-op members in the pews remained quiet. Daniel was known to be a thinker, but this was his first time to speak publicly. He talked loudly and clenched his fists.

"I work hard with my few coffee trees," he said looking around, "but someone else takes the profits." All eyes stayed glued to him. He seemed to gain confidence. "I want to buy shoes for my children. I want my family to make it through this year without being hungry. I want the money I earn. And I am not alone." Heads nodded in agreement, and mumbling arose. He looked to where I sat on the edge of the communion step. I shrugged my shoulders and signalled him to go on.

"San Antonio is great coffee country," he said. "Many of us have a small but valuable product, but our kids go hungry. Coffee brings a good price. But because we lack money, we have to sell the crop while still on the tree, before it is even ripe, in order to eat. The rich person who buys it pays us about one third of the going price. Those few who can hold out until harvest and sell to a middleman still get only half the selling price."

"That's right," a voice said. "And the banks won't lend money to carry us over."

"We know all this stuff, Daniel," another voice said. "Tell us something we don't know."

Daniel looked at me. "You are doing great," I said. He smiled nervously. "Can you do anything about the situation?" I asked.

"Listen to me," he went on. "What we are studying makes sense. If we are willing to join together, we can have bargaining power and the same opportunities and benefits as large producers."

"They would never let us do it," a voice said.

"No?" Daniel answered loudly. "If there are enough of us, they won't be able to stop us. Not if we register with the government as a co-op and have legal protection. Then we can exert our power." I felt a shiver go through my body.

"Instead of selling to middlemen," he said, "we would be able to contract directly with an exporter. Look, I have some figures here." He pulled out an empty cigarette package with writing on the blank side of the paper. "If we can contract with an exporter, we will receive in advance up to a third of the agreed-on price. We would not have to sell our crop early, or even sell it to a middleman at harvest time. We would get full value, and some of us could raise our income more than a hundred percent the first year." Heads were nodding.

After more meetings and much discussion, the group formed an agricultural co-op. The members elected a board of directors, with Daniel as president. The co-op had to figure out how to go about making a contract with an exporter and how to carry a large sum of cash safely through the mountains. The members agreed that they would keep their plan secret, and that only the board would know who the carrier was.

The members of the board came to me and asked me quietly

to take on that task for the first harvest. Realizing the serious-
ness of the responsibility, I accepted and went about the job
carefully. I went to Guatemala City and looked up *Café* in the
phone book. Since Germans were known to drink the best coffee
and pay the highest prices, I decided to experiment with a German exporting company. I called for an appointment and was
told, "You are welcome to drop by our offices at any time." I
got there in ten minutes. The receptionist welcomed me cordially
and showed me into the office of the vice president. A very kind
and soft-spoken young man, he invited me to make my presen-
tation.

Coffee generally grows at altitudes of up to five thousand
feet: the higher the altitude, the better the quality. So when I
indicated on his topographical map that the coffee trees of San
Antonio were on small plots ranging from four thousand feet to
five thousand two hundred feet, the man was interested. "What
quantity are you talking about?" he asked.

"If the price is right and sufficient advance payment is
given," I said, "the first contract will be for one hundred thousand pounds."

"How can you guarantee delivery?" he asked. I did not know
what to answer. I said the only thing that made sense to me,
"By signing a contract."

"And what price are you requesting?" he asked leaning back
in his big stuffed chair.

I had checked around on prices. "Fifty-one *quetzales* per
hundred pounds," I answered, the highest price anyone had
received to date for that harvest.

"And how much of an advance would you need?" he asked,
without any discussion or bargaining on price.

"Ten *quetzales* per hundred pounds, or ten thousand *quetzales*." I said.

He stood up and said, "Please excuse me. I'll have my secretary draw up the contract."

I could not believe my ears. He demonstrated total trust in
me and never even tried to bargain. He had asked for no documents or identification, not even my driver's license. I had no
doubt that the co-op was being blessed. In a few minutes he

returned with the contract, which I read and signed while he went to a vault and took out packets of fresh bills in denominations of twenty, fifty, and one hundred *quetzales*. I stuffed the packets into my saddlebags and had no sooner walked out of the office than I began to feel fear. I never had any security problem or sense of need to defend myself, but now I had cause to consider that. I went to a friend and borrowed a pistol—the first time I had one in my hands. But I found that the gun represented more than protection for me and the money; simply carrying it gave an added sense of importance and urgency. I could see how I could use a gun as an answer for low self-esteem.

I felt okay on the drive through the mountains; I just never stopped. My horse stood at the usual place at the end of the road. I tied on the saddlebags, stuffed with more cash than the average man of these mountains could make in a lifetime, and then mounted. I had heard stories of people being killed on these lonely trails for very little money. During what seemed a slow ride I realized the gun failed to give me security; it gave me the option of fighting, killing, and of being macho, and it made me more nervous than carrying the money did. I knew that I had greater protection than a gun and wondered why I had forsaken it. In the future, I would travel unarmed. As it was, I arrived safely at the *convento* and hid the money in a top drawer of a chest, behind my underwear.

The board of directors called for a disbursement the following Sunday, a glorious day in San Antonio, as co-op members signed up or pressed their thumbprints on paper agreeing to sell their coffee and received an advance of cash toward the full price. As more members rushed to sign up, I went back to the capital, now with several board members, for an even larger sum, again without mishap.

It was a gala celebration when the first truck left for Guatemala City loaded with sacks of coffee from the *Cooperativa Agrícola San Antonio*. The kindness and unusual trust of the people at the German exporting house had paid off. The Germans were completely satisfied with our product and agreed to continue to contract for any amount at top price.

The poor *campesinos* were not the only ones finding out

what could be done through the co-ops. The large coffee growers, whose income was being affected, were among those watching. No one knew how far this cooperative process would spread; but clearly, as the co-op grew, it would have social and political influence. The number of people organized into co-ops already wielded a power they had never before imagined. Most villages, for example, lack any connection or communication with the rest of the world except by foot travel. One group requested, and quickly received, a telegraph connection to an isolated village where a number of co-op members lived. Simple as that might seem, it would normally have involved much time, politics, and payoff even to be considered.

But even as many hundreds of people were benefitting from the co-op, the majority of people could not participate, for they had no coffee to work with. They had no land on which to plant a money crop or even the staples of their diet. It was clear that no matter how far the co-op advanced, the situation could not be altered much until the poor had land. To come up with a plan for obtaining land was the real challenge.

I thought of the Boston-based United Fruit Company (UFCO), the largest landholder in Guatemala, with much of its land unused. On a visit to the capital I talked to a few knowledgeable people about the possibility of approaching United Fruit. All were amazed that I would bring up such a subject. One asked me, "Do you know how many people have died for showing interest in UFCO land?" Another told me, "UFCO keeps people in line with its own army and police." I was amazed when a university professor told me the following story: "The United Fruit Company has such powerful friends in Washington* that in 1954 our democratically elected government was overthrown by the CIA because our president, the only president of the people we ever had, initiated a land reform program.

---

* At this time I did not realize that Secretary of State John Foster Dulles had been United Fruit's legal counsel; Allen Dulles, CIA Director, was a shareholder in UFCO; General Robert Cutler, head of the National Security Counsel, was company director; and Spruille Braden, Secretary of State for Latin American Affairs, would later become its director.

That program was to appropriate from the largest farms a percentage of the unused lands and to compensate at the existing tax value. Landless peasants were being settled on that land when the CIA directed the overthrow and the bloody end of the land reform program. The United States government and the Church declared the president and all the people involved to be communists, and that charge still stands for them, and for you and for anyone who attempts to help the poor get land. Don't think of it," he said.

With my own awareness developing painfully, it was becoming clear that the structures of society, be they political or religious, existed primarily and essentially for the perpetuation of the structures, not for the welfare of those who believed in them, adhered to them, or whom they allegedly represented. And the representatives of those structures, be they bishops or presidents, had to be committed to the perpetuation of the structures and their historical tenets, notwithstanding their personal desires and enthusiastic articulations to the contrary, or they would not have been chosen for their roles or permitted to continue in their lofty positions. "We must use the existing structures until we can use them no more," I learned to say.

When that first shipment of coffee left for the capital, the talk of land was on everyone's lips. The next afternoon, I stood chatting with a few of the town fathers, none of whom was a coffee grower or member of the co-op. "You don't know what you are doing," one of them said. "This cooperative stuff will bring some good results, but in the long run there will be trouble. You cannot make changes like this without trouble."

I felt my fists clench at my sides. I was not listening to his message; I heard only his words. "No one pretends we will not have trouble," I said. "However, we will avoid it as long as we can and then try to be prepared."

"How can you prepare?" another asked. "You do not know when or from where trouble will come. You can know only that it will come."

I answered, "When trouble comes, if the people are willing to fight I will take up the machete at their side." The men looked at me curiously and said no more. I felt their gaze and thought,

"What do I know about this stuff? I shouldn't be shooting my mouth off."

A sign of progress came in the form of the large, battered old Caterpillar tractor pushing its way into San Antonio. I stood with the townspeople to welcome it and felt proud of the American-made machine that now joined us to the outside world. After two years of chugging along, breaking down, and running out of fuel regularly, it finally connected the Panamerican Highway to our *pueblo*. The road would have no drainage, gravel, or topping, and when it rained, landslides and deep mud would abound, but seldom would I again bring in supplies by mule.

A few days after the tractor arrived, a telegram from the head of the Maryknoll Sisters announced that a Sister Marian was being transferred from a parish in Panama to a permanent assignment with us in San Antonio. So Sister Gertrude packed and left for the city, and we awaited the arrival of our new associate.

Cathy, Isabela, Límbano, Julio, Gabriel, Chilo and I met the Jeep-bus as it pulled up in the plaza. Out of that dusty cramped vehicle and into our lives stepped a wonderful person. Sister Marian, raised on a farm in Minnesota, was in her late thirties. She was bright, friendly, personable, and lively, the new Superior of the two Sisters. Sister Marian became Marian. She had already changed from the traditional habit to skirt, blouse, and veil, and although some of our liturgical developments were new to her, she found disagreement with none. In fact, as we continued to change and grow, Marian was a leader, moving into our lives as if she had long known us and into the work with enthusiasm and acceptance.

Although my life was meaningful and enjoyable, one aspect of it that disturbed me, although I found it difficult to admit: I did not like or enjoy my house. The *convento* was a confusing assemblage of rooms that had been tacked onto the church. It was made of adobe, now cracked from earthquakes, and dark inside, damp in the winter, hot in the summer.

As a missionary, I thought I was supposed to be rugged and satisfied to live without the finer amenities. But Maryknoll was offering five thousand dollars to help with new housing for anyone who could demonstrate need. When I considered submitting a request, I had to deal with the guilt that arose from the belief that I should not live much better than the people. But, as I was finding with so many of my beliefs, when I dealt with this one the guilt and the belief disappeared, leaving me free to make the decision. With the support of Cathy and Marian, I applied for the money.

Building the new house was fun and good experience. Brother Placid, a loving and generous Maryknoll Brother and an engineer, helped design it. I hired brilliant and dependable Rafael, the same construction supervisor who had completed the church in La Libertad, at two dollars and fifty cents a day. We dug out and gathered the stone for the foundation and transported it in my truck. From the Peace Corps I borrowed a hand-operated brickmaking machine. By mixing the earth dug out for the foundation with lime and sand, Máximo and an assistant made several thousand bricks, one at a time, for the walls. The limestone used for mortar as well as for plastering the walls was mined locally, burned to powder in large stone kilns, and brought in by mules. Men brought sand up from the river, also by mules. I transported handmade floor tiles from Huehuetenango and aluminum windows and asbestos sheet roofing from Guatemala City. The wood for the beams and ceiling came from local sabino trees that grew along the river's edge.

The woodcutters, brothers named Pancracio and Elíazar, were likable young men, considered by many to be troublemakers because of their occasional heavy drinking and brawling. They lived on the outskirts of town and were accustomed to drop by the *convento* occasionally to say hello. A few weeks after I contracted with them to supply the wood, they came to me and said, "We would like you to visit the three trees we have selected before we cut them down." Surprised and fascinated by their warmhearted request, I agreed to accompany them the following day. The slope to the site by the river was so steep that I had to go down one step at a time, holding myself back by gripping a bush or a rock. Arriving at the bottom, we stood by the beautiful sabinos, tall, strong, and straight.

After admiring and examining the trees, I felt happy that I had accepted the chance to visit them. I thanked the men for their consideration and thought we were ready to leave, when Elíazar, the older, said, "Pardon me, but we would like to explain that out of respect for the trees, we have asked their permission to take their lives." I stood in silence. "If permission is given," he continued, "we will come back the night before chopping them down and place lit candles at their base, helping the tree spirits to leave."

I had never heard of any such custom. I was amazed and intrigued, and as I considered the idea, I began to understand. But I also saw a possible problem. I asked, "What if the trees don't give their permission?"

"Then there will be a sign, and we will not take them," Pancracio said. I pushed my hands into my pockets, obviously perplexed. He tried to console me. "We would then hope to find other trees that might be acceptable." He looked to the sky and added, "*Gracias a Dios*, there has so far been no sign."

I was worried. The construction was at a stage where the wood should already have been drying. Not knowing what to say, I said, "I wish we had consulted the trees before we started the construction." I was tempted to add that in an advanced society, such beliefs would never get in the way of progress.

Elíazar broke the silence, saying, "You cannot be expected to know these things, *Padre*, for you do not live close to our Mother Earth. And if we speak to you of such, we are not sure if we are intruding." I knew he was right.

Pancracio stepped to my side and said, "We thought it might help if you prayed for a blessing on the trees and asked permission of their spirits." I considered what my former teacher Benito would say, and then I knew that God speaks to us through the trees. I was willing, and if need be I was willing to give up the three sabinos.

I knelt at the base of the center tree and touched my hand to its rough and mossy bark. After a few minutes I collected my thoughts and said, "Oh beautiful beings that have sprouted from small seeds along the river's edge into powerful giants of the forest, as you have brought God's message and blessing to us I beg God's blessing upon you. You have been on earth at least twice as long as I, yet I have the arrogance to ask the end of your earthly life in order that I may live in greater comfort. I have not considered the birds whose homes have been in your branches, or the squirrels that play in your heights, or the bushes and flowers below that need your shade and will miss your company; and, regretfully, I have not considered you. I am not sure that what I am requesting is correct for you or me or the earth, so I humbly ask your permission. And if that is granted and you become the roof supports over my head, I will be aware of your presence and will place my house at the service of people who live close to our Mother Earth."

I stood, feeling elated by the experience, only sorry that I had never before sensed such a relationship with nature. I leaned down to the river, scooped up water with my hand and splashed it on the three trees, then directed the sign of the cross to each, saying, "I ask the Creator's blessing upon you and ask the blessing of your spirits upon Elíazar and Pancracio." The woodcutters, having stood silently by with hands folded before them, said, *"Amén."*

A few nights later, about eight o'clock, they came to my house to get candles. I was unsure what I would do if the men found a sign against permission, but I did know that the outcome would ultimately be the best for me, and that I would abide by the decision. Then close to midnight I heard a knock and opened the door. The two men greeted me with big smiles. Elíazar extended his hand and said, "We left the lit candles. In the morning we will confirm the license with the mayor and begin cutting." And so it happened: the sabino trees were felled and hewn, and beautiful beams and boards came forth.

A few weeks later I was in the clinic unpacking several large cartons of sample medicines from Maryknoll headquarters in New York when I heard a scream. I looked out the door to see Rafael falling off a ladder. Working on the asbestos sheet roofing, he had lost his footing and dropped about ten feet, landing on his back on the hammer that hung behind on his belt.

When I got to him he was neither moving nor making a

sound. I knelt and asked how he was. He looked at me but did not speak. I took off my shirt and put it under his head. He whispered, *"Gracias, Padre."* Rafael was not a Catholic. He normally didn't use the title *"padre."* His workers rushed to his side, and some neighbors came running. When someone was hurt or there was an emergency, everyone available turned out.

I took his hand in mine. "Are you all right, Rafa?" I asked.

"I cannot move," he said slowly, barely moving his lips.

"Squeeze my hand, Rafa," I said. I waited but felt nothing.

"I cannot squeeze . . . not move my hand," he said. He was paralyzed. I didn't know what to do. There had been too much rain to consider taking him out by road. "What will we do, Límbano?" I asked.

"Probably get him out of the sun and make him comfortable," Límbano said. Then someone whispered something to Límbano, to which he answered, "Good idea." He leaned towards me and asked softly, "Do you think that perhaps *Doña* María could help?"

I repeated what he had said, "Good idea. We need to make a stretcher to carry him." Winding a blanket around a short ladder, we lifted the perspiring Rafael onto it and carried him across the plaza to the house of *Doña* María. No one was home, so we entered and put the stretcher on top of her stick bed as someone went to find her. The house was made of sticks sunk in the ground and tied close together, supporting a straw roof. The dirt floor was impeccably clean. Little was in the room but a few gourds and pots hanging from a stick beam. I wiped Rafa's brow. Except for a clucking hen in the corner with her chicks, everything was quiet. This was an important event for all of us, for *Doña* María was a *curandera*, a native healer. Everyone knew that the Church had forbidden her practice and thus Catholics could not morally accept it. I was delighted by the opportunity to have her share openly with me.

The elderly woman entered the hut-like structure with her hands folded around a small bottle and her eyes cast to the ground. She nodded to me, looked at her patient, and asked for his clothes to be removed except for his shorts. She stood at his feet, uncapped her bottle of herbs and oils, rubbed some on her hands, made the sign of the cross, saying, "In the name of Jesus Christ," and began massaging his feet. She explained that she would massage from his toes up, forcing the infirmity out the top of his head. We watched in silence until she finished. Capping the bottle she said, "I will rub him three times a day, and on the third day he will be walking." There were some smiles from those who knew this was not supposed to be. I, however, knew that it was to be, and I knew that if Rafa believed it, he would heal.

I was on a ladder, helping out in Rafa's absence, when someone called. I felt disturbed that anyone would bother me at that time. I looked around and was amazed to see Rafael standing below, grinning from ear to ear. "A bit stiff," he said, one hand cupping his mouth, "but almost ready to work." It was the third day after his accident. I climbed down, congratulated Rafa, and went to the plaza to thank *Doña* María.

The plaza was one of my favorite spots. And one of my favorite pastimes was sitting on the high curb with anyone else who happened to be there, watching the flow of people and animals. In an area without television or movies, the curb took on special importance. One day Tomás, one of the poorer residents of town, came and sat at my side. A bright fellow, he went around in tatters and usually looked malnourished. He asked about the co-op, and during our conversation I said, "Tomás, how about buying some seed from the co-op and starting a garden?"

His answer came so quickly that it appeared almost rehearsed. "For three reasons," he said, counting on his cut and callused fingers. "First, I don't have money for seeds. Second, I don't have water to grow seeds. Third, I don't have land to plant seeds." He stated his poverty clearly. That started me thinking, and my thoughts ended the next day with a visit to the lush corral that belonged to the church. The level, fertile, walled, and fenced land, with running water piped through it, a veritable jewel among people without land and running water, was perfect for vegetable gardens. I then went to see Rubén, the tough and stern butcher with whom I liked to sit and chat as he went about his skillful task, amazing me by not wasting one bit of an animal. Rubén was a philosopher, and I learned a lot while bouncing ideas off him. That day, sitting on the little stool he always gave me, watching the people go by, I said, "Rubén, I would like to turn the Church corral into a vegetable garden."

He kept cutting meat away from a large bone. The bones got sold also. "A little salt in the water with them, and you have a tasty soup," he once told me. He kept cutting, as if he hadn't heard me, but I knew he had. I waited. He wiped his hands on the same dirty old rag as always, lit a cigarette, turned to me and said, "You can't." I furrowed my brow and waited. After a few slow puffs, he said, "Your horses will get thin in the dry season." He was always watching out for me.

"True," I said, "but maybe I'm willing to let them get thin, like everybody else's."

"You won't be able to ride them much, and certainly not ride them hard," he said.

"Perhaps I'll have to walk," I answered.

"And what about the *Madres* and the *Señoritas?*" he asked as he began sharpening the blade of his long knife.

"Perhaps they will be willing to walk also."

He started spreading salt on the greasy counter. What didn't get sold got salted, and the sun was getting low. "Okay," he said, "and who will eat all those vegetables?"

"That's where you come in, Rubén. I want you to head a committee to decide how many family vegetable gardens can be put on the land, and then select from among the most needy families which ones will have gardens. Perhaps they can talk to the co-op about getting seed and paying for it by selling part of the produce."

He looked at me curiously, as he frequently did, then nodded his approval. Rubén was a responsible man who kept his agreements. I knew that was the last I would have to do with the project. Fourteen of the poorest families in town went to work. Each time I passed the land I would look over the wall and have a warm feeling as I saw line after straight line of healthy vegetables growing where my horses used to feed.

12

BIRTH CONTROL

If Christ were walking today amidst the teeming hovels of Guatemala, I wonder if He would castigate those considering the use of birth control. My thought is that He would probably weep at the sight of the wretchedness and perhaps even take a whip to those who have imposed such poverty for the sake of profit, those responsible for such sickness and hunger, those who command in His name that the destitute and impoverished continue birthing infants condemned to an early death or a life of hunger, sickness, and misery.

Administering baptism became for me a time of reflection. I would look at the mothers, frequently young girls, malnourished and weak, and know that with each baby their bodies became less prepared to have another, and that each baby would have successively less chance of a healthy life. But they kept giving birth, and I kept pouring the water of baptism, although in time I came to wonder if by this act I was truly serving God and the new-born children.

I came to see that at the baptismal font I was acting from blindness and ignorance, receiving beings of total innocence and divine perfection as if they were sinners and outcasts from God's kingdom, and supporting a belief that it was fine to bring babies into the world that would not survive infancy so long as they could be baptized. Of all the Church doctrines I had questioned, baptism remained aside. I hesitated to enter the realm of the untouchable belief, the sacrosanct of dogma—namely, that an infant was lost without the saving waters of baptism. But when I did raise the question, remembering that infant baptism was not a part of the early Church teaching, I had to wonder why we fail to take into consideration the absurdity of a belief, even when the belief is religious, long-held, and demanded or imposed by an accepted religious authority. I knew that I was responsible before God for my beliefs, and that as "only doing my duty in obeying my legitimate superiors" was rejected by the world community as a defense at Nuremberg, so it should be rejected as irresponsible at Rome.

It was time for me to recognize that for human behavior and relationships to be based on love and respect, we would have to be willing to deal with old religious, authoritarian beliefs, beginning with the belief that humans come into the world spiritually lost, basically bad, and alienated from God. Knowing that it was not the time to bring up such a question in San Antonio, I never stopped doing baptisms. I saw the ceremony as beautiful, but the beauty got lost in the belief that the perfect child was defective, and that I, in all my imperfection and limited love, by pouring water and saying a few specific words, would save the infant from being cast aside by God. Today I marvel at the strength of the tradition that for so long controlled my beliefs and moved me against what any unindoctrinated but clear-thinking person would know: that there was no way for those little beings to be offensive to God.

Today I am grateful to be able to recognize God's goodness in each new child, and I refuse to insult the Creator by calling the newly-arrived divine image a sinner, a lost soul. I welcome the opportunity of participating in a ceremony of accepting and welcoming a new-born child of God into the community of the world, committing to it our love, protection, and truth, and, since it is closer to Divinity than any of us, asking its blessing.

But in Guatemala I saw that these innocent new beings became burdens to their destitute parents, who were prevented by Church doctrine from deciding when it was appropriate to bring them into the world. Tentatively, gingerly, I approached the problem.

IT HAD BEEN RAINING all day and was late afternoon when Chilo the groundskeeper arrived at my door. "Come quickly, *Padre*," he said, with trembling lip. "My woman is very sick. I think she is about to leave me. What will I do with our five babies?" Even though he was earning higher than average pay at five *quetzales* a week and was one of the few men fortunate enough to have a steady income, Chilo lived in deep poverty, and his family suffered constant malnutrition. Although I had visited thousands of homes and seen rampant squalor, poverty, and sickness, never mind the lack of privacy, water, and sanitary facilities, that rainy day at Chilo's house the message from the people that they needed birth control began to scream at me.

"I am sad to hear that, Chilo," I said. "You go ahead home. I will be right along." I got my medicine kit, ritual, and holy oils and walked through town to his house, arriving just after dusk. Chilo, holding a screaming baby in his arms, opened the door made of sticks and hinged by string. He had bought a candle, which he lit as I entered. There was no fire, and the damp, cool night made everything feel wet. Three of the children lay on their bed, a small straw mat on the floor. The eldest, eight years of age, bathed the mother's forehead with a wet rag. The mother, a woman in her mid-twenties, lay on the bed of sticks, propped up, pallid, drained of strength, with a burning temperature. Death was near. She looked at me and tried to smile.

I gave her medicine for the temperature, anointed her, then sat on the bed beside her. She leaned against me, resting her head on my shoulder. I held her, feeling her pulse waning rapidly. "You are a good person, Alicia." I said. "God our Creator is also good, and you will shortly be with Him." She showed no response. I put my lips to her ear and said, "You are leaving us, Alicia. Your passage from this life will be gentle, and Jesus and Mary will be waiting for you." Despite my words, I tried not to think of her dying. I wanted to see her alive and vibrant. I wanted her to heal.

I don't know how long I sat holding Alicia. I did not realize she had died until Chilo, tears streaming down his face, tapped me on the arm and told me she was gone. Death had come as I held her in my arms. She had slipped away without my knowing it. As I laid her down, the children huddled together in the corner. And each time Chilo looked at them, he would say through sobs, "I don't know what to do with my babies. It is my fault that they have to endure this."

Later that evening, after he and several of the neighbor women had dressed and arranged the body, he said to me, "I have felt guilt each time I made love to her, thinking she might get pregnant. But I needed to love her. If only I hadn't loved her so much, she would not have died."

I wished the Pope, the person for whom she died, could have been present for Alicia's death. Sometimes it takes personal pain to shake a person from arrogant righteousness. I wished he could have held her in his arms. I wished he could spend a day in the hunger and squalor of her home. I wished he knew that these extraordinary people, who were truly looking for spiritual growth, had gotten stuck in an uncaring religious system that equated obedience and submission with spiritual development and love of God. I knew that those who insisted on the system that delivered this poverty and death were responsible before God for what I was witnessing. I wanted to scream at them that if they wanted to talk to the poor and uneducated about sin, let them first confess to the world, this, their own most grievous sin.

Anger filled me. The Church had obstructed all practical approaches to birth control and condemned them as evil. Most couples, like Chilo, could not support themselves on their income, yet they were expected to go on having families, and frequently large families. The resulting devastation confronted me more and more clearly every day after the death of Chilo's wife.

I wanted to write to the Vatican, but I knew my message would be discounted or would lead to being silenced or ostracised. I considered writing to the bishop, but I knew that would be a futile act that would lead to trouble. I asked what Christ would do. The answer was clear: Support the people, not the structure. The Sisters were in full agreement.

During the next pre-marital class, where the Sisters and I attempted to prepare young couples to be partners and parents, I asked those present, "Would it not be good if a married couple could choose when to have their children?" There was a moment of silence, then smiles and laughs and funny comments. They knew I had to be joking.

"*Bien*," I went on seriously. "I want you to think about this for a moment. If there was a way for you to make love, and still choose when you would have children, what would you do?" They were quiet. I had led them into a totally unfamiliar arena. I stood in silence as they looked around at each other and shrugged. "Alvaro," I said, directing myself to a young man who was not afraid to speak out, "would it be to your advantage to choose when to have your babies?"

He looked to his fiancée, Teresa, a very cheerful and bright young woman. They smiled at each other. "If we could choose," Alvaro said, looking nervously around at the others, "we would not have our first baby until I had found a place to build my *ranchito*." Teresa nodded agreement. Most of the others in the class did also.

"But what if you could not build your *ranchito* for five years?" I asked. Alvaro thought for a moment, looked at Teresa, who mumbled a few words in his ear, then smiled and said proudly, "We might be fine without children for five years."

"Who would not wait until they got their *ranchito*?" I asked.

There was whispering and chatter until Gregorio said, "My parents say it is a blessing to bring children into their small *ranchito*. But I think it is sometimes a burden. If we had to wait ten years for our own *casita*, we would think about waiting ten years for our first-born." His bride-to-be looked at him, amazed. She was not agreeing. But when the chatter quieted down, there seemed to be much agreement.

"Is there anyone here who needs to have a baby now?" I asked. All eyes looked to the two couples who already had babies on the way, who in turn blushed and grinned. One of the men spoke up. "We are looking forward to the birth of our child, but if there was a way to have waited, we would have waited."

I asked, "If there was a way of controlling births, so that the number of children, as well as when to have them, could be decided by each couple, how many of you would like to learn about that?" No one hesitated. I saw nods and statements of agreement as everyone answered affirmatively. But none of them had any sense of any form of birth control.

The Sisters and I began gathering data. At every opportunity I brought up the subject and asked questions. At a meeting of the Agricultural Cooperative, with more than a hundred members present, almost all men, I found that no one knew anything about birth control. All knew, however, that nursing a baby could inhibit pregnancy. Some spoke of a potion that was used in the old days; none knew what it was. None had heard of condoms, birth control pills, the IUD (intra-uterine device), or the diaphragm. All were interested and wanted to talk about the subject. I began explaining forms of birth control to the co-op members. They had no problem with the information. I was always amazed at how easily new ideas were considered when they came from the mouth of the *padre*. The Sisters likewise took every opportunity to bring up the subject with the people and came up with the same lack of information and eagerness to learn.

We were determined to find a way but knew that, for the present, condoms and pills were too expensive; "Vatican roulette" was impractical; the diaphragm would be unsanitary in the people's present living conditions. So we wondered about the IUD. I discussed it with a medical doctor in Huehuetenango, and he agreed that the IUD would be the most practical approach.

"It is about time someone did something about this horrible situation," he said. "If I determine that a woman you send me is fit to receive the IUD, I will insert it and will charge very little. But you people must be willing to educate the wife and the husband and do the follow-up."

And so began what we called among ourselves, "St. Anthony's Birth Control Clinic." We let it be known that there were means to control birth and that we would discuss this with any couple. We moved cautiously, not only because the idea was new to the people and very delicate but also to keep it secret from the ecclesiastical authorities. An obvious human need had to be met. It took little study to determine that it was not God's doctrine but man's that legislated against that need, and that none of those ecclesiastical legislators ever spoke from the experience and responsibility of having had a child.

As I continued to visit the homes of the poor, I felt increased anger toward those who legislated in favor of procreation at any cost, knowing that they lived in palaces, ate and drank very well, and were childless. I knew that peasants and workers, held for so long in poverty and without human dignity, had to be permitted a choice in bringing more lives into their hovels. They had to be freed from the doctrine imposed by those who had unjustly expropriated that right of choice. So we made birth control information available, and poor people with strong and loving family ties concluded with little problem and no guilt that birth control was a need, a right, and a responsibility.

The first couple, good and loving souls, devout parents, presented themselves with their three children. "We can barely feed our family," the husband said. "At times we go hungry. We do not want more children. I cannot afford sandals for these three." I felt humiliated. It was as if he were begging our permission to not have more children and more poverty.

The wife said, "The births have not been easy. My body is weak. I do not want to die and leave my three babies." She pulled her blouse aside and gave the infant her breast. "We are only learning now that God does not demand many babies. Perhaps our three will satisfy Him." She started to sob, saying, "Please, God, do not make me have more." I looked at the Sisters. They had tears in their eyes.

For such a couple to take the bus to Huehuetenango and

pay the doctor was an expensive venture, far beyond the means of many. We considered asking the United Nations for assistance but knew that if we did, the Church hierarchy would step in and reverse our meager start. But the word was out and spreading fast, and it was accepted: "God wants you to have only the children you want and can provide for." The unfortunate part was that only from the mouth of the *padre* was this acceptable.

For two years we ran the ungraded Church school for children along with a great variety of courses for adults, while also instructing in the public school. By then we had sufficient experience to conclude that our ungraded school was a weak link in the chain of education, taking too much time for what it contributed. After many discussions we decided to discontinue it and to emphasize brief courses for more people. Since I was using the Church building for co-op meetings and any large gatherings, the beautiful school building had lost most of its usefulness.

In sharp contrast, the deteriorating public school in town overflowed with children. Its few windows were made of broken shutters, not glass panes. The floors were dirt, not tile and concrete. The chalkboards, like the walls, had cracked heavily. The children, unlike those who used our individual desks and chairs, sat on benches and wrote on boards. The public school stood on the town plaza, adjacent to the *municipalidad,* exposed to all its noise and traffic, with a small dirt playground completely devoid of trees and grass; the parish school, with freshly painted walls and large windows for light and air, was a palace compared to it. Father Ed had gone to great expense and done a fine job with the construction of the Church's school. Situated in a quiet area of town, surrounded by giant shade trees and with a large grassy playground, it was a wonderful physical plant.

When Marian, Cathy, and I talked about what we could do with our school to best serve the people, Marian's answer was quick in coming: "Give it to the public school." That really made sense. Since such a handing over of Church property had never been done, we had to devise a plan. One thing was clear. In order for us to do it, other priests and nuns and the bishop could know nothing. Taking great caution, we hand-wrote invitations to a meeting at my house without stating its purpose; we had them delivered personally to the public school teachers, the town officials and elders. On the assigned night, the living room was filled with the invited guests, none knowing why they were there. I stood nervously before the group.

When there was quiet I began, "The Sisters and I appreciate your willingness to be with us tonight. We also appreciate your willingness to let us be a part of your community and your lives." The group sat impassive, expecting such words and waiting for me to get to the point. "We are living here in San Antonio in order to learn from you and to cooperate with you. One of the ways that you have permitted us to do this is by letting us participate in the education of your children." *Don* Lencho, the principal of the public school, a wonderful man and a devout Protestant, sitting directly in front of me, gave a big smile and nodded his head. I smiled back and tried to relax as I moved to the purpose of the meeting. "I hope we have contributed with the lives we live and the words we speak. But we want to go further in providing facilities for the education of your children. If you are willing to accept our offer, we want to give the parish school, the building, the furniture, the utensils, and the property to the *pueblo* of San Antonio Huista as a public school."

There was silence. No one moved. They continued to look at me knowing there had to be a catch. "That's it," I said; "that's the purpose of the meeting. The Sisters and I hope you will accept our offer." The Sisters started nodding their heads and looking around; that broke the spell in the room. The principal, a bright and articulate man, remained frozen until the group began to applaud. Then he stood up and accepted our offer graciously. One of the town fathers stood and suggested that the meeting be considered a town meeting and that the minutes be recorded.

The next day, in the office of the mayor, we drew up an official document, and he and I signed it. In order for an exchange to take place, the *pueblo* granted the *convento* the right to free water forever. The mayor shook my hand and thanked me again. I said, "I hope you will one day also acknowledge *Padre* Eduardo, who made this all possible, and the many people who volunteered their labor in the construction of the school." To as many of them as possible, I explained why we had given it away. I asked that they show the same generosity in giving the school to the *pueblo* that they had shown in giving their labor to the Church. Although a few were displeased, most agreed with the decision.

13

CELIBACY

Clearly, in accepting the Church's approach to sex I did much damage to myself, and it was my responsibility to find the appropriate means of healing. I was to learn that an intense and unchecked fear of sex could dominate my life, leave me sick and powerless, a helpless victim; and that the only way to deal with the fear was to confront the cause. My decision to deal with the issue initiated a continuous process that has been liberating and healing.

Today I know that celibacy is of value to those who freely and honestly choose it not out of obedience, not from fear, not for an ulterior motive, not as an escape from themselves or a relationship, but because they are in touch with a part of their consciousness that of itself transcends sex. At this point of development, celibacy is not forced and is not difficult. For celibacy to contribute to spiritual growth, complete freedom of choice is essential.

Those who enter into the celibate state for an ulterior motive, rather than experiencing life to the point that celibacy becomes a viable and valuable choice may well spend their lives avoiding sexuality until it becomes a major, even pathological, factor in their lives, detrimental to them and to the community.

My present work has demonstrated that as a person learns to love, she or he enters a deep spiritual process based on truth, and the hitherto confusing drive for sex diminishes. While many may confuse romance with love, romance lacks the truth, openness, and vulnerability of love. The romantic relationship is one that seeks excitement, the sharing of pleasure. The growth relationship leaves the romantic stage to pass through the initiation trials of love. Love seeks further truth, further sharing of self. The quality of love for and from another depends on the depth of appreciation and love for oneself, attainable through acceptance of self, including one's sexuality.

My closeness to my Guatemalan friends inspired me to examine my true feelings about celibacy and to question for the first time whether I used celibacy as a shield against the intimacy I feared. A serious reconsideration of my views about celebacy culminated in a vivid sexual dream that helped me see sexuality in a new way. Now, as a psychotherapist, I know how important dreams are in resolving issues, and I help clients use them to work their way out of problems.

DON RAMIRO was a big man. I stood five-eleven but still had to look up at him. At seventy, he was slightly more than double my age. I visited him at least once a week in his corner store, where he sold matches, kerosene by the ounce or gallon, and hand-rolled cigarettes as well as individual cigarettes removed from the commercial package. But what was most available at Ramiro's was the latest news and a good game of checkers. He often asked me for English words and said frequently, "I think I'm ready for you to teach me your language." During our games I usually sat cross legged on the rough counter. He would rest his body against the other side of the counter, leaning his big frame over the checkerboard, brushing back his white, silken hair between moves, occasionally adjusting his eyeglasses while commenting with a laugh on each move. I always felt at ease with Ramiro and comfortable in his refreshingly cool store.

It was a Thursday afternoon when Ramiro asked his compelling question. I had returned from four days in the villages.

We were into our second game when he inquired, "Is it difficult being celibate?" while double-jumping me and taking my only king. I felt shocked by what I believed to be an inappropriate question but tried to pass it off, pretending that his unexpected jump had caused my sudden awkwardness.

"Great move, Ramiro," I said. He knew I was avoiding his question. But how dare he speak to me that way? Celibacy or the vow of chastity was part of my personal life that no lay person had a right to question. Everyone should know that good priests do not think about sex enough to cause their celibacy to be difficult. Yet Ramiro had probably considered his question for a long time. I jumped one of his pieces and removed it without saying a word, my heart having gone out of the game. I knew I had to say something, but what? That I was angry at the intrusion?

He double-jumped me again and, for the first time since he had asked the question, took his eyes off the board. He looked at me and smiled. "Ah, *mi Padre* Arturo," he said, as he so frequently did, "you don't know how to answer." He laughed, but he was not mocking. He cared deeply about me. I felt afraid, afraid to let him be close. I wanted to leave the store. Ramiro, accustomed to sharing his intimate and interior life with me, was inviting me to go further in sharing mine, further than I ever had or ever thought I would. He was probably trying to help me face what was really going on in my life. I lowered my eyes, knowing that I had failed to be truthful with myself and therefore could not be truthful with him. I felt upset that I was unprepared to speak freely to such a good man.

Ramiro saved me. He interrupted the silence saying, "*Padre*, I already know the answer to my question." I looked up and saw his beautiful face and found myself smiling through my fear and embarrassment. He put his hand on my shoulder. "*Está bien*," he said. "I am also a man. I understand what you must go through. And you are my friend."

I lay awake that night. I wanted to let Ramiro know of my inner feelings. I had never shared these with anyone. Sharing was too fearful. Maintaining a comfortable distance from my emotions had influenced my decision to enter the seminary. I thought that if someone truly knew me I would no longer be me. But then I wondered how much I knew myself. Maybe Ramiro knew me better than I knew myself. Always willing to help, and forever reaching out to me, possibly Ramiro even loved me, but I used my clerical position to keep him distant. He possessed wisdom that could come only with age and experience. He was bright and understanding and, despite my hiding, I knew that he already knew me. It was up to me to know myself and be truthful with myself about my feelings and my celibacy, and to share the truth with Ramiro.

I went back to his shop the next day. "Checkers, *Padre?*" he asked, reaching hopefully for the board.

"Ramiro," I said, and stopped. I didn't know what to say. Just saying his name made me feel like crying. I pushed down my emotion, swallowed and went on. "I want to thank you for yesterday." He came around the counter, stood before me for a moment, then opened his long arms and gave me an *abrazo*. He held me tight against him and rocked slightly, my face against his chest. I could feel his warmth and smell his sweat. I started to sob. He was behaving as a father should. He held me for a few moments, and then took my hand in his and led me behind the counter and out the back door to his flowered patio. He told me to sit on an old stool, then went inside and got a beat-up old chair and sat facing me.

Everything seemed quiet. I looked at him. His eyes were moist and smiling. "Thank you, Ramiro," I said. "I have been hiding, but you have made me see myself. I am willing to begin evaluating my celibacy seriously and truthfully." He listened carefully and was thoughtfully quiet. When he saw that I could say no more at that time, he began repeating stories that he had told me before, sharing deeply of himself and of his relationship with his wife. I was able to relax and listen. When he stopped and looked at me, I knew it was time to risk.

I took a deep breath and sat up straight. "Ramiro, I am ready to say the words that answer your question." He said nothing. "The answer is that celibacy is really tough." He nodded and lowered his eyes. "Companionship with women, as with the Sisters, is rewarding," I said, "but I feel a great void. I miss

171

intimacy, even though I do not know what it is. To live alone is difficult. Not to have a partner is lonely." I hesitated and then made myself face the truth directly. "To not share sexually is to abandon a part of myself. Right now the desire for me, a priest, to be sexual is my biggest personal problem."

He raised his eyes, and I saw that he understood. After a few moments he simply said, "I know."

In the ensuing days, the fact that I had told someone of my problem allowed me to begin living with the truth and to be more open to my needs. Yes, women had been calling themselves to my attention, sometimes strongly. The prominence of women in my mind had become more noticeable with recent visits to Guatemala City, where I went every few months to take care of any business, to shop, and to have a couple of days of vacation. Away from the parish, I had been letting down my guard, appreciating women, letting myself observe their beauty. I looked into many pretty faces. I felt tingly in the presence of female bodies. I was attracted to those with fine clothes and enticing perfumes and cosmetics and to the natural beauty of those in traditional Indian garb.

I had been hiding from sexuality all my life; but now I could be open. I was looking, and I was questioning. I realized that what I had learned in childhood and what I had believed all my life about sexuality was nothing more than the Church's desire to control its followers through fear. Sex was not bad, not wrong, not against God, as the Church would have us believe. Sexuality was a good and important part of life. Christ did not advocate celibacy. Much later the Church imposed the vow of celibacy on those wishing to attain the priesthood, but once a man had entered it, maintaining the vow was not required for continuing as a priest; at that point engaging in sex was considered simply a serious sin that required confession. I had taken the vow to a controlling hierarchy in order to be ordained; I wanted and needed to free myself from it. But I had gone so far in avoiding the truth, in confusing the beliefs of others with the truth, that I wondered if I could ever bring balance into my life, if I could ever overcome the deeply inbred guilt that kept me from experiencing the truth.

In the freedom of the city, the urge to be closer to women grew stronger. I wanted to follow it. I needed to do something. I needed clarity. Seeing the prostitutes on the street corners, I thought they were my only recourse and no longer averted my eyes. Seeing men stopping to talk to them or pick them up, I felt envious. I did not know how much longer I was going to resist, yet I resisted. My mind worked it over from every angle. I was not free, and I knew eventually I would have to break free. But guilt and fear kept me from taking the next step.

On one such trip to the city I was sitting in the recreation room of the Maryknoll Fathers' House passing the evening with other priests over a few drinks. The conversation and the company was enjoyable but did nothing to furnish the gratification I needed. About nine o'clock I had the courage to get in my pickup truck and drive downtown to have the pleasure of at least looking at the women. Even the act of driving became a part of the excitement. My body felt electrified. I drove fast to prevent guilt from taking over.

Downtown, on many corners, there they were: a woman alone, or two together, or in groups of three or four, chatting among themselves, posing, leaning against lamp posts, acting seductive. Some were dressed in short skirts pulled tight; most wore low-cut blouses. I had never looked so closely before. As I drove by, I considered which one I'd select if I had the courage.

They looked at each passing car for a male occupant, smiling and waving, puckering their lips, and if a car stopped one woman would saunter to the curb to talk. I felt aroused when they waved to me or threw a kiss, but I needed to get closer. I parked the truck and began walking, passing close so that they would speak to me. The feeling increased. I stopped at a corner where a solitary girl stood. She had a scar at the corner of her mouth. I wondered what had caused it.

"Do you want something?" she asked. She seemed caring and warm. If I had the courage, I would choose her. My body began shivering. I looked at her, wanting to answer but afraid to do so. I continued walking. But I had broken a barrier. It had taken courage to stop. I saw two on the next corner. Again I made myself stop. They looked at me seductively, just as I wanted, and appeared interested in me, something that was itself rewarding. The excitement was incredible.

I moved on, knowing I would permit myself to go no further. Feeling cold, lonely and lost, I went to my truck and drove slowly back to the Center House. The excursion had been exciting but when it was over offered only frustration and guilt. I was beginning to realize that I could make myself sick over the issue of sex, yet wondered if I would ever have sufficient belief in myself to free myself.

I was not giving up the priesthood, as one would in marrying; I was willing to give up celibacy, but until I actually performed the act of having sex I would not be considered to have given up celibacy. Priests go to great lengths to get sexual gratification while still preserving the vow. No one considered it reprehensible, for example, that one of our older priests had an extensive library on sex. Another priest had simply been transferred for having had sex with boys. It is only officially that a celibate priest must avoid any opportunity for possible gratification. What is more important is that if he does slip, the laity must never know.

My fright about actually performing sex, after thirty-four years without having even looked at pictures of people having sex, or having read books about it, and without even having masturbated, was extreme. The thought of being close to a woman, actually lying down with a woman, was incredibly desirable and yet absolutely petrifying, not only because of the fear of sex instilled from an early age but because I knew little more than the basics.

Back at the Center House, I felt like a failure, wondering if I could experience my sexuality and go on functioning as a priest, thinking of myself as condemned to celibacy, programmed against sex with no room for change, wondering if I would make myself sick. I said good-night to the few priests in the recreation room and then went to the chapel and prayed that I might find resolution to my problem. I was surprised to have a sense that an answer was forthcoming. Going to bed, I fell asleep quickly and soon found myself in a vivid, colorful, and very realistic dream.

I was in my truck driving back from downtown, when ahead, on a corner on the left side, under a street lamp, standing alone, not in a sensual pose, not trying to look obvious, not in the expected dress, but just wearing a simple skirt and sweater, arms at her side, holding the strap of a small white purse as if she were waiting for a bus or to cross the street, and not paying any attention to me, was a young woman.

I felt my heart quicken. I could not tell whether this dream woman was a prostitute. I put my foot on the brake and started to slow down—a difficult decision. She still didn't look. I pulled to a stop, thinking that if she wasn't a hooker, maybe she would want a ride. Certainly, offering a ride was a legitimate reason for stopping. She looked at me. She didn't smile. She was small, about twenty, and pretty. She didn't speak.

Trying to sound sincere, gentlemanly, and casually interested, I asked, "Do you need a ride?" She stepped to the window as if she might accept a ride but wanted to check me out first. Her face was only a foot away from mine. I recognized her. She had a scar at the edge of her mouth. My heart pounded. I wanted to start a conversation, to talk about the weather, but could not say words.

"Are you looking for a girl?" she asked, still unsmiling.

My heart was in my throat. My body shivered. This was my chance. Could I do it? I began formulating words in my mind, but I couldn't get the words out. I cleared my throat, hoping to affect my most casual voice, but still no words. She hesitated. My body felt as if it were going to come out of my skin. I heard my pulse loud in my head. Then she turned and started walking. I thought I had screwed things up. Maybe I had to make an offer. I leaned my head out the window, but before I could say anything, she stepped in front of the truck, came to the passenger door, opened it, and got in. I froze. I didn't know what to do. It looked as if my decision had been made for me. I slowly shifted into gear and let out the clutch, and we drove on together.

I looked at her and smiled. She let a slight smile come to her lips. Although it might have been nice to just drive around with her for a while, I knew I had to do business. "How much?" I asked. The words came out easy. My voice sounded good, seemed as if I knew what I was doing, as if I was in charge. Like an old hand.

"It's late," she said. "Let's make it three *quetzales*."

I was torn. I wanted to do it and didn't want to do it. I needed no excuse to do it, but I wanted to make an excuse not to. She was making it impossible to come up with an excuse. If I said the price was too high, she would probably do it for less. In fact, I began to feel like a cheapskate, having sex for the first time for three *quetzales*. Making love with a woman, for three *quetzales*. Paying for this very important act, this long-awaited experience, this driving desire, and paying only three *quetzales*. This had to be worth a thousand *quetzales*, and yet it was almost free. It should be either a thousand *quetzales* or a gift, I thought. Three *quetzales* just didn't fit what was going on.

Instead of finding a place to go, I kept driving, keeping up a conversation. I was feeling excited and still not too threatened, until she said, "We can go to my place." She had cut off all escape routes. I had to make my decision and make it quick. I had to decide whether I was going to experience sex or not. I knew I had to then and there choose to be an ignorant, frustrated celibate all my life or permit knowledge of myself and what was behind my powerful feelings.

"Show me the way," I said, taking a deep breath. I had done it. There was no turning back. This girl beside me, who was really a very sweet person, was cooperating totally in making this life decision possible, and of course all it meant to her was three *quetzales*. I felt sorry for her. I wished she knew how much she was doing for me. And I wished she wasn't so in need that she had to sell herself. I wished I could tell her the truth about myself and wished that I didn't need to buy her.

"Take a left at the lights," she said. "Go straight for a while." I glanced around. Although the area had to be crime-ridden, I was unafraid of that. I was afraid of someone driving by and knowing me. I was afraid of my beliefs about sex and celibacy. And I was afraid of lying down with a woman. There were no cars on the road. No pedestrians. No dogs. She and I were the only ones out.

I pulled up in front of the very old, wooden house. There

were no lights on. We went in. I could hardly see. I stayed close, following her down a hall that ran the length of the building with many doors on both sides. We stopped before the last door on the left. She opened it, took one step in, reached up and pulled a piece of cord, lighting a small bare bulb, the only light in the room. The room was the size of a walk-in closet. To the left, a narrow unmade bed fit exactly into the width of the room.

She kicked off her shoes, took off her sweater, skirt, and panties, and put them on a table. I didn't look directly at her; in fact, I wished she had some interesting picture on the wall to distract me. She lay on the bed, knees raised, looking at the ceiling.

It was my turn. I took off my shoes and put them under the table. I wondered if people left their socks on but didn't really care, although I thought she might ask me to take them off. Remembering the money, I took five *quetzales* from my wallet and put them on the bureau. I hurried in taking off my jeans, shorts, and shirt, permitting myself no thought, no question, no guilt.

I slowly crawled onto the bed and knelt between her knees. I wondered if there would be a raid. Her eyes were closed. I put my hands outside her shoulders and carefully lowered my torso, wondering how I was ever going to find the spot to insert. She put her hand on me, sending a shiver through my body, and drew me towards her, and I knew I was entering. There was a burst of bright light. I was no longer a virgin. I knew I had finally altered early beliefs and the fears based on them. I lay there trying to keep my weight from pressing down on her small body. I didn't move. Then my body started to jerk. The feelings became intense. I was out of control. My body felt as if it were convulsing.

A long piercing cry came out of my mouth, and I opened my eyes. I was ejaculating, but I couldn't see her. I groped around, not knowing where she had gone, and then realized I had been dreaming. I was almost in shock. I couldn't believe the dream wasn't real. I got tissue paper and cleaned myself. I felt lonely for the girl and for the part of myself that had laid buried so long. I sat on the edge of the bed and thought about what had just happened. I knew there was more to intercourse than I had experienced, but I was grateful for the dream and satisfied with my experience. I knew it was much more than a dream: I knew it was an answer, a turning point, a declaration, an act of independence. I knew it had helped me to deal with much of my guilt and fear of sex and that I could now alter many more beliefs that lacked a legitimate basis for acceptance and that had restricted my life. It felt good to no longer think of myself as a virgin. I had a different sense of myself as a person. I would no longer need to watch the prostitutes. I knew that the time would come when it would be appropriate to make love with a woman who loved me.

I returned to San Antonio the next day feeling more confident, more assertive, as if I were getting a sense of who I really was. I felt more at ease with the Sisters and more accepting of myself. I knew I was able to make choices for which I could be responsible, not living by prohibition and demand. It must have shown.

One Sunday after Mass Ramiro came up to me on the steps of the church. He had a coy smile on his face as he shook my hand and said, "Ah, *mi Padre* Arturo, you look like you are really taking care of yourself."

14

RIGHTS

If the Church and the government of Guatemala were truly interested in the plight of the people, more than fifty per cent of whom are indigenous, they surely would have taken some remedial steps towards alleviation of the continuous deterioration of society. Not only have the lives of the people of Guatemala degenerated during the past five hundred years, they are in every sense more destitute today than they were even thirty years ago, and much worse off than they were ten years ago. Unfortunately, the legitimate authorities, heirs to those who initiated this insult to humanity, will institute only those changes that preserve or advance the affluence and luxury of the oligarchy—two percent of the population.

In turmoil since the arrival of the Europeans, Guatemala has experienced modern depression and hopelessness since the 1954 American-backed overthrow of a democratically-elected government that had intended to implement programs for the poor. Carrying on in the tradition of their forebears, the legal administrators of the country have since then wasted the national resources in an attempt to control those who, despite all odds, continue to try to recapture their dignity. In a repeat of history, the Guatemalan Government has destroyed more than four hundred and fifty indigenous villages in its war of oppres-

*sion, with uncounted numbers of earth people "disappeared,"
dislocated, and extra-judicially executed.*

*The greater responsibility for this outrage falls naturally
upon those collaborators who claim to represent God. It seems
obvious that if Christ were on earth today, he would distance
himself from the religious structure that has condemned His
poor for seeking their legal and moral rights while collaborating
with and blessing the oppressors. As a member of such a structure, I knew it was important for me, despite all rationale to
the contrary, to ask whether I was contributing to the suppression or the advancement of Divine Consciousness in the human
species. As the answers revealed themselves, I wondered how I
could have lived so long without recognizing that Church and
State support each other to the extent that they find the other
necessary in maintaining control of the poor population for the
purpose of enhancing the lifestyle of their benefactors. It became
obvious that the Church was committed to the ministry of the
wealthy, particularly by keeping the poor complacent.*

*With my growing conviction about the collaboration of
Church and State in oppressing the poor, I began to view the
actions of the Guatemalan revolutionaries in a sympathetic
light. Was it possible that through them I might find a path to
true spirituality?*

JULIO COMPLETED the year of work we had agreed upon.
He did a wonderful job, growing immensely. Although he
learned much about the parish and about working with people, he still knew little about the life he was choosing. Sitting
with him in my office, I congratulated him on a good job and
asked if he still wanted to enter the seminary. When he said yes
without hesitation, we began the preparations, and with the
start of the school year he left for the seminary in Quetzaltenango.

Julio and I exchanged several letters during the year, and
I visited him once. I felt like a father visiting his son, with a
sense of clerical reproduction, and realized how gratifying the

involvement can be for the priest who will never have his own children and who directs a young man to follow in his footsteps. Julio did well his first year and then returned home for summer vacation. I offered him a summer job at the *convento*. One day while we were on the trail to a village he said, "There is something about which I need to talk." Since we had already been chatting as we walked, I knew this was something important. We stopped under a shade tree and sat, each breaking off a long blade of grass to chomp on.

"I wonder if you won't be disappointed in me," he began. I looked at him and shook my head up and down in a way that says "perhaps yes and perhaps no."

"I have come to a decision," he said, and then paused. I waited. "I want to serve God and my people in the best way possible."

I chewed on my grass and looked at him, his eyes showing apprehension. "And how do you propose to do that, Julio?" I asked.

He hesitated and then said, "I want to be an agronomist."

I let out a "Yahoo!" jumped to my feet and gave him an *abrazo* that lifted him off the ground. He was delighted at my enthusiasm for his decision. He went on to request and receive a scholarship to a United Nations-sponsored school of agriculture. I had no doubt that God and Julio's people would be well served.

In the meantime, newspaper reports indicated more and more action on the part of the revolutionary movement. It appeared that the guerrillas were expanding their efforts and gaining strength. I respected them as people who were willing to struggle against the unchanging structure. The reports frequently quoted the Archbishop of Guatemala, Mario Casariego, condemning the revolutionary struggle, although in his statements he failed to condemn the obvious injustices and inequities of the government and the wealthy that the revolutionaries claimed to be fighting against. In the South American country of Colombia, however, a priest was reported in the press as condemning the violence of his government while calling attention to the plight of the people. The priest, Father Camilo

Torres, a man long committed to economic and social progress, even joined the ranks of the Colombian revolutionary forces. As a guerrilla fighter he posed many questions not only to his oppressive government and the wealthy but to the Church's stance of support for corrupt and violent governments. The hierarchy condemned Torres for his involvement. I felt angry about that. The Church had always sent its chaplains into the armies of the wealthy and their representative governments, no matter who the enemy or what the cause, but never once sent its chaplains to minister to the military forces of oppressed people struggling against injustice and repression.

Our co-op meetings and discussions regularly brought up the same point that Camilo was making: that only land was going to make a difference in the people's lives. Without land the changes the co-ops were facilitating would remain superficial. The coffee co-op members, although small landowners and poor people, differed in that they had an independent income. Others, having nothing on which to base a cooperative, struggled against the process of becoming poorer. They had no bootstraps with which to lift themselves.

In one of our discussions someone mentioned that if we had only been organized in the past we could have used the communal lands of Santa Ana. Santa Ana was the largest municipality of the parish and had the smallest population, meaning much land there lay open to use. When I questioned that, members gathered data about it. We found that long ago the government had set aside great tracts of land in various parts of the country, including Santa Ana, for the general use of the people. Anyone, for a small fee, could get permission to graze or farm this land for a season. The land could not be bought or sold. So what happened to the land?

Questioning revealed that a small part was still available for public use while the rest remained in the hands of wealthy families, fenced, held by illegal deeds, and accepted as private land. We talked of the possibility of landless people getting permission to use some of what might still be available, and our talk quickly became a threat to those who held communal land.

A bright young law student named Héctor came to San

Antonio for a weekend, visiting his girlfriend, one of the volunteers. He stayed at my *convento* and took meals with me. I decided to bring up the topic of communal land and our desire to use it. He had no information regarding the subject but agreed to investigate. A few days after returning to the capital, he sent a telegram saying, "Research indicates project Santa Ana feasible. Would facilitate matters if legal body could be formed, an independent cooperative, to deal with local and federal government. Project has basis in law. *Saludos*, Héctor." I read the telegram over and over, not wanting to get my hopes too high but knowing we had found a possible breakthrough. I went to Santa Ana and talked to everyone I could find about forming a land and agricultural co-op. Word spread rapidly. Excitement reached new heights.

The next weekend Héctor returned beaming. "It looks as if we can do it!" he yelled when he saw me. We stood in the patio as he explained, "A few of my colleagues and I found apparently unused legislation to the effect that, with the affirming vote of the majority of the population of a municipality, a legal organization of the people can supervise the use of all common land." I let out a shout that brought Isabela out of the house, and the three of us hugged with joy.

"I cannot believe it, Héctor *hombre*," I said with tears in my eyes. "We might yet do the impossible."

I returned to Santa Ana that week. Large crowds showed up for the meetings we held. The people talked excitedly. For many, this was the first time life offered such hope. After lengthy discussions, we took a vote on whether to form a co-op. The result was unanimous. Members elected a provisional board. I gathered the necessary data for Héctor to write up the by-laws.

Some weeks later, a bigger body of people gathered at the large church and accepted the by-laws of their cooperative. Many of the signatures affixed to the statutes that night were thumbprints. I again sent the paperwork off to Héctor. A few weeks later a telegram arrived, "Looking good for project. Statutes and by-laws approved. *Saludos*, Héctor."

On his next visit to San Antonio, I asked Héctor to go to Santa Ana to talk to the people. A messenger left that night to announce his visit and to call for a meeting. A horse was ready for him early the next morning. Héctor cared deeply about his people. I knew he would do well and looked forward to his return.

That evening he came back exhausted but exhilarated. "A huge crowd turned out," he said, "probably five hundred people. We spent the day discussing the difficulties, the problems, the dangers, and the procedures involved in gaining legal control of the common land. I must have answered a thousand questions." He talked right up to and through dinner without losing any of his enthusiasm. "I suggested to the people that we prepare the way and make matters easier by having a representative group pay a visit to the governor to let him know what we are doing." He held his fork in his hand, using it for emphasis, saying, "We have to get to the governor before the people holding the land do. We have to make sure he knows that it is totally legal." He put some food in his mouth and added, "You know, I like this guy, Cristóbal, the president of the co-op. He has a lot of confidence and character." I nodded agreement. Héctor went on, "Cristóbal spoke right up while others were deliberating and said he would organize the visit. And then he floored me by asking if I would accompany them to the governor's. I don't know where I am going to get the time," he said with a laugh, "but I couldn't refuse."

"You are doing great," I said, "and you are right. Cristóbal is unusual. He is not poor, but he is not wealthy; he is honest. He has land and animals and rides a beautiful stallion. He has always shown interest in what the co-ops were doing, but until now he never had any stake in joining one. For some reason, this is his project." Héctor was nodding. I went on, "And you know, he is not a religious man. I have never known him to enter the door of the church. But he comes to the *convento* to visit and talk, always presenting intelligent and well-thought-out questions and suggestions. What amazes me is that he seems to have no selfish motivation."

After dinner I walked across the plaza to the telegraph office on the second floor of the *municipalidad* and sent a telegram to Governor Rios Mont requesting an appointment for the group.

He had always been very cordial to me. Like all governors, ours was an army colonel appointed by the president.

On the designated day and at the agreed time, Héctor stood waiting outside the Government Building when Cristóbal and the full board of directors arrived. They again went over their plan and then nervously went in for the meeting.

Héctor had agreed that after seeing the governor he would return to San Antonio to give me a report. I heard someone enter, knew that he was back, and ran to the door. Without any greeting, he walked in and slumped in a chair, put his head in his hands and spoke softly with a trembling voice. "The governor is a goddamn bastard." I had never heard Héctor use that kind of language and knew we were in trouble. "He welcomed us cheerfully," he went on without looking at me. "He asked how the *padre* was. Several of the men and I sat in the few chairs available. Cristóbal, who had agreed to do the talking, stood, introduced himself and the group, and began a clear explanation about the purpose of the co-op. He had only briefly sketched the plan when the governor interrupted, and Cristóbal never got to say another word.

"The governor yelled at Cristóbal, 'Who do you think you are?' Looking from one to another, he screamed at the whole group, 'What do you think you are doing? You have come to me to present a plan that is unthinkable.' He then pressed his two fat palms on the big desk as if to lift his four hundred pound ass from the overstuffed chair and barked, 'As far as I am concerned, this is the end of your plan. I do not want to hear more about it from anyone.' " While Héctor talked, I stood silently, but my body was getting hot. I felt like grabbing a piece of furniture and throwing it against the wall. I wanted to hit the governor. I wanted to scream.

Héctor, his eyes bulging and piercing, looked up at me and in a pleading voice went on, "I then spoke for the first time. I was bewildered, but I knew I had to open a dialogue. I said, *'Por favor, Señor Gobernador.* These are our people. . . .' But the governor brought his fat fist down on his desk, shouting, 'I do not want to hear more. Keep on like this and you will be communists.' The son of a bitch's face was as red as a tomato as he pointed to the door and said, 'You may all go.' "

Héctor and I spent much time discussing the visit. We both saw that it made painful sense for the governor to oppose any plan that might infringe on the wealthy: he himself was at that very time taking illegal title to a large tract of uncultivated land. Everyone knew where the labor would come from that would eventually make his land productive. At any rate, feeling dejected but not wanting to give up, I went to Santa Ana the next day. The board of directors and a number of others gathered at the church in the late afternoon. Despite the governor's humiliating denunciation, Cristóbal remained resolute and continued to take his position seriously as he led a lengthy discussion. As the talk went on, most people worked through their discouragement and reaffirmed their determination to use any legal basis possible to continue with the plan.

I talked later with Cristóbal. "I have to admire you, Cristo," I said. "I don't know what's got into you, but you certainly have taken a courageous leadership role."

He smiled, looked around, and said, "Finally I understand what you are doing, *Don* Arturo. It never before made sense to me why you would involve yourself in these projects. But now I think I am benefitting in the way that you do."

Cristóbal truly wanted to keep the people interested and get the plan off the ground. But what he did one week later was truly unexpected. Cristóbal offered one of his own tracts of land to the co-op to be worked collectively. I couldn't believe it. Everyone was amazed. The wealthy were horrified. Cristóbal sought nothing for himself. "It's like giving away the parochial school to help education," he told me.

With a lump in my throat I said, "We gave away Church property, but you are giving away your own property. You are truly a Christian." He held up his hand to protest. "No," I said, stopping him. "I can understand that you do not want to be called a Christian, but I mean in the sense of acting Christ-like." He shrugged his shoulders.

Naturally, news of our program spread and aroused interest

in other towns. People said that if the poor of Santa Ana could succeed in gaining control of land in a legal manner, they could probably do the same in their municipalities.

Although we were working on a small scale, the potential was great. And no one recognized this more than the landholders. Threats were made. I received an anonymous and menacing note. An unidentified group began harassing and scaring people. Tensions increased. But the courage and determination of the people continued to grow. Opposition seemed to be causing a tighter union among them.

It was a Saturday morning. I had just returned from a short trip to a village and was tying up my horse when I saw Miguel, the vice-president of the Santa Ana co-op, approaching almost at a run. Something was wrong. I felt my body tense. As he got close he blurted out, "Cristóbal has been murdered."

I stood with my mouth open and said nothing. I could not speak. Miguel stopped about ten feet from me. We looked at each other. "What did you say?" I asked, knowing I had not misheard yet hoping I had.

He nodded his head. " . . .Cristóbal is dead," he said. Then shaking his head from side to side, as if refusing to accept what he was telling me, he added, "Beaten to death . . . on a trail . . . near his home."

I could not believe it. That beautiful man could not be dead. I dropped the bit and bridle to the ground and sat on the stone wall. I had felt something like this might happen but could not accept it. This was the logical outcome to the choices we had made. The wealthy could not be expected to stand by idly as we took away their means of exploiting people. I knew the repressive history of the wealthy of Guatemala. Anita had told me I would learn; now I was experiencing it. The power structure acted quickly, efficiently, and mercilessly. I felt angry and scared. Deep down I had known that we would find no legal answer to the problems of the people; I had just refused to admit it. I had kept making it important to continue trying, pretending that eventually we would find something that worked. But we only had shown that, although we were acting legally and responsibly, the result of real progress is real violence. I stood and hugged Miguel. He was sobbing. *"Gracias, mi hermano,"* I said. He did not answer.

I rushed to the telegraph office and wrote out a telegram to Julio César Méndez Montenegro, the President of Guatemala, decrying the murder and asking for an investigation. I also sent one to the governor, beginning it, "Cristóbal Hernández, who recently arrived at your office to describe a land reform program. . . ." That was the first time I had been willing to use the words "land reform," words that were unacceptable to the power structure. I sent another to the Chief of the National Police.

I announced that I would hold no Sunday Mass in San Antonio and invited everyone to Santa Ana for a Mass in honor of Cristóbal. Límbano and I set out early Sunday morning to meet with co-op members before the Mass. It was a dismal occasion. The murder succeeded in stopping the land project. It made sense that no one would be willing to be president of the co-op, or even to sign his or her name to any future paperwork.

Cathy, Marian, Isabela, and a procession of scared and somber people arrived. A crowd of forlorn mourners, many of whom I had never seen at Mass before, gathered in the immense, dark colonial church with its dirt floor and five-foot-thick adobe walls. It was not a requiem Mass. We celebrated a Mass for the living and those willing to live, "in honor of our beloved brother Cristóbal, who lived fully."

My eyes moistened as I gave the sermon. I had no idea where to go or what to do or what to say, but I said, "Cristóbal is an example to all of us. He learned how to love. He was truly Christ-like. Let us learn from his example. Let us go on. There has to be a way. To the murderers I say, 'You have taken our beloved in order to stop our progress, but you have only altered our course.' "

Cristóbal was buried. The mayor of Santa Ana refused to investigate or cooperate and recorded the cause of death as "natural." The only reply to my telegrams came from President Mendez Montenegro promising an investigation. A few days later Límbano found another anonymous note near my doorstep.

He brought it to me, his hand trembling. I read it. *"Reverendo Melville. Stop now, or you will get what you deserve."*

"What will we do?" Límbano asked.

I put my hand on his shoulder. "I wish I could stop this, Límbano," I said. "But I cannot. And if we continue, we may get hurt." He looked at me with the sincerity that I saw so frequently in his clear brown eyes. "Límbano, you do not have to go on," I said. "You have your mother and brother and sister to take care of." I wanted to add, and you are like a son to me, and I do not want to lose you.

He took my hand from his shoulder and held it in his. "I will not quit if there is another river to swim or another mountain to climb," he said softly. I wondered why I deserved such people in my life.

Since I could not know where or whence a threat would arise, I tended to suspect it everywhere. I began to notice details about people, their activity, and their behavior, and also noticed my fear gaining its own momentum. Límbano was afraid for me. He would not leave me. He asked if I could get him a gun. I told him a gun would bring more trouble than it could prevent. He reported any movement in the *pueblo:* a stranger in town was a possible spy; a soldier or policeman was to be watched. And on and on. I spent many restless nights.

Thirteen days after Cristóbal's killing, a medical examiner arrived, as President Méndez Montenegro had promised. The young doctor visited me on his way to Santa Ana. He didn't know what to expect and asked if it was safe for him to go there. I reassured him and lent him a horse. He said, "Most violent deaths never get investigated."

In the late afternoon the doctor visited me again. The body of Cristóbal had been exhumed and examined. He said that death had resulted from severe blows to the head. He said he would register his findings with the appropriate departments in Guatemala City and that we could await a further investigation. But none was to come. We would never know if the bureaucracy simply swallowed the case, or shelved it, or if there was some direct intervention.

A month passed, with the daily parish work continuing. Friday afternoon was a time when couples with a marriage problem would come to see me. I had already seen three couples that Friday in August when late in the afternoon another knock came on the *convento* door. I thought I would see more sad or distressed *campesinos*, but to my amazement there stood four young men, obviously not *campesinos*. From their demeanor and dress, I figured they came from Guatemala City.

One spoke up, saying they were students from the National University traveling throughout the State and asked if I would have time to chat with them about the area. I introduced myself and invited them in. They presented themselves as: Roberto, a student of business administration; Chico, a student of the school of dentistry; José, a student of psychology; and Fredi, a recent undergraduate drop-out. As we talked, I answered their questions and saw that they were sharp, interesting, witty, and full of good ideas. After almost an hour Roberto said, "Well, it's about time for us to move on." The others nodded agreement and lackadaisically started to get up.

It was almost dusk. "Move on to where?" I asked, thinking they were holding back from asking for lodging.

Roberto answered with a laugh, "Move on down the trail and see where it leads."

"That is crazy," I said. "You guys don't know the trails or the people. It will soon be dark out, and there aren't any hotels. And besides, I rarely have visitors, and I'm enjoying you. How about spending the night?"

They looked at each other with apparent indifference. "Let's stay," Roberto said. The others agreed.

Isabela heard the conversation. She appeared from the kitchen and asked if she should prepare food for all, saying it would take her a while longer. I went to the kerosene refrigerator and took out five beers. At dinner the hungry foursome finished off everything Isabela could put on the table.

Back in the living room, we continued our conversation. They talked about their lives and activities and asked if I knew about Sister Marji and the student group she had organized in Guatemala City. I had heard of her from Cathy but had never met her. I had heard mention of the student group from Father Blase Bonpane, a dedicated university chaplain in Guatemala City, whom I had known in the seminary. Marji was a Maryknoll nun who had taught previously at the Maryknoll Sisters' school for girls of wealthy families. She was a dynamic person with a reputation as a social organizer who had a way of getting things done well and fast, despite protests from her religious superiors.

Roberto explained that they were part of the group of students that Marji had formed, a group called The Crater. It had started as a discussion group dealing with relevant social issues and looking for ways students could participate in a movement of social awakening. As a result, some of the students were planning on taking time off from their studies to visit remote areas. Marji had suggested that they visit the parishes of the Maryknoll Fathers in Huehuetenango to evaluate social programs and offer their assistance. The four had volunteered to scout the parishes to see where students would be welcome. "You are our guinea pig," Roberto said. The others laughed. "We chose you to experiment on. We heard that there would be parishes where we would not be welcome."

They had questions about every aspect of the parish. I talked myself hoarse explaining in detail what the people were like and what went on in their lives, the success of the co-ops and the failure in Santa Ana. I told of my aspirations in coming to Guatemala, what I had expected, and what I had found.

The conversation became more politically broad as we went on. We discussed Viet Nam, Algeria, various countries of Latin America, the Beatles, the Civil Rights movement in the United States, and the movement to resist the draft. I loved the talk, since the four were informed about issues with which I was mostly out of touch.

On Saturday they had a chance to meet Cathy and Marian. They also saw the clinic in action and met many people coming in from the villages for a general meeting of the agricultural co-op.

Wanting all four to have a chance to participate, I invited them to stay over until Sunday afternoon. They accepted. I asked if one of them would like to speak at the Saturday co-op meeting. Fredi, who had been rather quiet, accepted eagerly. I asked who would like to speak at the Saturday evening Mass. They all laughed when José accepted quickly and then put on an act of embarrassment.

Fredi's talk at the co-op meeting was unexpectedly strong and somewhat humiliating for me. He talked of cooperation being a Christian virtue, of the need to struggle, and of the unjust control of Guatemala by the United States. He said that eventually America would have to give up its self-appointed role and let Latin America determine its own participation in the world community. This was new talk for the co-op members, who sat in awe throughout, and although I thought he was correct, I felt no awe.

At Mass I introduced the students and then, with some trepidation resulting from Fredi's talk, invited José to come to the sanctuary to speak. He spoke eloquently of St. Paul's explanation of love, commending the people for the examples of charity he himself had witnessed since arriving in San Antonio. I was impressed.

After a long day we settled down for another night of conversation. They were excited about what they were seeing and proposed that Crater members come to San Antonio to expand and accelerate the reading and writing classes in the villages. I felt enthusiastic about the idea and encouraged them to develop a plan and start sending students as soon as they were ready.

At the Sunday Masses I introduced the four students again. They helped out at baptisms and in the clinic, walked through the open-air market, and horsed around with neighborhood children. The people found it interesting that young educated men from the city would come into the back mountains and show such good will. We had spent so much time together and shared so well that it seemed logical on Sunday afternoon that I should suggest that they spend another night. They were delighted to accept.

The beer had run out. I got my half bottle of Scotch from the closet. It was Sunday night, and we were talking like old friends. It seemed that any topic was open for discussion. I told them about an American colonel coming to my door and asking about guerrillas and if I knew anything about revolutionaries running guns. They laughed. I told them my favorite line from the colonel: "You missionaries in the boonies have to be the eyes and ears for us in the capital." In turn, I asked them if they had had any contact with the revolutionary movement.

With that, something happened to the group. I wasn't sure what it was. There was an instant of silence, and then a slight tension. They answered by speaking of a few guerrilla actions in the capital that they had heard and read about, but the conversation was not the same. Chico, whose lisp got stronger as he drank, began doing most of the talking. I asked more questions, and although they answered they did so without their accustomed enthusiasm.

It was about eleven o'clock. Fredi yawned, said he was tired, excused himself and went to bed. About five minutes later Roberto said he was going to turn in. Chico said he thought that was a good idea, tipping up his glass and taking a last gulp. José and I sat alone. He was finishing a cigarette, apparently going to leave as soon as he put it out. I said to him, "José, do not go to bed yet." He looked at me cautiously. "We all shared well this weekend and became very close." He nodded agreement. "Now you all feel uncomfortable about something and want to withdraw. As a result, I am also feeling uncomfortable." He didn't take his eyes off me. "You are hiding, José. There is something that is not being said." He lowered his eyes. "If you can't tell me what it is, just say so, and I won't proceed any further. But this running off and hiding is not acceptable, especially if you have any intention of coming here to work with the people."

He pondered for a moment, took a long drag on the cigarette, and crushed it carefully in the ashtray. He glanced at me, took a deep breath, and let out a sigh. Looking at the floor, he said, "Let me talk to the others," then got up slowly and left the room. I could hear muffled talk as I waited.

About ten minutes later the four returned and sat in their same places. Except for glances to check me out, no one made eye contact with me. A heavy silence prevailed. I waited, unwilling to help by starting the conversation. After a long moment that seemed like an hour, José moved to the edge of his chair and played with a dead match in the ashtray. "I am going to answer your question," he began. "But in doing so, we will enter into a most serious conversation, a conversation that could have terrible consequences." He was speaking with authority. He looked around. I felt my body stiffen. The others listened attentively but without being at ease. I thought that maybe I didn't want to know what they were hiding. José went on, "You have noticed that at times I have been quiet. The reason for my caution is what I am about to share."

I looked at the others. They seemed somewhat anxious but in apparent agreement. José cleared his throat, looked me in the eyes, and said, "I am a member of the Rebel Armed Forces." Silence followed. My temples felt hot. He reached into his shirt, pulled from his belt a large pistol, and put it on the table in front of him. "I am committed to the revolution. If I am recognized by the authorities, I will be shot on sight." I felt my heart jump. No one moved. "But I will not be taken alive. Those who are in my company are therefore always at risk."

I wondered if I could trust him. I had read in the newspaper about the F.A.R., the *Fuerzas Armadas Rebeldes*, the guerrillas, and had heard about them on the radio. I thought of the time of the shooting I had witnessed in Guatemala City and the feeling I got as I looked up at the small hill where the army and police had a band of guerrillas surrounded, and the plainclothes policeman said, "We leave no wounded."

I had read about the F.A.R.'s *comandante*, Luís Turcios, a rebel Guatemalan Army officer trained by United States forces who had died recently in a mysterious car accident. Everyone knew that the Army and the police were fighting the F.A.R. tooth and nail. Any captured member or even suspected sympathizer was murdered or disappeared, most probably tortured and killed. I had found it interesting that in their communications, leaflets dropped in the streets of the large cities, the F.A.R. addressed clearly some of the problems I was encountering. Although the organization's information was vast and provocative, I questioned much of it. I knew also that to counteract the revolutionary propaganda, the government and the

Church had long been waging a successful propaganda campaign that left most people, including myself, in confusion and with great fear of anything that was not part of the status quo. American military officers were being gunned down in Guatemala City, raising doubts and questions for Peace Corps workers as well as for ourselves.

José broke the silence with, "We have heard of the work being done here in San Antonio. It looks good to us. We think your goal might be the same as ours but believe it will not be accomplished without a struggle." Hesitating a moment, he said, "Even if you don't agree with us, we think we have your confidence, and as a result we are willing to share." I nodded. He lit a cigarette. The others seemed to relax. Chico emptied the last few drops of Scotch into his glass. José went on, "It was our intention to check you out. That is why we are here. As we got to know you this weekend, we thought we could trust you. We wanted to discuss our work with you, but we were not yet in agreement as to how or when. You surprised us in bringing up the subject." He moved the pistol to the side, then thought better of it and put it back in his belt. "And now that we are clear with each other, we look forward to exploring the possibilities of mutual support, and possibly of cooperation. We want to see if at any level we can join our campaign with yours."

The room was charged. I felt a trembling in my body. I knew that this meeting and connection held importance. I sensed that I had wanted something like this and yet had no idea how I could ever bring it about. I could hardly believe what was happening. I felt convinced that it was needed but had always been afraid to say so. I sat with my legs crossed, trying to appear relaxed. Without shifting my position, I asked, "What do you hope to get from me?"

José again hesitated, and then answered, "As you can see from your own experience, no one, at any level, can bring about legal change in Guatemala." I nodded agreement. "If the revolutionary struggle is to be successful, the campesinos themselves have to be the base. But they have been so intimidated that they find it almost impossible to participate or to trust those of us who are willing to fight. They have been taught that any change is inspired by communists and that those involved will lose all they have. To bring about change they not only have to overcome those beliefs, they have also to be willing to risk the most intense horrors that official oppression saves for those who are inclined to transformation." I found his choice of words, "overcome beliefs," intriguing. He played with the match.

"It is our belief that people like you," he went on, "who have already earned the confidence of the people, and who believe in the need of changing the structure of society and yet recognize there is no legal way of doing so, are to be contacted, supported in any way possible, and encouraged to participate with us."

I hesitated, then said nervously, "I am interested," and after a pause added, "but even if the people enter the struggle and ultimately win, they have no guarantee of a better way of life."

"There can be no guarantees of anything," José said, looking around at the group. "If enough people enter, and the United States withdraws its support of the oligarchy, we will eventually succeed. As to having a better way of life, a person or a group will have a voice in the future according to their participation. It is not our intention that the people be further exploited."

Although nervous, I was determined to go on. "Every successful revolution becomes totalitarian," I said. "Successful revolutions change the quality of exploitation, but they still exploit."

"Arturo," he said, losing his serious demeanor and beginning to smile, "there was a revolution in 1776 that overthrew the exploiters, and the successful revolutionaries went on to give the world a constitution that to some of us seems inspired, and a bill of human rights that we would like to emulate in Guatemala."

Needless to say, none of us had any need to sleep. No one even yawned. The night was long and lively as we discussed and argued, touching on goals and possible means to attaining them, as well as hopes, beliefs, problems, and contradictions. I had many doubts and endless questions. But I was not just looking for information. I was studying the four people who had been living amidst revolution all their lives, a politicization I was unfamiliar with. I asked each to address his own beliefs and motives.

Chico had recently left the School of Dentistry in order to be a part of the revolution. His family were workers. He was about five feet-seven, plump, with a heavy beard and a sing-songy voice. He kept a smile on his face and apologized frequently. It seemed important for him to please people, and his joining the revolution may have been an offshoot of that. Chico was pleasant, courteous, low in self-esteem, a follower. He seemed more fit for the role of a priest than a revolutionary— but that was based on my narrow belief of what a revolutionary should be.

When I asked Chico why he had joined the movement, he said with unusual clarity, "I felt guilty going to the university, preparing to enter the higher social class, and seeing my family and my people underprivileged and lacking."

"Where do you stand on communism?" I asked.

Nodding to the three, as if asking permission to speak for them, he said, "We have all studied Papal Encyclicals, the New Testament, the Constitution of the United States, as well as Lenin and Marx. Some of our companions have studied in the United States and Canada, others in Russia, others in Cuba." He was now drinking ice water. He took a sip, as if gathering his thoughts. "We do not espouse communism," he went on. "We are not communists. But our people have to eat, and that means there has to be a change. The United States opposes the change we need. To whom can we turn for help? Whoever helps us will obviously be a factor in determining our future course." I remained silent.

"Look, *hermano*," he said, raising his arms as if in exasperation, "the government of the United States has no interest in our people. It has its own goals and will distort facts and information and use any means, including the slaughter of our people, in order to attain them." I felt hurt and defensive. "And the innocent people of the United States, good people, Arturo, just keep giving their money, without any idea of the way our generals become millionaires. But how long are we expected to go on forgiving the people of your country for their ignorance?"

I did not answer. After a moment of silence, I turned and asked, "What about you, Roberto?" A twenty-year-old undergraduate in business administration, Roberto was short of stature and strong of build. He was an avid bicyclist and sports fan. Roberto came from the upper class. He was good-looking and friendly with a quick and pleasant smile. He was also courteous, but more, he wanted to appear cool. Although he frequently acted and spoke maturely, Roberto seemed to doubt himself, as if not expecting others to take him seriously. Despite being a newcomer to the movement, he seemed committed to it. He also seemed committed to José, and I wondered if this were not the stronger commitment. As I thought about it, I doubted the purity of motivation for entering any profession, movement, marriage, or religion. As one became a priest, a parent, or a politician from mixed motives, I wanted to give the same grace to a revolutionary.

"What is essential for Guatemala is an equitable program of land distribution," he said, knowing that also to be my conviction. I nodded agreement, but that triggered something in him. Appearing to be angry, he asked, "What do you know about land reform in Guatemala?" Before I could answer, he went into a lengthy account of the subject from 1950 to the present. As he spoke about American involvement, at first I felt intimidated. Then I realized his anger was not directed at me personally. At times he spoke so excitedly and quickly that I had trouble following him.

After ten or fifteen minutes, appearing to have finished, he closed his eyes and rested his face in his hands. Then suddenly he stood, and with even more intensity added, "If the United States did not involve itself in Guatemala, our people could begin to develop and gain some dignity." He looked around as if surprised at himself, then lowering his voice, went on, "Land reform will never come through the ballot box or legislation. If you, Arturo, know that as truth, then you can share it with those who need to hear it. If you decide to be with us at any level, it will be of great help. Not only do many peasants know and trust you, but you, as an American participating in our revolution, can make what is happening here known to your people. They have to learn that they are not supporting a war against communism but rather an unjust war against the poor. If the United States would give up the belief that it has to involve itself in the way we run our country, we could free ourselves without turning to Russia or anyone else."

He looked around again, apparently embarrassed that he had held the floor so long. But when his companions saw he was finished, they yelled "Bravo!" and clapped their hands. Roberto blushed, excused himself, and went into the bathroom.

Fredi had been in the movement longer. He was short and stocky, and his head was disproportionately large. Although friendly to me, he was clearly fed up with Americans. Fredi had a deep, strong voice and a powerful laugh. He was bright and articulate and had completed several years at the university. I asked him to tell his story. He said, "I no longer want to talk about what the United States has done. I will participate in making our revolution. The U.S. will do what the U.S. has always done. There will be no discussion until we have won. I have come here to San Antonio because I am interested in my people. I find it unusual that you, an American, have not exploited them. Whether you, an American priest, join our movement or not, is of no particular importance or consequence to me. It is important that I and my people make revolution." I felt hurt but said nothing.

José, their leader, was about five foot ten, slender, muscular, and agile, twenty-three years old, the son of a mechanic. He had been graduated from the university with a double major in psychology and philosophy. José had good looks and, like the others, fair skin. His short hair was close to blond. He had an attractive personality and easily drew attention, especially that of women. He avoided pushing himself onto others, but others seemed to push him into leadership. He was intelligent, quick-witted, and articulate. He had seemed more shy and hesitant in the group, but in quiet conversations during the weekend José had been sharing his personal life with me. He said that people were not indifferent toward him; they either liked or disliked him. He added that although it made him uncomfortable, he was accustomed to have men compete with him. I guessed that many men would be jealous of him.

He began speaking. "My studies led me to the conviction that for personal fulfillment I had to share with the community of mankind. I learned that freedom and democracy were essential. In the process I became convinced that revolution was a prerequisite to attaining human rights in Guatemala. That fact makes me sad, but I know there is no other way. If I die working for human rights, I will have lived well."

He looked around the room. We waited in silence. He shifted the gun in his belt and went on, "I have been involved in the movement for some time. That led me to the F.A.R. I have just completed a four-month stint in the mountains. I was the personal bodyguard of *Comandante* Turcios, whom I will always hold in great respect. I would have been with Turcios at the time he died in the automobile crash and fire, but he wanted to be alone with a woman that night."

José went on to talk of exploits of the F.A.R., stories that were most stirring. He spoke sadly of his companion, Otto René Castillo, who with his girlfriend had died a torturous death by fire at the hands of the *Policía Nácional*. He promised to get me a copy of Otto's last poems.

"I am always looking for ways to increase support for the movement," he said. "I went to a student gathering at The Crater to meet people. I met Sister Marji there. I knew that if members of Catholic religious orders got involved, we would overcome much of the prejudice and propaganda built up against us. I also met these companions there." He looked at the others and smiled, then raised his hands, indicating he was finished.

I sat somewhat stunned, my head reeling. I had had enough. It was almost dawn. We gave *abrazos* and retired, but I could not sleep. So many of their phrases and statements kept echoing through my mind. I had so much to consider.

At morning Mass I looked at Límbano, concerned for what he would do if I joined such a movement. I shrank from thinking about that. I wondered if I could make a free decision without unduly influencing the people I had spent years trying to influence. I wondered if a decision I made would lead these people to suffering and death, broken families, the loss of what little they had, with possibly nothing gained. On the other hand, my joining the movement would affect the stigma that Church and Government had imposed on the revolution. If a member of the clergy joined, the power structure would find it more difficult to label revolutionaries as misfits. I might be able to speak to the people in the United States in a way that "the oppressed of the free world" had never been able to do, possibly influencing the selling of arms and equipment, the training of military and police, the sending of Green Berets and advisors. And it might be difficult for the United States to kill one of its own.

As I looked at myself standing at the altar, I wondered what my role really was. Priest! What was a priest? It seemed that many of us led lives of hypocrisy and escape, accepting an outmoded structure and committing ourselves unquestioningly to its perpetuation, a structure that not only failed to serve people but demanded continued submission. And as I stood there, I knew I had been offered the opportunity of a lifetime. The revolution could probably embrace the values, desires, and needs of my priesthood as well as those of the people.

Yet my motivation remained unclear. I was aware of a subtle desire to gain respect, power, and fame through a very exciting experience. I had a sense of the reward to be gained from living in close companionship with people of mutual trust and struggling for a common goal. I knew that the romance and heroism of the movement could look inviting to one whose primary goal had become empty or frustrating, and that some who would enter naively would live or die regretting it.

After breakfast my four companions left looking confident. I knew they would return shortly. They knew they were welcome; we had established a strong and significant bond. I spent the day reflecting on what had passed between us, questioning myself, doubting and re-doubting what had been said, thinking I was being led or misled or used, wondering: Where was I going? What did I truly want in life? Was there any other way for the people? Could I accept violence as a part of my life?

I knew there was no legal way for the people to progress,

and by living in Guatemala I was accepting officially-sanctioned violence. Was I willing to stand up to the violators? The question haunted me. I asked repeatedly for divine guidance. And it began to filter into my thoughts. I heard such messages as: "Be with the people." "Listen with your heart." "The existing structures produce violence and oppression."

Although I had always desired it intensely, I never thought I was succeeding in developing true spirituality. The teachings of the Church, so dominant in my life, had led to religiosity and devotion, inhibiting the free development of spirituality. Now I was on my own, without a Church, still wanting to grow spiritually, yet wondering if I trusted myself enough to create the opportunity. Yet I now appeared to have done just that.

I was not sure how Marian and Cathy would respond to this sudden twist, but I needed very much to confide in them. I thought Marian would be inclined to support me in whatever decision I made, while Cathy, who was presently in Mexico City for a workshop, would find it difficult. I went to my confidante, Marian. I am sure she noticed my nervousness. I found it difficult to open the subject. But as I shared some of the weekend conversations, I eased in bits of the critical topic. At each point of the discussion, she showed interest and responded favorably. I went on step by step and finally felt relieved when I had shared all. Throughout, she kept her brow furrowed and moved nervously in her chair as she presented her own questions and problems. But it was as if she had expected this turn of events and lacked only the sufficient data and the opportunity for it. Realizing I had such a supportive companion, I felt a shiver go through my body.

In the ensuing days, instead of visiting the villages I limited my activities, only writing out my thoughts and ideas, meditating, and meeting with Marian. After many discussions, covering and recovering each and every point, Marian and I concluded that if the facts proved out as we believed them, both of us would join the revolution. I said, "If I hold back, it will be only out of fear." She agreed, saying, "And that is no reason or excuse for holding back."

15
DECISION

I found myself doing something that a short time before I would never have considered: in search of support for the people, I was exploring the thoughts, motives, and behavior of those considered by Church and government to be militant enemies. It took no great insight to realize why the power structure viewed such people as enemies; but to my amazement, as I familiarized myself with the revolutionaries and their ways, I did not find them to be enemies of Christ or of His people.

Meeting with them helped me to evaluate ecclesiastical and social teachings that had obscured certain truths—for example, that women are true leaders. I came to see that without women in leadership positions, no organization or movement can claim to represent the truth or hope to have a positive and widespread spiritual and social impact.

Entering onto the personally uncharted and critically dangerous course of assessing United States doctrine forced me to conclude what previously I hadn't even wanted to consider: that the democracy we have attained is for the wealthy, and that God is not on our side. Democracy is a goal still to be sought, and of course a first step in developing true democracy will be for women to participate in the leadership of all elements of society.

Thinking of the wars my country had participated in and the way I had always been led to believe that God was on our side, I realized what an affront to our Creator that view represented. That our Source would take sides in a struggle, or fix upon a particular human approach as the absolute truth, or support one social element in defeating another are beliefs that clearly reject the nature of God.

I had entered a very unusual school, learning unusual lessons that eventually led to further conclusions, including these: God has no enemies; God does not interfere in our choice of friends or enemies or the way we relate to them; it is truly up to human beings to choose to work out their differences responsibly or irresponsibly; God has given us free will, and no matter how we use it or abuse it, that gift will not be violated or retracted.

I used my gift of free will to seriously consider supporting the people through the Guatemalan revolution.

A WEEK LATER when the knock came at my door, I knew who it would be. I had been waiting for them. José and Chico wore big smiles, although they had walked some distance and looked tired. I asked about the others. They said Roberto looked forward to returning to San Antonio, and that Fredi had gone on an assignment and would not be seen for some time. I never heard of him again.

I told them of my conversations with Marian and of her response. José jumped around like a child and said he could hardly believe what was happening. He asked when we could all get together. That afternoon I invited Marian to join our conversations.

The four of us discussed what was going on in the parish as well as what was happening with the movement on the coasts and in the capital. José spoke of surveillance and suggested some precautionary measures. He also said that another nun was already committed to the movement. Marian and I knew immediately that he meant Marji. José and Chico talked about her work with the students, saying she was already preparing a group to come to San Antonio to view our projects and work with the people. They pointed out, however, that these students would not be committed to the movement, nor would they necessarily know anything about it.

I asked about my friend, Blase Bonpane, and his work with university students. They said they knew him as a good and sincere man, interested in change and revolutionary causes, but in his zeal he had made contact with people at the United States Embassy, and for that reason it was difficult at that time to confide in him. I felt sad. One of the few priests in whom I had confidence, Blase was a man with whom I had wanted to discuss my views. José and Chico participated in the weekend work and had several more conversations with Marian and me, then left Sunday afternoon. On Monday, Cathy returned.

I had missed her, but I also realized how important the revolutionary movement was becoming for me by how little I had missed her. She bubbled over as she showed Marian and me snapshots and spoke excitedly about the workshop, her travels, and the people she met. We were interested, but our preoccupation did not let us share in her enthusiasm. We slowly began to reveal some of our discussions with the students, prepared to stop if she showed any objection. I wasn't sure how I wanted her to respond. I stayed jittery throughout the conversation.

She showed interest, appearing wary of our enthusiasm and, while not opposing our ideas, presented a number of questions, which we spent hours answering. Her nervousness was obvious as she said, "I am happy at the course you are taking, and that neither of you is ready to make your decision. I want to be part of this process of gathering information, but I'll be in no hurry to come to a conclusion." She smiled at each of us and then touched Marian's hand, saying, "As always, you can count on my support, but I don't want you guys getting ahead of me."

Marji began occasional visits to San Antonio, driving upcountry with a Jeep full of interested students who wanted to spend a weekend or some vacation time among the villagers. Not long after, the students were involved in literacy programs and producing a good response from the *campesinos*.

On one of José's visits to the parish, he had just arrived when he eagerly asked me to sit down. "I have much to tell you," he said. Isabela brought us a pitcher of ice water and two glasses. I asked her to go buy some fresh bread, knowing she would dilly-dally in the market. "First and foremost," José began, lowering his voice, "I want you to know that I talked to Camilo Sánchez, the new *comandante* of the F.A.R. I told him about you and your work and of your interest in the movement. Sánchez said he wants to talk to you personally." He had a big smile on his face. I didn't smile; in fact, I felt shocked. I had never expected to know a person such as Sánchez and was not sure I wanted to. In fact, I found it difficult to believe José's words. I said nothing. His smile faded.

But he talked on, and as he did, a meeting slowly began to make sense. I felt my interest being aroused, and my body began to tingle with excitement. I knew I was going to have to make an important decision, a decision that would force me to confront head-on some old beliefs. And I did not want my feeling of romantic excitement or of fear to sway that decision. I said, "I need time to think. I have to be clear about my motivation." For several days I considered the idea, talked it over carefully several times with Marian and Cathy, and the night before José was to leave I told him with some trepidation, "Yes, I sincerely want to have the meeting."

He was delighted and had the details of the meeting ironed out. He explained them, saying I should follow the instructions exactly, tell the plan to no one, and commit nothing to paper. On a particular day, at a specific time, I alone was to drive in my pickup, with no baggage or cargo of any type and with no tarpaulin or cover, to a fixed point on the road above Lake Atitlán. From there I was to proceed at thirty kilometers per hour to another point where I would park for five minutes, as if observing the scenery. I was then to drive at thirty kilometers per hour back past the original point on the road. He said there was nothing else I needed to know, but if at any time anything suspicious arose I was simply to drive into the town of Atitlán and enjoy the day. Just before he left we went over the instructions once more.

It was a bright and sunny morning. The highland lake set between two volcanos is one of the most beautiful spots in the world. I loved the lake, but on that day I hardly noticed it, so intent was I on the specific details of my instructions. My timing had to be accurate. I was to demonstrate absolute caution. I had to be clearly observed as alone and with nothing in the vehicle. There could be no room for betrayal or mistake. If there was, people were going to die, including myself. I knew that the exercise was helping to clarify the extent of my commitment.

I did everything exactly as prescribed, feeling tense and awkward while trying to appear relaxed and casual. As I sat for the five minutes, I let my eyes glance around. I saw nothing. No one. Back on the road, I shifted up to second and kept it there where it was easier to maintain the prescribed speed. I wondered where they were, if they would come through, if they were simply testing me, if something had got screwed up, if. . . . I passed the original mark again. There were no further instructions. I didn't know if I should turn around and go back again. I kept on at thirty. I looked in the mirror and saw a car approaching in the distance. It came up fast. I squeezed the steering wheel tightly, pulling to the right to let it pass, but it slowed behind me. My heart pounded. Then it pulled alongside. I felt my palms sticky on the wheel. I looked out the window. There, driving a new BMW, was José. The man beside him looked at me seriously. José waved for me to follow. They went on a short way and then pulled to the side onto the gravel. I stopped behind them, wondering: What do I say? I had no instructions. What do I do? I decided I would follow their lead.

They sat in the car for about ten seconds, then both got out. José was smiling. He waved to me and yelled, as he did so frequently, with his hands cupped to his mouth, "What a perfect day!"

I got down from the cab and walked toward them. I smiled, but only to cover my fear. They walked toward me. The stranger was not smiling. José put out his arms for an *abrazo*. We hugged like old friends. I followed his lead as we both said how happy we were to see each other. I was wondering about the introduction. There was none. As we ended the embrace, the stranger held out his arms for an *abrazo*. He wore a blue two-piece pinstriped suit. He was of medium height, solidly built, with black hair and eyes, dark skin, and a rugged face. He hugged as he looked.

The three of us chatted small talk for a moment, looking around and pointing to the lake and the volcanos as if admiring the beauty. Then José began to wander off, and the stranger, nodding to me, took a few steps toward the beach. I did the same, and then we were both walking toward the water, acting casual, asking and answering irrelevant questions about the family, the ride down, and so on.

An Indian fisherman's rowboat, old, virtually without paint, sat on the beach. He pointed to the boat, and we walked to it, stepped in, and sat, he choosing the back seat, facing the road. I sat on the middle seat facing him and the water. He glanced around as if still admiring the scene, then confronted me squarely. I dug my fingernails into the bottom of the seat, feeling as I did when I had faced Virgilio. This was one tough man.

"My name is Camilo Sánchez," he said looking into and beyond my eyes. I am pleased to meet you, Arturo. José has told me about you." He paused, looked to the beach, probably at José, then asked, "Has he told you about me?"

"No," I said, forcing a nervous smile. "He has told me only that you are the new *comandante* and that you asked for this meeting." He acknowledged with a nod of his head and began talking.

Aware that my back was toward the road, I felt tense. If anything was going to happen, it would come from the road. But I knew that if there was a hint of anything's happening, Camilo would react quickly. He had the eyes of a cat and missed nothing in our surroundings. From the corner of my eye I saw something move to my left. I looked. José was sauntering down the beach, hands in pockets, kicking a stone. I knew his sharp senses were on total alert.

"José will take care of things," Camilo said, opening the button of his suit jacket, revealing the big, shiny, bluish-grey pistol stuck in his pants. He touched it gently, as one might a beard. "We never relax totally," he said, "but it is important to know how to ease off without becoming careless. It would be foolish for me to forget that the most powerful and highly skilled forces of the hemisphere are at this moment searching for me. Yet I must be able to live with myself."

I looked beyond him to the calm blue water. For a moment I let myself see the beautiful scene with the volcano in the background. He knew I felt nervous and tried to put me at ease, speaking in a soft, firm voice, a voice that I knew could also scream, curse, and rip.

"We are in good shape here," he said. "This meeting has been well planned. The area has been under surveillance for days. Even now we are being watched by our own people, dedicated people, people willing to die in order to keep you and me and José alive, people who at this time have no idea who you are but are playing their practiced role to the utmost." He looked toward José and then continued, "We take no unnecessary chances. We are good students, studying every possibility before making a move. We are patient, and then we move like the coyote."

On the far bank I could see some Indian fishermen, patient people. I wondered if they had been too abused to move like the coyote.

"We have struck terror into the government forces," he went on. "They never know where or when or how we will show up. That is why they wipe out whole villages, hoping to eradicate one or two of us, expecting to intimidate the people to turn against us."

The water looked incredibly refreshing. What a place to be with a man I would not choose as a friend, but a man on whose side I would want to be in a fight. This man was a killer. He would stop at nothing to get what he wanted, including using me. If he were a policeman, he would be and do the same. How did people choose which side to be on?

"Some of my family have been killed," said Sánchez, shaking his head. "I hate what goes on. I would love to spend time with my children. But we cannot stop. My children will either suffer under the system or fight against it." He was pushing his right fist into his left palm and twisting it. "Never in history have the wealthy stopped to look at the problems they create. They are totally irresponsible as they send their children to expensive

Catholic schools." A chill ran up my spine. Although I agreed, what he was saying felt like a lecture. I did not want to interrupt. He seemed to get a sense of my discomfort and smiled, obviously in charge, as he went on speaking of the struggle, the gains, the losses. He spoke of the difficulties, the horrors of living like an animal in the jungles and mountains.

I realized why he was *El Comandante*. He talked and acted like one who had grown up in the *barrio*, who knew the streets and the alleys, who had fought hard and knew how to command, who did nothing part-way and would accept nothing less than winning. This was a no-nonsense man, a man not to be joked with unless he chose to joke. He was about thirty years old, self-educated but well educated. I listened to every word, but I also needed to hear myself say something. When he paused, I interrupted with, "Why are you doing this, Camilo?" Hearing my own voice helped relax me.

He took a deep breath, turned his face to the side, and looked at me out of the corner of his eye. He had black circles under both eyes. I wondered how long he had been on the run, how long he had gone without a bed, how long since he had eaten in a restaurant. He was being patient with me. He was not this way with everyone.

"All my life I have been abused and looked down upon. I was taught that I was not good enough, that I did not matter, that I was to keep out of the way and to serve others if permitted. As you can see from my skin and features, I have Indian blood in me—something they taught me was not good enough, and to deny in order to be acceptable. They taught me to work hard, and I have. For nothing. My family lives impoverished. They will never get ahead." He paused and looked around. "It has been this way for centuries and is getting worse. Why not fight? In fighting, I feel as though I have some dignity, some self-worth. I will die fighting." He glanced toward José, and when he looked back I thought I saw sadness in his eyes. "My children will know, and perhaps my grandchildren will speak of me proudly. I will not be just another unknown slave to a system that grinds unknown bodies into poverty."

Captured by his intensity, I had not noticed my hand over

my mouth—a pose Indians frequently hold when someone like myself talks to them. I became aware of my hand, realized I was showing my fright, took it down, and tucked it under my leg.

"You are a religious man," Sánchez continued. "I used to be. Religion is part of the system. It enslaves and grinds. But now I realize that I am a child of God, that I have dignity and creativity and the right to express my creativity. I create the way for people to free themselves and feel dignified in doing so."

He was obviously intent on influencing me. But these were not pat answers, such as we had developed for questions like "Why did you become a priest?" I knew I faced an inner contradiction as I listened to a man who had brought many lives to an end now speaking sincerely about bringing life to people.

"I have not talked to a priest since I was a boy," he said. "My family left the Church because the priests were rotten on the inside as they spouted words of being nice and quoted scripture to keep people in line. Such shit! The world is awakening. Individuals who have any sense of themselves will realize that to find God, they must free themselves from religion." He shook his head and asked, "How can any thinking person believe that God has a religion?"

I thought he was not simply feeling me out but perhaps trying to shake loose any ties I had to the structure. I looked at him, trying to show no expression on my face. He studied me with his penetrating eyes, searching to find out who I was and how I was reacting. I stiffened as he put his hand on the pistol. Without pulling it from his belt, he shifted it to the other side. I realized how uncomfortable it must be to sit with a heavy piece of metal pushing into one's stomach. He watched me watching him. "Made in the U.S.A.," he said with his first laugh.

I had pieced much together since I first met this group. I was aware of the motivation that comes from high excitement, of the gratification that comes from seeing one's name in print, of the sense of fulfillment that a leader feels in having gained power, of the reward that the martyr enjoys. I knew also that the pattern of rebelling was as strong for some as the pattern of conforming was for others. I looked into Camilo's eyes and saw the killer, the brutal man opposing brutality. I saw a man in charge who needed to be in charge. I saw a capable revolutionary leader, and I knew that he wanted to recruit me. Like the missionary priests who recruited boys to the priesthood by telling missionary stories, Camilo told me revolutionary stories.

"We went into an area where there was very little water," Sánchez began, "but where a wealthy landowner had a stream on his large property. The peasants who worked his land and lived in the surrounding area were not allowed to use this water but had to walk almost a kilometer to fetch their water from another stream, the one that the animals of the landowner bathed in and drank from.

"Six of us waited in the bushes one day, and when the *patrón* came out of his *hacienda*, we stepped forward, armed to the teeth. In our conversation with him, we told him the water belonged to everyone. He said that was right. I asked him for a drink. The *patrón* was glad to dip cool water from the spring for all of us. He even filled my canteen. We then told him he had to permit the people to freely enter his gate and take water. The *patrón* said there was no problem, that there was plenty of water to go around, and that he would be glad to even take down the gate.

"We borrowed his watch, some money, and some food, and told him we would be back if any problem befell the peasants. As far as I know, the water is still shared, and there has been no problem." I was smiling. He went on, "Look, Arturo, if the people had taken water before our visit, they would have been mistreated and possibly killed. We simply balanced the power."

As Camilo talked, I could see José walking about, occasionally picking up a stone and spinning it across the water's surface, never quite taking his eyes off us. At one point a car pulled to a stop on the road above. Camilo went silent, but did not turn his head. I did not look either, but I could see José. He continued walking, head intentionally down, shoulders slouched, facing in the direction of the car. I saw him adjust his belt, knowing he was fingering his pistol. I knew he was competent and confident, and I felt reassured by his presence.

The car doors slammed, and the engine started. As the

sound died away, Camilo relaxed and said, *"Turistas."* He wiped his sweaty brow and continued, "We don't always have such easy successes as in my water story. Once we went into a village and visited some of the houses, talking to the people about their problems and how they might be resolved. We stayed a couple of days. Not long after we left, the Army came in, directed by several of your countrymen, Green Berets. They called the people together and questioned them while making them watch the torture of several of the village men. Later, they assassinated every male in the village, young and old, more than a hundred of them." He looked around, stretched, rested his forearms on his knees and asked, "And you, Arturo, where do you stand as regards to our movement?"

I swallowed and wiped perspiration from my forehead and neck. "I have come a very different road than you, Camilo, but our roads have intersected. Basically, I support the revolution. I am interested in what you are saying, but I am afraid of two things." He was listening intently. "I am afraid of leading people into violence they have not chosen to risk." He nodded his head in agreement. "And I am afraid of a communist takeover."

He wanted to answer but waited. I went on hesitantly. "I am afraid of making a mistake. I have chosen to be a priest. . . . The people have accepted me. . . . The role of the priest may ultimately be that of a revolutionary. . . . I guess the only mistake would be to be ahead of my time. Or maybe to miss my time." He smiled again.

I squeezed the thin wooden seat tightly and continued, "But I am also afraid of people like you abusing your power." He frowned, as if hurt. I felt more confident and relaxed my hands. In fact, I raised my hand and watched my finger point at him as I said, "There is no reason for me to think that you would not use people, just as the wealthy are using people. You are as convinced of your approach and goals as they are. I am afraid of participating in something that becomes more important than the people, as has happened with the Church."

Sánchez held up his hand. I paused. "Pardon the interruption," he said. "I have to answer before we go astray. First, you know as well as I do that the people already are and have been

213

for centuries suffering under a violence they have not chosen. You will not lead the people into more violence. It is coming no matter what you do, because the oppression has heightened to the point that people throughout the country are at a stage of revolt.

"And I agree, the only mistake would be to miss your time. This is a historic moment. Members of the clergy hold the only power that, united with us, can combat the wealthy and their army. We will fight anyway; but if priests and nuns join us, we will together bring justice and dignity to the people. Not to act now would be a major mistake. In the future, the official violence will be too widespread for you to join." I sat pensive.

"And the only way you are going to influence this movement from being taken over by communists is for you to participate. That's how you get a vote, have some influence, and give some direction. If you are not a part of it, you can do as the other pompous asses, including those of the Communist Party, who sit by and tell us how we could have done better. Communists are not running our show. We don't need Russians or Cubans telling us how to live or what is best for us, any more than we need Americans."

His voice got sterner, "And as for my using the people, if ever you don't like my leadership, simply show yourself more capable, smarter, tougher, with the troops willing to follow, and I will also be there for you as *comandante*, or for anyone else."

He took a deep breath, looked to the beach, and went on, "José is very capable, but he is still learning. I think some day he will make a better *comandante* than I am. When that time comes, I will accept and support him. Meanwhile, I like my job. It's better than being a *presidente*. But if anyone can do better than I, he or she will find that I am first of all a revolutionary, willing to give up my position if it supports the revolution. You know that there are always people that could be a better *presidente*. But did you ever hear of a *presidente* acknowledging that someone else could do the job better? You may not believe what I am saying, but that doesn't matter if you are on the sidelines."

I did not believe that he would readily give up the power. In my mind I was thinking that I already knew that I would join the revolution and, like Camilo, subject myself to an early death. I also knew that I was unwilling to substitute one demanding authority for another. I needed more thought and information.

José had told me of the strict rules of the F.A.R., which left no room for weakness, disobedience, or vacillation. He said tribunals were held to consider infractions, and that the death penalty had been imposed on several members. I knew I could never participate in such actions. But I also knew I was living under a government that was assassinating anyone who sought the improvement of the peasants' lives. I sat pondering the words of a man who had committed violence not only against the Army, the government and the wealthy, but also against his own comrades. I was amazed at myself that I would consider joining him. But only a moment of reflection showed me the other option.

Sánchez interrupted my thoughts, saying, "Those who choose our way choose perhaps the most difficult road." He looked around and pointed to the steep volcano. "One must be prepared to climb that mountain with fifty pounds upon the back. One must be prepared to set up camp, only to tear it down and march on, to where one does not know—possibly through the night with no trail, through harsh rains, with the best-armed mercenaries in the world not far behind and itching to practice on human flesh." He looked at me with sad eyes, and said, "If you join us, I can promise you nothing more than comradeship."

I sat silent. What does one say to such a person? I said, "*Gracias, Comandante.*" We both knew that was the first time I had used his title.

As if reciprocating, he said, "You let José know what you decide, *Padre*. For my part, I have made my decision. I accept you."

He stood, looked about, and stepped from the boat. José began walking our way. We returned to the cars and gave *abrazos*. I felt Camilo's body warm from sitting in the hot sun with a suit on, but I also felt another warmth. We looked each other in the eye.

"*Que te vaya bien,*" he said.

"Igualmente," I answered.

José waved and smiled as he got in the car.

I drove slowly out of the lake area, then stopped and pulled off the road. I was exhilarated and confused. If Camilo was telling the truth, then he was a highly committed man. I sat and thought and prayed and took the notebook from the glove compartment and wrote, although in very indefinite terms. Writing was relaxing. After an hour or so I got back on the road and continued on, mulling over and over all that had been said. If I had any doubt, both José and Camilo made it clear that I would be valuable to the movement. But I also knew that I would be at least as valuable dead in the struggle as alive.

I was home only a short time when Cathy and Marian came to the door. They could not wait to get details of the meeting. We talked for hours. They offered support—particularly Marian. She and I seemed to be very close.

The work went on, but much that would be considered my work as a priest now seemed secondary. I visited the villages, administered the sacraments, had sessions and meetings, but my mind was on the revolution. I considered each village and looked at each person from the perspective of the struggle. With each child, I asked myself what influence the struggle might have on his or her life. With each man I talked to, I wondered how much he would support or oppose my involvement. With each woman, I considered how important her participation would be. My training made it difficult to imagine women in the front lines, so I tried to think of other ways they might participate and how they would react to my involvement or to their husbands' and children's. But ultimately I knew that without the participation of women, the struggle would not succeed.

To those few in whom I had the utmost confidence I began to put forth my views as opportunity presented. I could not risk speaking to anyone else. On their part, although with doubts, fears, and reservations, they agreed with my entering the revolution, and all spoke in some way of their willingness to support. I wondered how much I had influenced their conviction, but also, although we were only at the level of discussion, I recognized the courage of people willing to face all odds to risk bringing about change.

I had many discussions with Jesus and experienced Him close by. Talking to the Sisters, to José, Chico, Roberto, Límbano, and others, I worked slowly through my doubts and got answers to my questions. Finally I reached a place of clarity and felt ready to make the toughest decision of my life. I walked into the church. It was empty. I knelt before the altar, bowed my head, and committed myself to the revolution. I knew it was the only thing for me to do at that time and in that place. I knew that the process would be unpredictable and that it would frequently go in a way different from the one I imagined or wanted. But I knew it would go, and it would have a direction, and that I could influence that direction. And I knew that at times I would wish I were back in the security and comfort of my parish, free of intense fear and responsibility, free of accusations, criticisms, and judgements, just being a priest in the protective structure of the Church. I also knew that despite suffering and pain I would never regret the decision I was making; that it would be a step in a long, unpredictable process of growth; that I would always be grateful for the opportunity to make such a decision, that it was part of my priesthood and what I had been looking for in becoming a priest.

On a damp, misty morning in August I walked down the uneven cobblestone street, across the little bridge that had been there in one form or another for centuries, jumped up the rock wall I had helped build, and knocked at the door of the Sisters' *convento*. It was as if they had been waiting for me. They could see I had made my decision. I must have looked happy. I put my arms around the two of them and hugged them. They simply smiled, and tears came to my eyes.

We sat at their large table and had another of our quiet subversive talks, Marian and Cathy both saying they were each close to making their decision. I knew the grueling process that had to take into account all contingencies and options and said they would have my love and acceptance no matter what their decision. I knew what Marian's would be. Over a second cup of coffee we reviewed the speculative plan we had been working out: that an autonomous front could be formed based on the example of the Man who took a whip to the moneylenders, a front willing to negotiate with, coordinate with, and make agreements with F.A.R. and eventually with another revolutionary front called MR-13, a front directed by *Comandante* Marc Antonio Yon Sosa.

A few days later Marian came by my *convento*. The purpose of her visit was obvious. I felt nervous. She did not sit down but stopped just inside the door, smiled, and said, "I am complete in my mind and heart and know that my vocation includes the revolution. I am committed." My body trembled with joy. I felt love for her.

A few days later, Cathy did similarly. She found me in the *bodega*, a small storeroom on the edge of the patio. I was kneeling on the floor, working on the carburetor of the generator. She entered smiling and said, "*Hola*, Arturo," as she always did. I knew her purpose. I stood up, afraid to say anything. She stepped close and leaned casually against a low workbench. I wiped my hands on a rag. In her inimitable way she said casually, "The process of my life will make sense only if I take the next step." She hesitated. We looked at each other. I was afraid. I didn't want her to say the rest of it. She looked beautiful. I felt proud of her, like a brother of his sister.

She smiled, scratched the back of her neck nervously, and said, "I am committing to the revolution." I forced a return smile and felt conflicting fear as I wondered if any of us knew what we were doing. "I will not participate in any fighting," she said, "but wherever I am, I will gladly serve in the capacity of a nurse." Again I felt my body tremble as it did with the experience of unusual joy.

Then a voice called out, "*Padre*." Both of us jumped. "*Padre*," called the voice again.

"Here I am in the storeroom," I yelled out. In stepped Eladio, the secretary of the co-op.

"Excuse me, *Madre*," he said to Cathy. "*Perdone la molestia, Padre*, but the typewriter ribbon is stuck again." We were trying to re-form the cooperatives independently of the Church. The Sisters had given a used typewriter to the co-op, and Eladio was using it to formalize the records in the newly rented co-op office across the street from my house. Unfortunately, I had not used or taught good bookkeeping methods, and now we were doing everything to catch up. I had fixed the typewriter that morning and told him to call me if there was another problem.

Cathy accompanied me to the co-op office. I found it difficult to concentrate on the typewriter and on what Eladio was saying. I felt so much distress, knowing that she could be killed, knowing that I loved her, and knowing what I did not want to know: that I could not commit to the revolution and maintain my feelings for her.

That night, as I had so many nights, I lay awake thinking and exploring ambivalent feelings. I felt happy about Cathy's decision, yet I also felt sad. It seemed appropriate for me to risk my life in the old martyr spirit of the Church, but I hated to think that others whom I loved deeply would be risking theirs. The possibility of others dying hit me hard. At times I felt overwhelmed. I pulled the covers over my head, wanting to hide. Yet I knew I had to live with and get used to the idea of others possibly dying along with me.

For days I was distracted by the thought of Cathy's possible suffering. I told José. He listened, taking my words seriously. "Do not worry, Arturo," he finally said. "All this will pass." But I knew it wouldn't. If I was this concerned without any real danger, what would be my anxiety under pressure of combat?

By the following day I had gained some clarity. I said to José, "I do not think I will be able to be with Cathy in the movement." He frowned. "My thinking seems to have the same basis as the Church's teaching on celibacy," I said. He laughed and slapped me on the back. "You see, José," I went on, "I have never before cared so deeply about a woman." He was serious again. "Yet having chosen the revolution, I have to figure a way to handle my relationship with her. . . . Separate units, or whatever way we could handle it."

"I do not know," José said. He rested his hand on my shoulder, "You have to make your choice, Arturo, and I will support you in it."

The next day I went to Cathy. She was sitting at the Sisters' long dining room table cutting articles from a newspaper. She smiled her incredible smile and said, "I was just thinking of you." I shivered at hearing those words and wished I didn't have to say what I was going to say. She saw my distress. I felt sad to see her smile disappear. I pulled out a chair and sat across from her.

"Cathy, I am torn." She put down the scissors and reached out to me. I touched her hand, felt its warmth, and then withdrew my hand. I knew I had to get this done. "My feelings for you have not diminished. If anything, they have intensified. I am committed to the revolution, but I do not know how I would respond to that commitment if you were in danger." She was nodding her head in acceptance. "If we were to go into the same unit, I don't know what would happen, but it would be incredibly difficult."

"I know," she said. "I agree that it would not work. I have also given this some thought." She raised her eyes to mine and said, "I know now that your love for me is very deep." She then lowered her eyes and added, "I accept your love and am willing to be apart from you." I reached out and touched the hand still extended on the table, knowing that the vow of celibacy had been easier.

16
DOUBT

Doubts were keeping me awake at night, sometimes making me nervous for days on end. I struggled to know whether I was remaining true to myself and my spiritual process. Yet I knew I had to keep on evaluating my ambiguous position in the violent and continuous power struggle between the Church, the government, and the revolutionary forces, all three claiming, as if by some divine right, control over the minds, hearts, and bodies of the people. I knew I could easily get caught up in the same current and become an abuser of the very people I had come to Guatemala to help. To think there was a simple solution would be to err. To think there was one right answer would be stupid. To act only if there would be no risk, no mistakes, no casualties, would mean not to act. I tried to listen to others for possible options. But if the revolution really intended for the poor to exercise their God-given rights, I had no other option except to join. I realized I not only had to deal with my own doubts but to make my own decisions and follow through with a willingness to be responsible for them.

I concluded that for a person to speak relevant truth and be heard, she or he must be willing to step outside any controlling structure—not an easy task for the socially oriented. The nature of a structure like the Roman Catholic church is generally to manipulate and co-opt borderline members and to punish and humiliate those determined to leave. Letting go of the structure of Church frightened me, perhaps as a child is frightened when leaving its parents, or an adult in letting go of all security. Despite my disagreements with the Church, it had been the focal point of my upbringing, education, and career, and it still held a strong bond for me. That it is called Holy Mother Church took on deeper significance for me. I was rarely without doubts.

Today I have deep empathy for those who choose to leave a dysfunctional family system, social structure, or religion. Recognizing the dysfunction and making a conflicting healthy decision is difficult, no matter how painful the abuse or deprivation one may have suffered. But the real test is the definitive act of cutting off and leaving whatever has been the destructive foundation of one's past, a foundation that normally permits no change. Because of my own experience in tearing myself from the former foundation of my life, I appreciate the privilege of my present role in supporting people in a process that includes doubting themselves in their decision to heal and be free.

EVERY DAY THAT Marian, Cathy, and I put off our move, we risked detection. Yet too much was at stake for us to rush into our new life. We tried to calculate how much time was needed and came up with a date. I felt sick to my stomach as we made the decision. On Friday, December 29th, we would disappear from our beloved San Antonio. Less than four months away, it seemed at times like years, at other times like the next day. But it was the date on which we agreed to give up our past, family, friends, pets, Church, lifestyle, and possessions, and enter the most unpredictable of lives. That day, we would slip away to a training base in the wilderness, not to be heard of again until we came back as part of a fighting force.

But until that departure we would do our best to go on with the parish work while preparing ourselves physically, mentally, psychologically, and spiritually, orienting everything toward our goal; we would heighten prayer, meditation, and daily exercise, as well as sleep on the floor and walk great distances through the mountains carrying daypacks.

Límbano was accustomed to opening the front door and yelling, "José is here." Everyone had come to accept José as part of our family. He came and went as he wanted, sometimes going on village trips with Límbano and me, and sometimes I accompanied him on his trips to the city. Having borrowed my pickup truck for one such trip, he had just returned. He stepped inside the door, said "Hi there," in English as he liked to do before going into Spanish, and then after a few minutes of small talk asked, "Can I talk to you?" I knew something was up. Cautious, we went outside and sat on the stone wall.

"I have some news," he began. Then smiled, took a deep breath and said, *"El Comandante* wants another meeting with you." I felt honored and acknowledged, but I gulped, never ceasing to be surprised at the turn of events. I was still working on the last conversation with Sánchez, jotting down ideas and getting insights, and felt perplexed that I might suddenly have to deal with more.

I asked, "What does he want to see me about?"

Still holding his smile, he said, "Arturo, you are so serious. Relax! It's something good. I think you are going to be offered a trip to Cuba."

I was amazed. For years I had been interested in Cuba. I had always thought communism could have been avoided there. I felt that with proper American support, Cuba could have gone another way and possibly still could. At times I wished I could talk with the Cuban people to see and hear what had happened to them, what the revolution had and had not produced. But I had always thought that verifying my ideas by a visit to our island neighbor was never a possibility.

"Come on, Arturo," José said, slapping me on the back. "What are you so pensive about? This could be great for us and a good time for you."

"I think the idea is terrific," I said, "and I would love to go. My problem is that any association with communism would be to the detriment of the movement."

"Oh, *Dios*," he said. "How is it that you see the violence, the inhumanity, and the injustices of capitalism and are not afraid to associate with capitalists?

"That's foolish," I said. "The capitalist system permits freedom of speech, movement, and disagreement."

He shot back quickly, "The benefits of capitalism are for you and your people, not for us." Then slowing down, as if teaching, he said, "Both communism and capitalism enslave the Third World, only in different ways. We look at which system enslaves us and, without being taken over by the other, see how we can use it to free ourselves. There is no alternative. Without help from the enemies of the United States we cannot advance, we can do nothing. It is a big risk, but it is our only chance." I sat thinking.

"Camilo favors the formation of our independent front," he continued. "He is willing to help with anything that promotes the revolution, and I have convinced him that we can contribute." He interrupted himself to say *Buenos días* to Isabela and waited for her to pass.

"But look, *hermano*," he went on, "as we discuss Cuba, remember that a revolution needs outside help. Even that famous one of 1776 would probably not have succeeded without help from France. Coups overthrow a government, but they do nothing for the people or for the changing of structures."

He looked around and lowered his voice, "We may have our heads up our asses for trying, but no one has ever been able to form a Christian revolutionary group. And Camilo thinks it will help our cause to show the Cubans that the potential for such a group is real. We have to make friends where we can while maintaining our own beliefs and values."

"But the negative side is so strong," I said. "Risking any association with communism could be our downfall. The Church would use such a visit to destroy me and my participation in the movement. If we could eliminate that risk, I might seriously consider going."

"You worry too much, Arturo," he answered, nudging me.

"No, not too much, José," I said. "Look at the way the Church works. It offers corn and beans, a sense of belonging to its protective structure, and eternal life. To get the goodies, the people say 'I believe' and attend some functions. If they continue to behave and conform, there may be education and even financial benefits. The only thing is that they get hooked. They come to get acceptance and goodies and they end up controlled, manipulated, judged, and guilted until they are willing to die for the structure."

"So what?" José said.

"So communism does similarly. It offers rice and beans, a protective structure, and life here on earth. All you have to do is believe and attend some functions, and if you really behave, you get guns and education and financial help. But in the process you get hooked and begin to think that communism is the way, and soon you are dying for it."

"*Bien*," he said. "But we are too bright to fall for that shit."

"For how many generations have we fallen for that shit?" I demanded. "For how long have I fallen for it? The Church and the government are correct in their opposition to communism, but in their pretense of supporting us, they hook us, then suppress us, and then will do anything to maintain that control. They desperately need the power the people give them and will never freely give that back."

"So what?" José said.

"So if, by a trip to Cuba, they learn we are pulling away from their controlling structures, particularly if they think we are being influenced by communism, they will do everything from maligning to killing in order to stop us. We will be declared anathema before all their faithful, the very people we want to influence."

He paused a moment while an elderly couple walked by, then said softly, "Wait a minute, Arturo. If we were to fight only with the very machetes the *campesinos* now possess, the Church and government would claim the machetes were made in Moscow and came through Cuba, and your countrymen would believe it." I nodded. "That being the case," he said, "we have to take the machetes where we can get them. We do not have to be taken in by the gift-givers, nor do we have to surrender to another controlling structure."

We sat in silence. "Well," I finally said, "that's my concern. However, whether I go to Cuba or not, I guess I can at least profit from another meeting with Camilo. What data do you have on that?"

It did not take long for my role to affect my ego. I began to feel a false sense of importance and knew I had to be careful. My desire to be acknowledged and accepted by a guerrilla leader could be as damaging as dependence on validation and approval by a Church leader. I wanted to put an end to my immaturity.

On the appointed day, at 1:45 P.M., I stood on a street corner in Zone Two of Guatemala City trying to appear inconspicuous. Wanting to get my mind off the frightening meeting, I was studying the graffiti scribbled on the walls when I was brought back abruptly to my task by a young man pulling up to the curb on a motorcycle with a leaky muffler. I looked at him and felt paralyzed. He took off his helmet, leaned the bike towards me and said, "Hello, today is Wednesday."

I jumped. I could not believe I was hearing correctly. My instructions were that when someone spoke those words, I was to respond, "How are you? Yesterday was Tuesday." I took a step towards him and hesitantly said, *"Como está? Ayer fue martes."* He watched my mouth as if reading my lips, then pushed down the kick-stand and stepped off the bike, leaving the engine running, and shook my hand. I was amazed that any of this stuff worked.

He was about seventeen, very serious, and intent on business. "Do you know where El Dorado Restaurant is?" he asked over the noise of the engine.

"No. I have no idea," I told him.

He carefully told me the address and drew a map on his hand with his index finger. "It is not so far," he said. "You are expected there by 2:45. When you enter and they ask whether you want a table or a *casita*, say that you have come for a glass of white wine."

He asked me to repeat it, which I did. *"Bien,"* he said, "and you are aware that none of this should ever be written down?" As I nodded my head, he glanced around, shook my hand, said, *"Cuídate,"* shifted the bike into gear, and was gone. I didn't even say thanks. It seemed so strange to just let him go out of my life. But I was learning that it had to be that way. We would probably never meet again, and he would probably never know who I was or the significance of his message. He was just doing his job.

I followed the directions exactly, worried that I might get lost and be late. But the El Dorado was not difficult to find. I arrived at 2:30. It was a rustic and romantic place, made up of individual huts with straw roofs. I wished Cathy were there to share it with me. I entered the gate to the main hut. A man dressed in black said, *"Buenas tardes, señor.* Do you want a *cabaña?*

I knew I was supposed to be asked if I wanted a table or a *casita.* I felt confused. Hoping I would not create a problem, I answered, "I just want a glass of white wine."

The man smiled and bowed slightly, saying, "Follow me, *compañero,"* and led me to a small hut. A waiter stood inside, and as we entered he buttoned his white jacket, concealing a pistol in his belt, and left without saying a word. The first man pulled back one of the two metal-framed chairs from the small round table. I sat down and thanked him. "Your wine will be here shortly," he said and left with another slight bow.

At 2:45 the waiter entered the hut, smiled, pulled back the other chair and left. A few moments later I tensed as Camilo walked in, a day's growth on his light beard, and dressed in the same blue suit. It was wrinkled, as if he had slept in it. "Don't stand," he said, as I fumbled to push back my chair. He sat down, signaling for silence. He had even larger black bags under his eyes. The fingers of one hand drummed lightly on the table as he cocked his head to one side and listened. After a minute, he let out the breath he had been holding and relaxed somewhat. As he opened his suitcoat, I noticed that his pistol was of the same caliber as José's. I had practiced with José's several times and knew it to be a .357 magnum.

Camilo winked, put on a big smile, and asked, "How are you, *mi amigo?"* as he patted me on the back. Hardly waiting for an answer, he went on, "And how is your business going, *mi compadre?"* setting the light tone of coverup conversation.

I answered him in turn and posed similar irrelevant questions. "Have you put on a little weight, my friend?" I asked, laughingly pointing to the bulge over his belt. "Perhaps life is getting too easy for you," I said, my words coming out with difficulty.

Camilo laughed, leaned close to my ear and said, "Urban warfare can do that to you. I need to get back to the drudgery of the mountains."

The waiter appeared in the doorway. "*Perdónenme, caballeros.* Can I bring you each a *copa de vino?*" We both ordered a glass of *vino blanco.* The small talk continued until the waiter returned. He stood before us for a moment, put one glass in front of me, took a sip from the other and put it before the *comandante.* Turning to Camilo he said, "Business is very quiet today, *señor,*" and left.

We touched our glasses. In a soft voice Camilo said, "To the people of the United States and Guatemala: may we mutually create a free society." We sipped. I felt my nervous system calm down some. Camilo was ready to talk. He leaned close. "We had trouble in the city the night before last. We lost several *companeros.*" He bit his lip. "It was terrible. I don't know how I have kept this appointment. I think someone up there wanted me to see you." He looked at me as if wondering whether to explain, and then went on. "Our policy is that unless the fallen are dead, we are on full alert. If they live, they may give information. If there is a possibility of that, we must change all plans and residences." He took out a handkerchief and wiped his forehead. "We all know that once captured, torture comes quickly; and if a captive should survive torture, assassination follows. Although those captured know that death is unavoidable, it is almost impossible not to give information. Your brethren have developed and taught the science of torture. Very few can resist it. Fortunately the companions died of their wounds before they could be tortured." I wanted to ask how he knew they had died. And as if reading my thought, he shook his head and said, "We have informants."

He picked up his glass, looked through the wine as if not seeing it and, leaning close, said almost in a whisper, "The strug-

gle is in a particularly difficult phase. What happened the other
night has been happening often. With your countrymen shipping
huge quantities of new arms, vehicles, helicopters, and communications equipment, along with instructors, intelligence people, and fighting personnel, the police and army are stepping up
their activities and conducting more searches and arrests." He
cast a glance toward the open doorway. "Many relatives of com-
batants totally uninvolved in the movement, even suspected
supporters, are disappearing and being assassinated." He took
a small sip. "And of course, the insane *Mano Blanca* is out there
sanctioned officially to wipe out anyone who wants change." He
frowned deep creases in his forehead. "It makes it difficult to
keep up the morale." The *Mano Blanca* or White Hand, a terrorist group, acted for the power structure to suppress all dis-
sent.

Shaking his head and looking very tired, he went on. "But
our revolution has been through similar stages before, and we
know that the harder the government tightens the screws, the
more the people will join and support us. The only thing that
can stop us is genocide." He took a sip of wine. "It is not that
your government and ours are incapable of that," he smiled,
"but they are aware that we have popular support in many Latin
American countries and other nations of the world." He looked
at me as if wanting me to get a lesson, and said, "The people of
the United States do not realize that they are a lonely nation.
Their money blinds them and makes them think they are respected and acceptable. If the United States goes broke, the
world will then gladly enlighten them." He took a sip of wine
and asked, "Do you think other priests and nuns will join the
revolution?"

I knew that José was telling him of the great benefit of
winning over members of Catholic religious organizations, a concept I myself did not agree with. I answered, "I would be hesitant to trust any of them." He looked surprised. "But generally,
nuns are more dependable than priests. They are more mature,
more in touch with the people, and probably more able to endure
hardships." He was nodding his head as if understanding. I
wondered if he had found it to be that way with women in the

movement, but he was still listening, wanting me to continue.

"When I was ordained in 1961, the Maryknoll Fathers were celebrating their fiftieth anniversary. However, 'the golden boys,' as we called ourselves, were not considered to have come from the traditional mold. Older priests were calling us the 'new breed.' We were different. We wanted more freedom and were willing to question many of the old, unquestioned approaches." We each sipped our wine. "I am not sure that the Church can change," I went on, "but it either becomes the voice of the people of the twentieth century, and not of the first, second, or tenth century, or else many priests, nuns, and lay people will be leaving, and some will be joining the revolution." He nodded his head as he raised his glass. I took a sip also and went on with a thought I had prepared beforehand. "I feel very sad that our land program came to a halt with the death of Cristóbal."

Camilo touched my arm and said, "I remember the first time a friend of mine was murdered. It is difficult to accept. But we learn. Your friend's death is not in vain. It is the seed from which will grow a strong vine. Wait and see!" Then as if to lighten the conversation, or at least change the topic, he said, "But how are you and the *compañeras* doing?"

Amazed at his willingness to talk of any subject, I told the story of Marian's and Cathy's and my own decision to join the movement and our progress in preparing to move out. He looked delighted. Never taking his piercing eyes off me, he listened carefully as I talked of the importance of forming an independent front. He showed no resistance. I knew he was not hearing any of this for the first time.

He asked many questions, ending by saying, "I am sure that all this can be arranged. José speaks highly of you people. You have a good man in José. I am sorry he will not be with me, but we will participate with you and offer any help and training we can.

"I do have a suggestion," he said, touching my hand. "José tells me you run a short-wave radio. If you can have one to take with you when you leave on December 29th, it will be of great help. Can you imagine yourself talking about our revolution from some mountain encampment to radio aficionados around the world?"

He went on to say that when we had completed basic training he would try to arm our original group "with some of the best of American weapons" and offered several suggestions where we might begin to train. He said, "But such logistics will be handled in due time. Things change so quickly in our business, it is impossible to make anything certain ahead of time."

The waiter stuck his head in the door with questioning eyebrows raised. I held up two fingers. He was prepared for that and immediately brought in two new glasses of wine. He stood again by the table. Camilo and I watched as he took a sip from one glass and set it in front of Camilo and the other in front of me. Taking the two empties, he left without a word. "I do not ordinarily consider that my wine might be poisoned," I said with a smile. "But maybe when I am with you I ought to bring my own bottle."

Camilo laughed and said, "It is more of a gesture to remind me that I am *el Comandante* and that everyone in the movement will do anything possible to protect me."

I was enjoying being with him, and it seemed that the feeling was mutual. I raised my glass. Raising his, he said, "A toast to *los Padres* and *las Madres de* Maryknoll who have the courage to stand at the side of the oppressed." We touched glasses and sipped.

Suddenly putting down his glass, he said, "*Dios mio*, I am nearly forgetting my main topic." He lowered his voice and asked, "José has talked to you about a trip to Cuba?" I nodded. "What do you think?"

"I feel excited about the idea," I said. "If we can iron out the problems, it would be fantastic. I've had time to think about it and have discussed the pros and the cons with José and the Sisters. All three will support my decision. I would like to see at the grass roots how the revolution has affected the life of the Cuban people both positively and negatively, and how popular the government is. But. . . ."

He held up a finger and interrupted with, "But . . . you do

not want to be associated with communism." I nodded. "I understand, and do not blame you," he said. "It is unfortunate that there is no other alternative." Patting his pistol he added, "But eventually those exploited by both systems will create something new. I know it's a risky business playing with them, but for now we either take that risk or continue on with the present oppression and violence.

"If you can see your way clear to going, I guarantee you that no one will try to convert you, although I do not think you are susceptible, and only a few of us will know of your trip." He took a sip of wine. "Your visit could be important to the movement. There is someone there for you to meet who will be beneficial to us. You could stay as long as you think prudent, and we will pay your way." I was nodding my head in agreement. "Now," he said, lifting his glass, "are we ready to toast a successful journey?"

"My problems are as resolved as they will ever be," I said raising my glass and touching his. "I too consider the trip important. I am happy to go. And I will pay my own way." I figured that would give me more control, and I was also thinking I would be taking a direct flight from Mexico. I went on to say, "In order not to attract attention, I will have to return to my parish within a month, my allotted vacation time. I still have much to do there and cannot risk blowing my cover."

He said, "You can leave when you are ready, only letting me know the date of departure a few days in advance. The same day that you leave Guatemala, check into the Santa María Hotel in Mexico City and wait to hear from a contact named Carmen. She will take care of all arrangements." Our conversation was finished. Camilo touched his pocket and asked, "Do you have need for a *pistola?*"

I thanked him and said, "No, not yet."

"*Bien,*" he said. "We will protect you to your car. Then you are on your own." I reached for my wallet, but he put his hand on my arm stopping me, saying, "They are pleased to serve us." We gave an *abrazo*. "You leave first," he said. I stepped out of the hut. The waiter was sitting ten feet away facing us. At the front the man in black bowed and opened the gate. A waiter standing just outside the entrance nodded. I walked to my truck. A young man was leaning casually against it. As I approached, he smiled, unbuttoned his jacket and stepped away. I swung onto the highway and looked in the rearview mirror. The young man was watching.

Back at the parish I went about my work distractedly in anticipation of the trip. A few days later I sent a note to the bishop saying I would begin my vacation on September 16th and would be traveling in Mexico.

My plane set down in Mexico City at noon on that date. I took a cab to the designated hotel, checked into a room on the fifth floor, and sat waiting for the contact. A big military parade was in progress on the street below. I had forgotten that the sixteenth of September was Independence Day in Mexico. I was there only a moment when the phone rang. I picked it up immediately. A woman's voice said, "My name is Carmen."

"Please come up," I said, trying to contain my nervousness.

Carmen was in her mid twenties, slightly over five feet tall, well dressed, attractive, serious, and sharp. She never told me anything about herself. I saw a strong, tough, and determined woman.

Carmen began explaining that a problem had arisen with the flight from Mexico City to Havana. The C.I.A. was photographing all passengers and had an agreement with the Mexican Government that any American who took that route would not be permitted to return via Mexico. She said that I would have to go to Paris and Prague and then back to Cuba, and that I could not go beyond Paris under my own name in case the C.I.A. was checking flights into Prague. She said that, if I was in agreement, I would use a fictitious name on a falsified American passport that she would have made up for me. We lined up a series of meeting places for the following days, beginning with a meeting the following morning at ten to have coffee and then to have passport pictures taken.

We met on the seventeenth and parted after getting the snapshots. The next day we met again. Details were still being worked on. The next day, the same. We met each day for a week, and details were still being worked on. I reminded her of my limited time and asked, "Are you sure your people have the ability to pull this thing off?"

She reassured me, saying, "Given sufficient time, the underground can pull off anything. Our forger has run out of United States passports and is waiting for a package of them. They should have arrived long ago." When there was no news after a week, I told her I was not going to hang around waiting but was going to Cuernavaca to the Center of Intercultural Documentation run by Ivan Illich. If necessary she could reach me there. If I did not hear from her, we would meet in one week at a specified site in Mexico City. I took a bus to Cuernavaca and a taxi to the Center.

For many years Ivan Illich had had a powerful influence on me. From the time of my first year of theology I had been interested in his insightful and confrontive writings. A former priest, a revolutionary within the Church, he had resigned from the priesthood rather than give up his teaching. Illich was an outspoken critic of society and the Church, an outstanding educator. I felt privileged to visit his institute. Fortunately, there was room for me there. I requested a moment with Illich but was told by his secretary that his schedule was full and that he was not making appointments.

As I sat in the lounge on the fourth night of my stay I was surprised when Ivan walked in, came directly to me and, pulling up a chair, sat down and introduced himself. I thanked him for making such a marvelous institution available, acknowledged him for his work over the years, and asked about his current writings.

He in turn asked about my work in Guatemala. I told about the co-ops and the work of Maryknoll as well as the social problems and the strife. He was listening, but I got a sense that he was not receptive. When I paused, he leaned his wooden chair back, looked up at the ceiling, and took me totally by surprise, saying, "The best thing you missionaries can do is withdraw." I looked at him. "Get out!" he said nonchalantly. "Go home! Your presence supports the status quo and slows down the progress of the people."

I had been playing the role of typical missionary, playing

it so well that, although I liked what he was saying and wanted to be in agreement, I felt offended and defensive. But, getting hold of my Jekyll-and-Hyde life, I adapted, saying, "I am surprised by your words. But coming from a person whose insight I have long respected, what you are saying has deep meaning for me."

He had not expected me to accept his words and looked at me skeptically. I was really wondering how he would feel about missionaries in the revolution. I could not ask him directly, but later I brought up Camilo Torres, the Colombian priest turned *guerrillero*. Ivan leaned forward, resting his elbows on his knees, gesturing with his big hands, and said "Torres is a Colombian fighting for his own people. I do not support violent revolution, but that is his business. It doesn't matter what kind of revolution a person is making or what a revolutionary's profession or vocation is. What matters is that it be his or her revolution.

"The second biggest mistake you Americans can make, after thinking you can understand and influence a foreign culture positively, is thinking you can be revolutionaries in a foreign country. What is the difference between that and what you are doing in Viet Nam? Are not Americans there believing they are helping the Vietnamese people, defending them, and teaching them what is best for them? Priest or soldier, in someone else's country it has never worked. It's about time you and the Russians and any of the other missionaries, whether military or clerical, got that straight." I felt like applauding.

He sat up. "If you people have a need to teach, convert, save, or defend, there is plenty to do in your own country. But you don't know how to clean up your own messes, so you pretend you can clean up those of others." He looked at me with piercing eyes and asked, "Have you been to Harlem recently? Or Washington, D.C.? Or to the Indian reservations? It's time to stop pretending that egotistical, righteous missionaries have any role in doing things to, for, or against Latin America."

I was being lectured and felt a bit defensive. But I knew that only Illich could give such a sincere, powerful, confrontive, off-hand dissertation, caring little what anyone else thought or said. Hearing him talk of revolutionaries, I wondered if I had somehow tipped my hand. But I did not wonder for long. "I know there are priests among you in Guatemala who are thinking of joining the revolution. Father Blase Bonpane visited here recently. He told me he thought he might have a calling to the *guerrilla*. That is more American foolishness and deserves to be put on the table and examined. I hope I discouraged him."

I felt discouraged. One of the few people that I considered to have enough experience and wisdom to speak about the Church and the problems in Latin America had just told me that no matter which course I took, it would be futile and foolish. But I still trusted my own experience and involvement with the people, and although I was being left with more questions, I knew I had to make my own decisions.

Back in Mexico City, Carmen said, "I am sorry. There are still complications. It only seems practical to call off the trip." Very disillusioned, I went to my room for my suitcase, took a cab to the airport, and headed back to Guatemala. Cathy, Marian, José and the others were also disappointed with the failure of my trip. I asked José what he thought had happened. He said, "We will probably never learn what was really going on." I asked whom I was supposed to meet in Cuba. He said, "I do not have access to that kind of information."

On October 2, while on an overnight visit to Jacaltenango, I was surprised by the arrival of my brother Tom. I was happy to see him but wondered about his purpose. He explained that he had sent a telegram to San Antonio advising of his visit, but when he arrived Isabela told him I was in Jacal. We returned to San Antonio together on foot. His visits were rare, this being his second since I had arrived in San Antonio. Ordinarily, I would have been delighted but, afraid that he had learned of my involvement, I did not look forward to our sitting down together. Our conversation was sparse along the steep and rocky trail. I wondered about Marji, who had a close relationship with Tom. She had asked me not to tell him of my participation. I agreed, thinking she would do likewise, or at least would consult me first.

Tom was involved deeply in alternative approaches to the

problems facing the people, but I had my doubts that he would be willing to make the type of commitment required to participate in the revolutionary movement. He had obtained government permission to utilize a large tract of land in the remote jungle of the northern State of El Petén, where he had initiated a marvelous colonization project. The colonizers cleared and planted a section of land and built housing, a difficult task and a daring adventure. But Tom was finding out that even in the uninhabited jungle, the government not only gave poor people the poorest land but impeded any clear title or guarantee. Although he left no stone unturned in his work for the people, I still wondered if he would be willing to take one more big step. But whether he would or not, I would permit no interference with what I had chosen.

I took his bag and led him into my new house. At the guest bedroom he leaned against the door frame, looked at me seriously, and confirmed my intuition. "Marji has told me everything," he said. I stopped, not surprised, and waited. "She told me about the movement, your participation, and your aborted visit to Cuba." I nodded my head. "I don't know what to say," he went on. "I came here to ask how you arrived at your decision and what is going on with you." I sat down on the bed, trying to think how to answer, but he continued. "I also want to say that I'm glad you didn't get to Cuba. They would have used you incredibly." I figured that he didn't have any information about the movement's relationship to Cuba and accepted his comment.

Instead of sitting down he stood with a worried frown on his face as I began to speak. I took him through the events of my years in Guatemala, knowing that he had many similar experiences. He listened intently, never interrupting or asking a question. I covered the unresolvable problems of the people, the early legal cases, my views of the Church, my growth with the Sisters, the development of co-ops, the attempted land reform, the resistance of the wealthy, the arrival of the students, my relationship with José and Camilo, and my decision. "Either I am willing to go all the way with these people, or I came here for my own gratification. The movement is a logical conclusion to my work as a priest." I paused. He was listening. I continued,

"It fulfills my vocation and my interpretation of the teachings of Christ. I do not agree with a lot of the ways and means of the revolution, and I wish things were different, but they aren't. This is my only real opportunity to contribute to changing the lousy situation our Church and the government have perpetuated." I leaned back with a pillow behind me. He was blinking a lot but didn't take his eyes off me.

I felt as if I were giving a sermon, but continued, "I expect to influence the process of change by my participation. I do not expect to see the conclusion of the revolution. I imagine Marji has told you about the involvement of Cathy and Marian." I explained how they arrived at their decisions and said finally, "I do not know how you feel about all this, Tom, but I have made my choice."

He sighed, walked to the other bed, and sat down. "Marji and I are in love," he said. What normally would have been shocking to me had virtually no impact. I listened. "I knew she was involved in the movement," he said. "She encouraged me to participate. I refused, even though I agreed with much of it. But the other day she told me she could no longer hide from me the fact of your participation. I was dumbfounded."

After a long silence, I said, "I see myself not as a military leader but as a soldier, using my role as a priest to further the revolution, as other priests are being used and use their role to inhibit revolution. I will make mistakes along the way, but I will still take action in doing what I consider prudently useful for the movement."

Tom spent two days at my house in a state of quiet—unusual for him. On the third day he came into my office and sat down. I looked up from my desk. His face was drawn, and he appeared tired. I knew he had come to some conclusion. I hoped there would be no pressure from him. He lowered his eyes and said, "The two people I love most are in the movement, Marji and you." I felt a warmth. "For that reason, and because the purpose is noble and the means are necessary, I am going to join."

I never felt closer to him. I was sure he would have no argument with the basic revolutionary cause, and I was happy with his conclusion. I stood up and went to him and hugged him.

He left San Antonio to prepare for departure. I wondered about his and Marji's ability to commit themselves to the movement while being together in their new love. I knew the excitement and intensity of a middle-aged man finding love for the first time. I was jealous of what they might have, especially since I had chosen not to have that. I did not yet share with Tom my conclusion that there was no way for me to commit myself both to the revolution and to Cathy. I knew that being brothers in the same business could make it tough; each of us would have to make his own personal decisions.

17

MASKS

An army officer masked his identity while perpetrating illegality, cruelty, and violence in one of the villages of San Antonio. The mask not only protected him from an unlikely prosecution but made it easy for him to be an actor and play a role. As I despised him for what he did, I began to wonder about masks and came to find that I had worn many of them and probably had never been without them. I wondered if I could ever remove all my masks and reveal my true self.

At an early age I lost my personal identity to a mask not of my choice, that of religion. I wore that mask dutifully into adult life, afraid of having any sense of who was under the mask and also afraid that others might know who was underneath. My only freedom was in the choice to put on one of many subordinate masks. Up to and through adulthood I presented whatever front I thought was needed, appropriate or acceptable. I had my athletic mask, my good-old-boy mask, my humble mask, my macho mask, my stupid and smart masks, my priestly mask, my devoted son and brother mask, and now my revolutionary mask. But as I considered the latter, I didn't know for whom I was wearing that mask. I was not a fighter and made no claim to be and wanted no one to think I was. I was not a killer, not even a hunter, and did not want to be. But being a revolutionary in Guatemala at that moment in time had a pull of its own, a meaning, an importance. It was not a mask. I came to understand that my actions need not make me what I was. I had finally undertaken to do something that meant being myself. I was not a revolutionary, but I was taking a stand for truth and justice, and revolution presented itself as the only approach. It was important that I be myself in making revolution, perhaps being true to myself for the first time, with a sense of myself that had always been missing and for which I had long been searching. It was strange, but finally I had it. My masks didn't matter much any more. What people thought of me, or how I impressed them, no longer held its former value.

As a result, I could more easily observe and study masks: police masks, army masks, nun masks, priest masks, prostitute masks, bishop masks; people taking on the facade of what they did, or wanted to do, believing the facade to be them, or wanting to be the mask, or believing they could or should behave in the mask's mode. The policeman with the badge and gun could be violent. The army with artillery and flamethrowers could wipe out a village. The nun in her habit could be asexual. The prostitute with her makeup and low blouse could be seductive. The bishop with his purple robes and large ring could be authoritarian. The priest with his Roman collar and breviary could be holy.

As I learned to distinguish between myself and my masks, I took delight in looking under the masks of others. I could see an abused and powerless boy playing policeman, a humble and destitute man playing soldier, an emotionally abandoned and lonely woman playing nun, a frightened and searching man playing priest, a poor and loving mother playing prostitute, an inadequate and frustrated would-be parent playing bishop. I permitted myself the fantasy that one day we could all appear on stage with masks of clowns and play that role to our hearts' content and then by mutual agreement remove our masks, face each other in truth, and experience the fear of being ourselves and letting others see who we truly are. The beauty of my work today is that it affords me the opportunity to continue to examine and drop my masks, including that of psychotherapist, and to support others who are willing to drop theirs.

LÍMBANO AND I WERE with a group of men in a village beyond the town of Santa Ana working on a proposed water project when a messenger interrupted us saying that Cathy was calling me on the telephone. This was the first time in six years that I was summoned from a village for a call, so I knew it was important.

"We better get started," I said to Límbano. "Sorry we have to leave," I said to the group as we started out, breaking into a downhill run to the river. Arriving at the plaza, we hurried across to the *municipalidad*. The *telegrafista* saw us coming and was adjusting the dry cell connections when we entered, then cranked the handle on the wooden box, talking impatiently to himself as he did. He handed me the receiver. I stepped to the mouthpiece protruding from the wooden box, and said, "Hi Cathy."

"Arturo, something terrible has happened," she said excitedly. "Santiago was kidnapped last night by a group of armed men."

I couldn't believe it. A half-dozen college students were teaching literacy classes in the villages, gaining social awareness in the process. None was involved in the movement. Large groups of *campesinos* gathered in the afternoons and evenings for classes and discussions with the students. Santiago had been living in the high mountain village of Roca Grande, doing a great job. Of course, nothing went unnoticed in the parish, and the work called much attention to the students and the classes. "My God, I don't believe it," I said. "Do you have any news of where or how he is?"

"Nothing. Only some details of the kidnaping."

"I don't know what to say, Cathy, except that we'll leave immediately and should be back in town in two hours." We started out of the valley, climbing hard, cutting all the curves short. I explained to Límbano what Cathy had said. After that we did little talking, my mind running wildly over the different possibilities. I figured the culprits had to be the National Police or the Army, which meant we were being observed and threatened by one or both.

Exhausted, we arrived at the *convento*. As we came through the gate we spotted Candelario, a gentle soul from Roca Grande. He jumped to his feet and started talking as soon as we entered the compound. "What can we do?" he asked, gritting his teeth and making fists. "It was all so crazy. We were sound asleep. It was after midnight. I had gotten up earlier to tend to the baby when the moon was not quite high. She has a hacking cough that was so bad last night that my woman stayed home from the literacy class to take care of her." He wiped sweat from his brow with the back of his hand. "I was not asleep long when they broke down the door. I thought the house was collapsing and jumped up from my mat to grab the baby. Suddenly there were these lights, and this man was pushing a rifle into my stomach and screaming at me to stand still or he would kill me." He paused, looked to the sky, and said, "I didn't know if I was in a dream. I stood still. My knees started to quiver, and I knew it was not a dream. The baby started to cry. My wife was screaming. Another man pushed a rifle into her and knocked her over. Blood poured from her nose. They made us all sit down. The *jefe* told my wife to stop the baby from crying or he would shoot it. My wife crawled to the baby, lifted it up and started nursing it, her blood running onto the baby's face." My heart pounded as Candelario continued. "They had powerful flashlights that they shone in our eyes. I looked away from their lights and at my other two children. They had tears streaming down their faces but were so scared they didn't make a sound. I thought we were all going to die."

"Goddamn bastards," I said, feeling the anger rise in me. But realizing I had to keep calm, I sat down on the ground and said, "Here, Candelario, sit here, please." We sat facing each other in the shade of the house. I took a deep breath. I knew I had to sort things out. "Límbano," I said, trying to keep my voice in control, "we'll be leaving for Huehuetenango. Get yourself ready and prepare the pickup truck." He was off and running. "And put Champ in the storeroom so he doesn't follow us," I yelled after him.

"Do you know who they were, Candelario?" I asked.

"I do not know. I have never known such people. They had masks covering their faces."

This was incredible. "How many were they?" I asked.

"Five men. All very angry. All moving much in a hurry."

"What else did they do?" I asked.

"They searched my *rancho*, throwing everything around. They broke both our dishes. They found our literacy studybook, called it communistic material, and took it with them."

"What were their rifles like?" I asked.

"Some had *pistolas* in their hands. The ones with rifles had *pistolas* on their belts. The rifles were like none I have ever seen. They were shorter and had big handles under them."

I sat thinking. Candelario interrupted my thoughts. "Will they kill Santiago, *Padre?*"

"Did you see them take him?"

"They asked where the teacher was. We did not answer. The *jefe* pointed his rifle to my eyes and said he would pull the trigger if I did not answer. I told him. As he turned to leave I said that Santiago was a good man. He did not listen. They left us and ran to the chapel. I watched from between the sticks of my *rancho*. I saw them push the door open. I heard Santiago scream. I heard their shouts and curses. They were throwing things around. When they came out, I think they had a rope around his neck. His hands were tied behind him. I watched them go down the hill. We did not know what to do. After a while a few neighbors came over. We sat in the dark and talked the rest of the night. Look, I am still shaking. I do not know if they will return. I was afraid to come and tell you. What should we do?"

"We are going to try to find Santiago," I said. "We will also try to find out who these bastards are and what we can do. Thank you for coming to the *pueblo* and waiting, Candelario. Go to your home. Take care of your family." We gave an *abrazo*. I stepped back, with my hands still holding his shoulders at arm's length, and said, "What we are going through, it is very difficult. But we are protected and guided. The bastards will probably not return, but stay close to your neighbors." I watched him leave, his head and eyes down, heart sad, feeling powerless, thinking hopeless, not knowing. I knew he carried another scar.

Límbano returned, wearing a clean shirt. We got in the truck. I drove fast over the muddy, winding road until we came around a bend on the other side of the village of Rancho Viejo. Límbano shouted *"Cuidado!"* and I slammed on the brakes, sliding into the branches of the fallen tree. It had come down with a small landslide. Límbano jumped to the ground, his machete swirling into the tree. I rolled rocks out of the way and used a piece of slate to shovel dirt. We were both exhausted by the time he had hacked through ten inches of trunk. We dragged the twelve-foot section to one side, opening enough space to pass. In the truck again, I looked at him, soaked with perspiration and covered with dirt. I never told Límbano that I loved him. I just felt it. When we got to the Panamerican Highway he pulled a cloth from his shoulder bag and took out cold tortillas. Not having eaten since the early morning, we gobbled them down as we bumped along.

At the State Building a secretary ushered me into the governor's office, but the governor did not want to talk. He may not have known anything, as he claimed, but I thought he was lying. His answers certainly showed he was unwilling to cooperate or involve himself. "I have no suggestions," he said without any concern.

We went to the police station. Límbano watched the truck. Hands clutched out as I passed the heavy wood-grated door of the jail. Men shouted. A woman looked out with terror in her eyes. I walked to the desk. "I am *Padre* Arturo from San Antonio Huista. I need to see the *jefe*."

"The *jefe* is busy," the clerk said. The office door that said '*Jefe*' above it was open. I stepped to the doorway.

"Pardon the interruption, my *jefe*," I said. I had never seen the man before. "I have an emergency that cannot wait."

"Come in," he said gruffly.

"Pardon the bother, my *jefe*, but I have an emergency." He gave me the look that wonders how much one is willing to pay.

I explained briefly what had happened. I saw him withdraw as I gave the details. He wanted no part of it, not even vaguely suggesting the customary payoff. "I hope you find the young man. Now if you will forgive me, I have other business."

I felt like screaming. I walked back to the truck. Límbano said nothing. He probably knew we would get no help. "Shit," I said getting in and slamming the door. "Let's go to the damn Army."

I drove fast out of Huehuetenango, back out the Panamerican, past our turnoff to San Antonio to the small army base near the Mexican border, two mountains away from Roca Grande. The road was closed to the public. As I swung off the highway I thought that sometime in the future we would be attacking this base. The guard at the gate stood there with his legs apart, holding a short rifle with a big handle under it. I saw Límbano's body stiffen and knew I could not permit myself to feel or show my fear. I had to be audacious. I pulled up to the gate, leaned my head out the window, and said, "The colonel is waiting to see me. Open the gate."

The confused soldier hesitated a moment. I repeated my words impatiently. Those who are impatient usually have some authority. The "colonel" part was easy: everything in Guatemala was run by a colonel. The young soldier swung open the gate with a look of bewilderment. I pulled ahead to the compound of small wooden buildings with sheet-metal roofs. I stopped in front of the larger building, stepped from the truck, and walked directly to the first door, entering without hesitation. "I have come to see the colonel," I said to the two startled men behind the low counter.

Both stood up. One stepped to a side door, knocked, opened it and said, "Someone to see you, my colonel."

I stepped to the doorway and stood at the side of the soldier. The man behind the desk, older and balding, smiled. I entered and introduced myself. He extended his hand. As I gave the details of the incident, he shook his head trying to appear sympathetic. I sensed that he knew, and I decided to go for broke. "So I have come to you, my colonel, to request the release of the young man." He did not answer. He put the eraser of his pencil to his lips and looked at me. I knew I was clicking.

"You want to talk to the lieutenant," he said pointing out the door with his pencil.

"*Gracias, mi colonel,*" I said, and returned to the outer room.

"I am to see the lieutenant," I said. One of the two soldiers led me to a back building. He knocked on a door and opened it. "Someone to see you, *mi teniente*," he said.

I stepped in and registered shock. It was the lieutenant I had encountered a few years before, back in La Libertad. He was tough; he had been mean to the people. I introduced myself. He did not offer his hand. He did not remember me. I decided to go for it. "Pardon me, lieutenant. I am the priest from San Antonio. I have just spoken to the colonel who has referred me to you. I simply want to know when the young man captured in Roca Grande last night will be released."

He leaned back in his chair, dropping his hand to his holster. He looked me up and down, knowing I was not macho, and said, "Listen, your university boy was teaching those people to read and write." A shiver went up my spine. I had hit pay-dirt. I nodded my head. "If they learn to read and write, they will only go on to stir up trouble." I was amazed. I knew of this mentality but never expected to hear it expressed so clearly.

I didn't want to get into an argument over the value of literacy or the rights of the people, but I wanted to go further. I simply asked, "But why did you wear masks?"

He smiled and answered, "That is the technique that your people have taught us." I thought of the folks back home and wondered if they would ever know the truth.

"What has happened to the student?" I asked.

"It is really none of your business," he said, "but I am willing to tell you that we gave your Santiago a good talking to and released him. I doubt that in the future the priest will find students willing to teach peasants."

I felt like spitting in his face. I looked him in the eye. I said nothing. I turned and left. In Guatemala you do not push your luck. You get what you can and get out, if you're lucky. Límbano was relieved to see me. I told him the story as we drove home.

I felt relieved, despite all the confusion and turmoil. "Take the day off tomorrow, Límbano," I said as we approached the *pueblo*. "Get some rest and have some fun."

"There will be time for fun," he said. The next morning he was at the house at six o'clock as usual.

I dropped by Ramiro's for a game of checkers and to see if there was any news. He looked sick and very tired. He did not mention the Santiago incident directly. He simply said, "I hear the students have been doing a good job." I nodded agreement. "Sometimes you can measure the effectiveness of work," he went on, "by how strongly the authorities respond." I said nothing. He smiled and said, "Well, I am happy for the way things turned out, and I am sad for my people." Such subjects do not get discussed openly. People generally pretend such things don't happen, or that they know nothing. What they do know is the penalty for getting involved.

"You look tired, Ramiro," I said. His face was pale, and he was breathing heavily.

"Yes, I have been feeling weak," he answered. "I do not get my strength back as I used to. Maybe just one game today."

As we set up the checker board, he said, "I will not be playing many more games with you." I looked into his sunken eyes and felt sad. He forced a smile as he said, "You don't have much more time to teach me English." I knew he was right. I was losing a good friend.

"Perhaps I will drop by the church for a confession," he said. "You could still do a confession for your old friend, could you not?" Confession was not a new topic for us.

"Ramiro," I said, "even if I were truly able to forgive sins, you have no sins to confess." He looked at me with a slight smile, as if wishing he could accept what I was saying.

I knew it was too late for the new idea. "Let us go to your patio, Ramiro. You can confess there."

"But you do not have your confessional stole," he said.

"You can let me borrow one of your neckties," I said, he being the only man in town to wear them.

He stepped into a room and brought out a stained red tie with yellow polka dots. "I do not have a purple tie," he said.

"Red and yellow works just as well," I answered, as I put the tie around my neck. He sat on the old chair and I sat on the stool, and Ramiro made his last confession.

I said, "If you leave us, Ramiro, you will be playing checkers with Jesus." He smiled and shook his head as he did whenever I spoofed him. "Whether you win or lose, Jesus will not care. He just likes to play. But if He double-jumps you, or you double-jump Him, either way, you are going to think you committed a fault and want confession."

He laughed and said, "Ah, *mi Padre* Arturo." But his eyes had lost the old sparkle. When we got back to the game he moved slowly and made mistakes. It was the first time I ever let him win.

Three days later his family and friends brought his simple coffin to the church door. I was waiting with my purple stole on. I read some prayers, said a few words, sprinkled holy water, and gave a blessing. I walked with the weeping widow, *Doña* Sylvia, behind the coffin. After the burial, when the relatives and friends were leaving, *Doña* Sylvia stepped to my side and gave me a small brown paper bag. "Ramiro said to give this to you," she said, still weeping. I took it and gave her an *abrazo*, and she left with the others.

I stayed behind wanting to be alone with my thoughts and for a few last words. I recalled how Ramiro had helped me come to grips with my sexuality and to feel good about myself as a man. I considered how I had to come to the mountains of Huehuetenango to have the experience of a man caring about me like a father. Ramiro and I treated each other like father and son, with frequent switching of roles. I thought of our conversations, and of the way we laughed during our checker games. I wanted to speak out loud to him. I did, softly, in English. "Ramiro, you have been more than a special friend. You have been my mentor and my father and my son." I paused, and smiled, and went on, "You used to say you wanted to learn English, and now I know you understand it." I thought he was hearing me. "You have taught me much," I said. "I have been privileged to know you. You are as a dear brother, Ramiro, and I love you. I will never forget you." I was about to leave. I turned back and said, "By the way, Ramiro, watch out for your kings. I've heard it said that He wipes them out." I started down the rocky trail to town, when I remembered I was carrying the bag. I opened it, chuckled, took out the necktie, and hung it around my neck.

Meetings and plans for making revolution went on. We discussed the pertinent issues for getting under way: methods of storing medicine and food, gathering and hiding arms and ammunition, obtaining money. And sometimes we simply had interesting and exciting conversations, almost cops-and-robbers stuff. But as time went by the discussions became more serious and intense. As we grew in size and maturity we handled such subjects as group decisions, recruitment, physical and military training, discipline, buying arms, insubordination, kidnaping for ransom, holding up business establishments, attacking isolated army posts, propaganda, communications, relations with the Church and media, the taking of prisoners, and torture.

I shut down on the last one. I could in no way approve of or in any way be part of such action. We discussed it; policy had to be established. The government, the police, the military, the United States trainers, the official rightist groups and guerrilla groups—all used torture as a matter of course. Someone asked why we should not use it in isolated instances if the lives of our people could be saved as a result. "I cannot approve, and I cannot participate in such action," I said, meeting my first major stumbling block. But I had known that at times situations would arise that I could neither accept nor agree with, situations that would be beyond my control.

Our ranks increased. Selected students and *campesinos* were being approached and generally found open to our invitation. I was afraid, however, that we were moving too fast and that people might be entering without sufficient thought and preparation. I put forth my view to José. "Clearly, we will be unable to continue recruiting for long without exposure," I said. "I think it is better to get away with a few people, but get away, and make our impact after the front is formed."

"I agree," he said, "but there is a momentum that is difficult to stop, although we can slow it down. And we have to discuss another issue: we need more time for logistics. We do not even have an area sufficiently known for us to survive in. As we are now, we would not make it in the jungle."

I agreed. We discussed this with others and decided to move our departure date back a month, and also to slow down the recruiting. There would have to be a consensus before anyone else was approached, and we would move into our new front at the end of January. Meanwhile, José and a companion would prepare to go to the jungle of the Petén to practice survival techniques and to evaluate the area for our first training base.

José and I had been making frequent trips together. We walked when going to villages and went in my pickup truck to different cities. On the road, any time we came to a police or army checkpoint I always felt tense. Sometimes those inspecting would just look in the cab and wave us on. Other times they would ask for my license or a cigarette, or inquire where we were going. If the tarpaulin covered the back, they might ask what we were carrying or take a peek. Sometimes they would joke, sometimes they were angry. Once a soldier reached in the passenger window and opened the glove compartment. He was inches away from José's pistol in his belt. I froze as I saw José jump. The soldier said, "Nothing to be afraid of."

I was frequently frightened when with José. On our first trip together he had said, "If I am discovered, you take cover. I will not be captured without a fight. I will always try to shoot my way out. If I can help you, I will. With luck, we might both survive." But José's identity was never challenged.

Once we were returning from a trip to the city, talking about, of all things, the Beatles. We went on to talk about Liverpool and the turmoil there. And then about Spain and José's ancestors and the revolutionary movement there. And about the Spanish coming to Latin America and Guatemala. I told him of a Spanish priest who had come to Guatemala some years before, who lived in the neighboring State of El Quiché. "His name is Padre Luís. He is well-known for his success in working with cooperatives and is considered to have a good understanding of what the people are up against."

"You think we could visit this Spanish priest?" he asked.

"We could go by his place and see if he is home," I said.
So we went to El Quiché, located the *convento* of the Spanish
Sacred Heart Fathers, and found Padre Luís at home. We introduced ourselves, told of our interest in cooperatives, and
asked if he had time to chat. He invited us in and was very
hospitable, gladly discussing with us his involvement with the
people and his view of the future of cooperativism. After a half-
hour one of his companions stuck his head in the room and asked
if we would stay for lunch. We were enjoying the talk and were
hungry, so we accepted gladly. The meal was pleasant and
hearty. Luís and his companions seemed to share well. After
lunch the three of us retired to Luís's room and continued the
discussion, which led to a variety of topics including the present
political situation.

Somehow José concluded he had Luís's confidence and said,
"You have told us about your work with cooperatives. Arturo
has talked about his. I would like also to tell you about my work."
Luís was obviously interested. I thought José was going to talk
about The Crater. He lowered his voice and began, "My work
cannot be done as openly as yours. My work is subversive."

I could not believe what was coming. I saw Luís frown.
José paused, looked at me, nodded to indicate that everything
was fine, and said, "I am a member of the F.A.R." I was amazed.
He looked at me as if pleased with himself, saw my bewilderment, and nodded again as if everything were alright. But I had
a sense that it was not alright. Luís gave a slight smile and
nodded his head. If he was surprised, he was not much surprised,
or he hid it well. Instead, he became enthusiastic and asked
many questions. With such apparent acceptance, José felt confident to go on to telling of my participation and our organization,
laying out our general plan.

Luís said, "This is good news. I had hoped that something
like this would eventually form." José's eyes lit up. He truly
wanted the movement to advance and thought that priests and
nuns could make the difference. He was not going to miss a
chance to recruit an interested priest.

I was angry. I did not join the talk. When Luís asked me
questions, I answered them simply. I didn't know what to do.

I felt nauseous, out of control, lost. I indicated that it was time for us to leave. Luís must have noticed my distress. As we got up he said, "Do not worry, Arturo. I promise security and secrecy. I also have much to lose; so do not be concerned about sharing your confidence. My lips are sealed." José nodded his head happily. Luís walked us to the truck. As we got in he said, "I am interested in the plan. I will advise you shortly of my thoughts."

As we pulled away, I barked, "José, what have you done?"

"Do not worry so much, Arturo," he said, relaxing into the seat. "He can be trusted."

For the first time I let myself express anger towards José. "You do not know that," I yelled. "I know priests very well. You do not. They are not trustworthy. And you have no reason to trust Padre Luís with people's lives and the success of our plan."

"Wait, you are getting too excited," he said holding up his hands in protest. "Luís is a very good priest."

"Bullshit. Good priests have kept the people in submission for centuries. Because he works in cooperatives does not mean he would be a good participant. And I will bet that if he is not right now telling some of the others of his community about our plan, it will not be long before he does so. Are you willing to trust the rest of those priests?"

He hesitated and then said loudly, "Social-minded priests may never have another opportunity to demonstrate alliance with the people. We have to make it available to those we think capable."

"No, José. Absolutely not," I said. "Once we are away and gone, *bien*. Then you can send engraved invitations. But not now."

"He will be fine, Arturo. In selected cases we have to risk. Now relax so we can look at his positive aspects."

Two weeks later Padre Luís reported that he wanted to be involved. He was welcomed unanimously. He was an important figure. That he was Spanish would bring the movement more into the international media. I still felt hesitant but accepted him, while continuing to push for caution.

We had people in different areas committed to our plan. Communication was ordinarily difficult; communicating about a subversive subject proved impossible. We needed a general session for purposes of getting acquainted and to discuss problems, logistics, and the many aspects of our work. We called a meeting for the end of November at a house made available in the city of Esquintla.

About twenty people met in secrecy. The meeting was useful. Discussions were provocative and helped to settle discord. We made agreements that alleviated fear, and we established basic strategy. We would keep our departure date for the end of January. I left the meeting feeling prepared for revolution.

18
ROOTS

My mother, a victim of childhood emotional abuse and neglect, found her identity in the Church and became the model of that Church to her future family. Her father, an unquestionable and untouchable Irish Catholic patriarch, was a faithful confidant of James Michael Curley, the famous Boston political boss, and beneficiary of his political system. Her mother, a depressed relic of the Victorian era, satisfied to submit to her husband's stern dominance, lived quietly in his shadow. Both were adamant in their defense and practice of the Catholic faith. Of the three boys and three girls they sired, the males all graduated from Catholic colleges. The three females never questioned their roles, one entering the convent and the other two, including my mother, going to work immediately after high school.

With a daughter a nun, the devout Catholic family went on to fulfill its highest expectation by sending a son on to the seminary and the priesthood. Father Bill (my uncle), pious and deeply caring but uninformed beyond baseball and unaware of anything beyond his ecclesiastical circle, became the nerve center of the expanding nuclear family. Only mother outdid him in constancy of devotion and subservience.

My father, although reared as only a nominal Catholic, followed Mom in her ardent and uncompromising daily observances. Every aspect of the lives of the six children they begat revolved around the beliefs and practices of the Catholic religion. The family never discussed or doubted what course to take or what decision to make and took no responsibility for the results; the Church had it all laid out.

The mettle of my relationship with my mother was once again to be tested as she, still wielding the unbending power of the family system, insisted on coming into my missionary life. Even from a distance I could feel the pull of the bond, the depth of the roots, and the manipulation of the control I had unwittingly ceded to her in my early years. I also felt the old fear of opposing or offending her and my need to take care of her. In dealing with her I was up against a force in my life second only to that of the Church, and in meeting this challenge I would take another step in further understanding both.

Today I realize that our family structure resulted from the actions of generations of unthinking and unquestioning followers. It was not the Catholic Church that determined the form of our family habits. Mom and her household would have followed just as devoutly and with the same compliance any other religion into which we might have been born. Never having learned to believe in ourselves or to question authoritative structure, we would have submitted equally to any inherited system, be it Jewish, Mormon, Muslim, or Protestant—any system that would similarly justify and give import to our lives while righteously making its beliefs and practices the correct approach to God and the absolutely dominant factor in determining our values, behavior, and beliefs.

Having freed myself from the imposed beliefs of Catholicism, I now consider myself fortunate to have learned the challenging lesson of respecting the beliefs of others. In this I remember the fallible origin of beliefs and the importance of not confusing them with truth.

A LETTER FROM MY MOTHER awaited me back in San Antonio. Over the years I had developed the custom of writing to my parents every week or two, sharing my activities and parish happenings. I had not, however, exposed them to anything of what was going on with me as a result of the movement.

Mom's letter expressed concern for my brother Tom. She wrote, "I gather from his letters that big changes are happening in his life. He talks as if he is involved in something that is causing him much concern and possible danger. Do you know what is happening? If you do, please tell me."

I showed the letter to Marian and said, "I'm going to write back to calm her fears, but I don't like being in the middle. You know, this reminds me of when we were kids. I thought it was my responsibility to smooth stuff out for my mother and Tom and felt guilty if I couldn't."

Marian said, "Apart from the issue of your mother, it will be a miracle if we ever get our front off the ground—people find it so difficult to keep their involvement to themselves."

I wrote back to Mom speaking of the plight of the poor, adding that "those of us who are involved in the social problems of the day are indeed endangering ourselves. And, yes, one day this involvement might call for Tom's and my giving our lives for the cause we believe to be just and true, and such is the duty and privilege of the priest and the follower of Christ."

That did not clarify what Mom was picking up from Tom's letters. She wrote right back, "What else is going on? I know that he is talking about more than social involvement. To satisfy myself and to be of any possible help, I am coming to Guatemala."

Mother, a woman whose longest trip had been from Boston to Niagara Falls for her honeymoon, who never went anywhere without my father, was coming into a strange country and coming alone. She was not asking if she could come; she was coming. I went to Marian and said, "I do not need more surprises, but I have one. Guess what."

"What now?"

"Mother is coming."

"Don't tell me," she said, looking skyward as if for help.

"It doesn't fit for her to leave her role of homemaker to try to understand what's going on here," I said. "Mother is afraid of everything. How will she adjust?"

I held out the letter. Marían read it and said, "You know, I think your mother has what this movement needs. With her kind of guts, maybe we should recruit her." I laughed. "Seriously," she said, "we will take care of her when she gets here. Don't worry about it. Tom will have to be responsible for what he has told her and what he is doing. We have too many preoccupations already. And we have to remain collected, or we'll blow the whole plan."

It was mid-December. Tom, Marji, Marian, Cathy, and I met Mom at the airport in Guatemala City. I had not seen her in a few years, but she was the same old Mom. She was unhappy, and she did not try to pretend otherwise. She did not want fun or enjoyment. She did not want to tour or shop. She wanted to see her sons in their role as priests and make certain nothing would interfere with the continuance of that. We put her up at the Biltmore.

While I felt sorry for both Tom and Mother and wanted to make the situation as easy and harmonious as possible, I also felt sorry for myself for being involved. We sat in her room for hours trying to make conversation; it was a disaster. At the first opportunity she confided to me, "I do not like what is happening between Tom and Marji. I see how she looks at him and how close they are. I'm afraid he might leave the priesthood to marry her." She did not try to hide her sadness.

"Mom," I said, "Whatever Tom does, it's his choice. He knows what he's doing. I know you don't agree. But you are just going to make it difficult for yourself if you try to control him."

"Do you think he will marry her?" she asked.

"I know this is sad for you, Mom. But if that is his intention, that is what he will do. He has not discussed such an idea with me. But I wish you would let him run his life." I didn't think Tom had any idea of marrying. Being in love was something I grasped easily. Needing official approval did not fit into my picture of what we were doing.

I felt so sorry for Mom I could have cried. In many ways she was like the parishioners that I wanted to free. She had no personal identity. The Church was her life. Her success was measured by religion. She had never permitted change. She never questioned. She never thought for herself. She had no belief of her own. She had no joy. At sixty-nine she thought no differently than she had at perhaps twenty-nine, or possibly even at nine, and was proud of it.

Tom had chosen to be a priest at a very early age, and Mom never permitted herself the idea that he could ever possibly want to change that. Now she thought he was betraying her in possibly doing so. I looked for an opportunity to pass Mom's words along to Tom. He wasted no time in sitting down with her, and in the presence of all he confirmed what she had suspected and had hoped and prayed against.

"Yes, Mom," he said, "I am in love with Marji."

She took a breath and said nothing. The tension hung thick. Everyone looked uncomfortable. I had to admire Tom. It took guts to go against the source of the tradition and beliefs that had been imposed upon him since his earliest days and that had run most of his life. He broke free, and he did it well. And Mom's frail body shivered, and she lowered her eyes, and those eyes rarely lifted again. There were no tears and there was rarely a smile. From that point, the already depressing visit went downhill.

Time dragged on. That evening we were still sitting in Mom's room. Her distress and sense of failure intensified our own pressure. I needed a break. Mom had already turned down the idea of going to a restaurant. I stood up and asked who would like to go out and get some snacks for the group. Marian volunteered quickly, looking relieved to be able to get away.

Getting off the elevator into the crowded lobby, I was taken totally by surprise when I nearly bumped into Father John Breen, the newly-elected superior of the Maryknoll Fathers in Guatemala. He, with two of his assistants, Father Rudy and Father Dave, were standing at the elevator waiting to go up. They were the last people in the world I wanted to see. But, accustomed to behaving appropriately in the midst of my secret life, I simply greeted them. They returned no smile. They showed no friendliness. Something was clearly wrong. I started to move on, but John called. I stopped and turned. He stepped up to me, the others staying right behind him, and said, "Go get Tom and bring him down. I need to talk to the both of you immediately."

"Sure thing, John," I said, trying to smile as my stomach twisted. Marian and I got back on the elevator. I pushed the button. We faced each other. It was an unusual experience to stand before that wonderful and powerful woman, to look into her eyes and to share such open and deep fear. It is a feeling I do not want to repeat, but was a moment of intimacy that I will never forget. Neither of us spoke. Her eyes were wider and bluer than I had ever seen them. She broke the spell, saying, "They knew we were upstairs and were about to come up."

I shook my head in bewilderment and said, "Looks as if they're onto us."

"I wonder how much they know," she said.

"And how they found out," I added

"Looks as if you and Tom are going to have to face the music first," Marian said. I knew she would have no trouble facing the music when her turn came.

"If they do know something," I said, "the problem will be holding ourselves together as we plot where to go from here."

We were at the door of Mom's room. "We'll find out soon enough," Marian said. And then, smiling her confident smile, added, "If it's to be, we'll make it happen." I opened the door.

"Back so soon?" Cathy asked. "Where's the grub?"

"Well, we've had a change of plan," Marian said.

"We met John Breen," I said as casually as I could. "He's downstairs with Dave and Rudy, all dressed up with suits and collars. They were on their way up here. They want to talk to Tom and me." I paused with what must have been an awkward smile. There was silence for a moment as it sunk in.

"Let's go find out what they want, pal," I said to Tom.

"Sure thing," he said with apparent calmness as he got up from a low bucket chair. "Would you like to come along, Marji?" he asked.

"Yes, I would," Marji answered.

We stepped into the hallway and took an anxious moment to try to figure out what was happening. We couldn't, except to confirm that it looked like a leak. We would have to play it by ear. We stepped out of the elevator. There was no shaking of hands or any form of pretense. John led us to the side of the lobby. The four of us stood in a circle, with Dave and Rudy silently behind John and on both sides of him, obviously there for support. John's jaw was sticking out and his lips were tight, as he asked, "Were you at a meeting in Esquintla?" There was a pause. We needed time. He was catching us off guard. We needed to ask questions, not answer them. I wanted to say, "Hold everything."

Tom answered, "Yes." I felt anger that Tom would give in so quickly.

John turned to Marji. "Were you there?"

"I was there also," she said.

Then John looked me in the eye. I saw his fear and his strength. I was never a friend of John's. At get-togethers, John would be in the center of a group that regularly discussed problems of the doctrine, difficulties with construction, parish problems. He joked and teased. He was loud and sharp and, as far as a priest can be, truthful. He had a soft heart and could be considerate and kind, but he usually covered it by brusqueness and macho. In my mind, he was the best choice for religious superior. I sometimes felt jealous of him. Tom had been John's assistant at the parish of San Pedro Soloma and was closer to John than I was. Alike in many ways, both needed to be strong and in control. They seemed to agree to compete, and for the most part, it worked. John and I just seemed to agree not to be close and let it go at that. I looked at John, knowing that he was no longer my Father Superior. I knew it was all over. I knew that our plan was uncovered. John looked at me. He was determined to take care of this matter, which could screw up everything he stood for.

I wished there was another way. I wished John would look at what he was part of. I knew he was threatened by what we were doing, but I also knew that he could offer no viable option for the people. "Were you there?" he asked me.

Wishing I could get out of the question, and now not having a way, I answered, "Yes," and felt my heart sink.

He took a breath and said, "I know all about the meeting. I know its purpose. I know who was present and what was discussed. And the *Policía Judicial* and the American ambassador also know." He looked from one to the other of the three of us. "You are to leave on the plane with your mother tomorrow morning."

I felt furious. I was angry at John and his two supporters, angry at whoever had betrayed us, angry at myself for getting caught. I was angry at the Church for its blindness, its lies, its control, its abuse of power. I was angry at a government that stood for business, for the wealthy class, for decimating those poor who sought human dignity, for spending the national treasury on United States weaponry in the name of God and democracy. My fists were so tight that my nails were digging into my palms. I felt like screaming and hitting, and knew I had to calm down. I had to stall. I needed time. Loose ends had to be tied up. People were now in danger and had to be warned. And I needed to protect my mother. I would not leave the next day. And if all else failed, I would take care of what I could and then go into hiding with the F.A.R.

I knew John's plan. He would permit no discussion. He would get us out before we could cause more trouble. He figured he had two tools: my mother and threats. He was using my mother to get us out. I decided to use her to stay. I would take my chances with the threats. "I won't go," I said.

"If you don't go," John answered back, "the *Policía Judicial* will pick you up, and the lives of people you are working with will be endangered." John was no dummy. I knew he had figured out his strongest lines beforehand and would use them as he needed. What he was saying was possible, and I had no way of checking its truth. But I thought he had played his strongest card. I decided to challenge it.

"I will not go tomorrow. And I will not let you use my mother to get me on a plane. She has come this far, and I'm not willing to send her back without seeing my parish. I'm going to take her there," something I had not considered before. He looked at me carefully. I could see he was willing to buy it if I was willing to make a concession. I did. "After that, I will leave."

He thought for a moment while staring into my eyes, determined not to blink. "I will give you five days to do that, if you will give me your word that you will not discuss this with anyone else and will then leave the country."

I wondered if I could get everything done in five days. I considered going for seven, but the thought that the *Policía Judicial* might be aware of what was going on scared me too much. "You have my word," I said.

He looked at Marji and Tom. They agreed.

"Okay," he said. "I will meet you at the airport on the twenty-first for the morning flight. I will have your tickets to New York."

We told mother nothing. We spent a little more time that evening with her, during which I said, "Mom, I have an invitation for you. Cathy, Marian, and I want to invite you to our parish. We want you to see what we have done and let you draw your own conclusions about the situation and conditions. Will you go to San Antonio with us?"

She raised her eyes and tried to force a slight smile.
"That sounds like a good idea," she said. "I think I would like that." I told her that along the way we could stop off at Lake Atitlán for a night and briefly described its beauty. She looked at me but showed no real interest. I told her we would pick her up in the morning, said good night, and left.

Since Cathy and Marian were not implicated, they decided that they would stay in San Antonio and keep the work going until they were ready to make their next decision. Marji, Tom, and I had some serious preparing to do, so we went our way and left them for the evening. We sat for hours in a car on a side street, trying to figure out where the leak was, how much of our plan and who of those involved were known, and what to do. We agreed that everyone was suspect until proven otherwise. We went through a process of elimination, starting with ourselves, examining each other, looking for a possible motive or mistake. We found none and started looking at the others involved. Father Luís was a prime suspect. I had a meeting lined up with him for Monday. I would keep that meeting and confront him. We agreed that whenever we met any other member of the group we would likewise immediately confront that person as a suspect and study his or her reaction. It appeared that the informer lacked information and therefore was not a person close to us. John evidently did not know that Marían had been at the Esquintla meeting or that she and Cathy were part of the group.

As we sat in the car trying to figure out our next move, Tom came up with an idea. "Look," he said, "what's wrong with our going to Mexico and organizing there?" Knowing we had to make quick decisions, we discussed the idea briefly, and then accepted it as the basis for a plan that Tom went on to unfold. "Anyone who is in danger here, or anyone who wants to join us, can go to Mexico and help organize and set up our front. When we leave Guatemala, we will be flown to the United States. As soon as we arrive, we can start looking for a flight to Mexico."

Marji said, "The people we have been working with need to get out for their own safety. We could meet the students and *campesinos* in Mexico, along with anyone else who has to flee or wants to join us."

We agreed on the plan and then decided on a series of specific dates and places in Mexico where others could make contact with us. Tom would go back to the Petén and talk with his people. He would also send out a scout to find José and Roberto, who were practicing survival in the jungle, advising them not to return to Guatemala City but to make their way to Mexico and one of the meeting points. Marji would advise and inform the students and people in the city. Cathy, Marian, and I would take Mom and set out for the lake and then to San Antonio. We would talk to our people over the weekend, and I would put Mom on the plane from Huehuetenango on Monday. Tom and Marji would meet her in Guatemala City and put her on her flight to Boston. I would drive to the meeting with *Padre* Luís, then on to Guatemala City. The three of us would reunite for any final preparation. We parted, very frightened.

The next morning the Sisters, Mom, and I set out for the lake. We got two rooms, had a late lunch, and sat in the midst of one of the most beautiful scenes in the world, unable to appreciate it. I looked to the shore across from us and reflected on my meeting with *el Comandante*. I wondered if I would ever again be able to relax and enjoy the lake. Time hung heavily. Cathy and I went for a swim. My attraction to her was so strong that I wondered how I was going to leave her in a few days. She performed beautiful dives, swam with grace, and—possibly because of her fear—laughed incessantly.

I looked at Mom and wished we could enjoy being together. As night was coming on Cathy and Marian went to their room, and Mom and I sat in silence for a while and then began walking across a grassy area to our room. I looked up and saw the moon, very bright, with a halo around it, and said, "Mom, look how beautiful the moon is."

Her eyes were cast on the ground, and she did not lift them. "I do not have time," she said. I put my arm around her shoulders. I knew her heart was breaking. I felt a pain in my own heart. I could do nothing. She was locked into her sadness and self-pity. Her world was falling apart.

In our room together, alone, we didn't talk. The occasion reminded me of my childhood. I had for six years been the baby of the family. When Dad left for work and the four others for school, she and I would spend many hours quietly alone. When she did the washing in the cellar, I would play there. The day she caught her hand in the ringer and screamed as her arm was dragged in, I ran to her and pulled the plug. She cried and said I had saved her life. That day the little boy knew she would always need him and made the decision that he would always protect her.

The moon reflected itself in the lake behind her. She sat in the dim light, saying her beads, her face wrinkled with age, her eyes closed and moist. I knew her thoughts were running wild as she tried to control them with prayer. I realized that she had been doing that her whole life. "Let's talk, Mom," I said, without having anything specific to talk about.

She looked up. "Is there anything to talk about?" she asked.

"Yes," I said. "I want to tell you about a friend of mine named Ramiro." She did not look especially interested. "We used to play checkers together in his corner store. . . ."

"Tom is leaving the priesthood," she interrupted almost inaudibly.

My heart went out to her. She could not get this off her mind. "Mom, you have to let Tom lead his own life," I said.

"Will you ever marry?" she asked.

"No," I answered. I was leaving the Church and the priesthood and going into the unknown and to possible death. Marriage had of itself no personal value or import for me. A relationship did. She made no comment.

I thought it was probably the best time to tell her what some of the future would be. I said, "Mom, I have a secret I want to share with you." Her eyes opened and even sparkled for a moment, as if this was some game we used to play.

"What?" she asked.

"I will tell you a secret if you promise not to tell anyone else, except Dad."

"I agree," she said.

"You know how I have told you about the poverty of our people?" She nodded. "You have seen some of that already, and you are going to see much more in San Antonio. That poverty is not necessary. These people could live well. They endure much suffering, sickness, and early death because the government of this country exists only for the wealthy, and the military of this country exists basically to keep the poor from rebelling."

"I think it's terrible," she said. "I think it's a crime. I feel sorry for the people. So what's the secret?"

"I'm getting to that," I said. "Tom and I have learned to love these people, and we have learned a lot from them. We are committed to them." She signalled agreement with a nod of her head. I continued, "You are aware that a revolution has been going on here for many years, trying to overthrow the system. It is only the United States that keeps the revolution from being successful."

"The secret?" she said.

"So the secret is, Mom, that Tom and I are involved in the revolution."

There was a moment of silence. Then she asked, "Is she involved in the revolution?"

"Mom, I asked you to leave Tom alone in his relationship with Marji."

She thought for a moment and then asked again, "Is she involved?"

"Yes," I said. "And you have to let that be okay."

There was silence. I was afraid to tell her what was coming next. I wondered if, on top of the sadness she was already handling, she could accept more. Something told me to tell her. I did, hesitantly. "Mom," I said, "this means we will be leaving our parishes, and it could mean the death of both of us."

She lowered her eyes. The beads began to move again. There was a long silence. When she raised her eyes, she looked different. She raised her head, sat up and said, "You know, I would consider myself privileged to give my two sons to the revolution."

I couldn't believe my ears. This woman could let her priest-sons fight and die. She could not let them marry. We sat in silence as she finished her beads. She put them in her purse, stood up easily, came to my chair, and put her hand on my shoulder. I looked up at her. She leaned over and kissed me on the forehead and said, "We have our secret." She went to bed. I sat up for a long time, stressed and confused. I did not tell her about our expulsion.

The next day we continued our trip. Mom never seemed bothered by the jolts and bumps of the four-hour ride with four of us jammed in the cab of the truck. She had no complaint or criticism, nor did she express any need, like a veteran of the unpaved back mountain road. Cathy and Marian were wonderful with her, and she showed her appreciation for them. We arrived at San Antonio about mid-afternoon that Saturday. Many people were waiting. I introduced Mom to everybody, and then Cathy brought her to their *convento* and left her there to rest. Marian and Cathy did as they always did: talked with the people and dealt with any issues and problems.

When I called Límbano into the office, I saw in his face that he knew something was wrong. The young man standing before me, who could hear the fire and wind speak, had no problem reading me. I didn't know how to tell him, so I did it as simply as possible: "They know about our movement, Límbano. I have to leave Guatemala."

He sat down on one of the small benches against the wall, hands clasped under his chin, silent, staring at me as I told him what had happened.

"We have much work to do and very little time," I said. "There are people I have to talk to. Those involved who are not already here, we will have to summon by messenger. We have to make plans and decisions. I am going to give you a little extra money for yourself, then tomorrow our job is finished." Tears came to his eyes.

"I never thought this job would finish," he said. I did not know what to say. "No more rivers?" he asked. I shook my head, a tear rolling down my cheek. "No more mountains for us?" he asked, the tears now streaming down his face. I had never seen Límbano cry.

I went and sat beside him. "Límbano," I said with difficulty, "I have never had a better friend than you." But then my sobbing took over. When I was able to go on, I said, almost one word at a time, "It is difficult for me to leave you. I can never thank you enough." He reached out and put his hand on top of mine. I went on, haltingly, "You have never faltered in guiding me. You have never misled me. You have done your job perfectly." Once more I had to compose myself before saying, "I will be going to Mexico. Our group will be preparing to come back to Guatemala as *guerrieros*. You must take good care of yourself. You will be in danger."

I put my other hand on top of his. We sat in silence until our tears stopped flowing. Then he said, "I have been afraid since you left on this trip to see your mother. I did not know if you were going to be killed. But now I know. You do not get killed." He paused. I waited. "You are right about my job," he said, looking as if into the distance. I waited. After a long moment he continued, "My job here is finished." He cast his eyes down as he said, "I do not have the words with which to say how happy I have been." I looked at his face and saw the pain. He went on, "For me, it could not have been better." He paused and raised his eyes to mine. "I do not want you to go, Arturo, but it is the time. You have been the teacher. I have been the guide."

Late into the evening, Límbano was sending messengers out to the villages and pueblos, and one by one and in small groups he received those privy to our clandestine work and ushered them into the *convento*. Well after midnight, people were quietly slipping in and out, sitting in the darkness of my living room, talking softly, answering each other's questions, sharing feelings, offering suggestions and support. I explained that I would try to remain in communication with a few key people, and to those few I gave the contact point for January 2, at 10 A.M. in the plaza of Comitán, the southernmost *pueblo* in Mexico, and two later contacts in case that one failed. I wanted to bestow gifts from my possessions to these dear friends but was afraid they would only be used as evidence against them in the future. When everyone left, I spent hours over the stove burning records, letters, and pages of notebooks with a brief history of my work, relationships, and ideas.

Sunday morning I celebrated the two Masses in San Antonio. The church was full as usual. Mom sat in the first pew at both. I introduced her as the one who set me on the path that led to San Antonio. The people applauded her. She had tears in her eyes. I knew she loved seeing me in the vestments, delivering the sermon, conducting the ritual, distributing communion, giving the blessing. She did not know that I would never celebrate Mass again.

Cathy and Marían were full of love and energy, sharing with the people, leading our favorite hymns. I spoke on social justice coming from the heart, the heart being the center of love and courage. Mom seemed to understand and smiled a slight smile the whole time.

After Mass I performed the baptisms as Marían and Cathy worked the clinic. I told Isabela that I wanted no breakfast. Afraid that she would tell others, I simply said that I was going to drive my mother to Huehuetenango, asking Límbano to tell her later. I saw a few more people with last-minute requests or questions. I patted Champ, who was jumping all over me, thinking we were going on a trip. I said a simple goodbye to Límbano and told him to hold Champ. Then I put my suitcase in the truck and left, stopping by Cathy's and Marian's to pick up Mom. After she said goodbye I gave Cathy and Marian a hug and walked to the truck. I did not dare look back. People along the road waved as they always did. I tried not to think about what was happening. I tried not to feel my emotions.

Mom said nothing as we drove. I was grateful for that, knowing that if I had to talk I would not contain my tears. We put up at the Zaculeu Hotel in Huehuetenango. When Mom was settled in, I drove to a secluded spot by the ruins and cried.

I returned, feeling less stressed, and sat down. Mom looked at me and said, "So tell me the story about your friend Ramsey, the checker player." I looked at her in amazement, and then told the story of Ramiro. She seemed to enjoy it. When I finished, she asked, "So what did you do with that necktie?"

"It's still hanging in my closet," I said.

"Good," she said, jokingly, "Leave it there. I don't want you wearing neckties."

The next morning I drove Mom to the Huehuetenango Airport. There stood Father Dave, leaning against the wall waiting for the plane. I had not seen him or any other Maryknoll priest since the incident at the Biltmore. The look on his face communicated the betrayal he felt. I wished we could have talked, but I knew that nothing I could say would make sense or be acceptable to him.

I hugged my mother and said goodbye. It took guts for this woman, who had flown only once before coming to Guatemala, to look at that runway and that plane and not hesitate. She was tired and worn out but content to be leaving. She kissed me and said, "Dad and I will keep the secret." At the top of the stairs she turned and waved. Then I was alone. I thought I might get sick.

19
FREEDOM

Justice Brandeis said, "The greatest dangers to liberty lurk in insidious encroachment by men of zeal, well-meaning but without understanding." Those of us who view freedom as a personal responsibility must evaluate the lives of those who demand conformity of belief. Some believe I will go to hell without their guidance and leadership, but that is simply their controlling belief. Their belief gives them no right to limit or judge my freedom and creativity, which are fundamental gifts from our Creator. Asking me how I enjoyed my freedom in the Church might well have been like asking the same of an animal born in captivity, trained and controlled by a master who believes the animal to be better off captive. Since all I knew was the controlling structure, I mistook that for freedom. My life would have been quite different if I had been exposed to varied and responsible thoughts and beliefs and then permitted to choose and develop according to my own needs.

The Church, fearing and distrusting thinking individuals, attempts to intercept them at an early age, manipulating their power and potential through the highly controlled body of church and clergy. In Catholic circles people say, "give me a child until it is seven, and that child will never waver." The supposition is that by seven the child will be so indoctrinated in the thoughts, beliefs, and values of the authority figure that changing would be difficult or even impossible. My training and teaching lasted four times seven years. Without the unusual path that my life followed I would never have freed myself from that authority. I would have refused and rejected any differing belief or teaching, resisting any attempt to dissuade me, even becoming defensive of my inbred position and therefore strengthening my resolve. When I sought the freedom of Guatemalan peasants from the legitimate authorities that judged, controlled, and condemned them, I entered unwittingly on the path to the realization of my own precious gift of freedom.

Lincoln freed himself by following his conscience and opposing the standard beliefs of the day. The slaves, even when freed legally, still had to free themselves by choosing to go or not go. Clearly, holding a person physically against his or her will is immoral; but it is at least as immoral and damaging to control the minds and souls of people, denying them free spiritual choice.

Children who are denied a healthy example of responsible choice and are simply trained to submit are robbed of their freedom and frequently lose the will to be responsible and creative. An animal kept in captivity is not free when released from the cage. Children raised in ghettos, in slums, and on reservations are not free, and it takes them little time to realize that if they are to attain freedom, they must pursue it themselves. But in attempting to live freely in an environment without adequate options, they become victims of drugs, alcohol, and crime—their poor imitation of freedom.

A person denied the opportunity to think or to believe as he or she chooses, manipulated by fear of punishment, is not free. Human beings prevented from developing their potential are not free. God cannot be attained except by free choice, despite the belief that the sacraments work their effects of themselves. The overbearing parent who continuously controls the child steals that child's most precious gift. The jailor who guards the prisoner is also a prisoner. Being unable to speak to God in one's own way, from one's soul, is being unable to relate to the Creator with the most magnificent of divine gifts: creativity.

I came into the world with God's gift of freedom to think, to believe, to be; with the instinctive potential to know right from wrong, good from bad, the deliberative from the arbitrary, truth from deceit, helping from hurting, teaching from exploiting. The domination of the Church stole that gift from me. For me to take back my identity, myself, from a Church that talks of the importance of conscience but not of freedom of conscience was to enter onto a path returning to and uniting with the Author of freedom.

T HE NOW DREADED confrontation with Padre Luís was to take place on the outskirts of Guatemala City in an area unfamiliar to me. My original request had been for a simple conversation and discussion in order for us to get to know each other better, but that was before the betrayal. Luís had agreed and suggested a spot reached easily from his parish. I had been driving for hours, thinking about him much of the time. If he was indeed the betrayer, I wondered: when had he made his decision? and would he show up for our meeting?

Lost in my thoughts, I missed a turn. When I became aware of my error I stopped and looked at my map and saw that I was coming out of the mountains on the wrong road, a good distance from where we were supposed to meet. I was going to be late. Exasperated with myself, I began to push, passing vehicles on each straightaway until I arrived at a section with many sharp turns. I settled in behind a Landrover, waiting for an opportunity to dart ahead.

As I watched the vehicle, I recalled that Padre Luís had driven a similar vehicle to the meeting in Esquintla. I wondered. I could not see clearly through the dust on his rear window, but the driver was his size and wore his style hat. But if it was Luís, he would be on another road . . . unless he was not going to our meeting. I found the coincidence difficult to believe. But if it was he, we were going to talk. I had to stop him, and soon, before the city traffic separated us.

I leaned on the horn. The driver looked in his side-view mirror, not sure what to do. I kept my hand on the horn. The car moved over. I pulled alongside and was amazed. It was Padre Luís! He was not going to our meeting. I knew this was not luck or coincidence. I knew we had to meet; for what purpose, I did not know. His jaw dropped. My heart pounded. I signalled with my thumb for him to pull over, then parked behind him. He sat for a moment and then got out as I walked up. "*Como está?* Arturo," he said, extending his hand.

His greeting just didn't fit the circumstances. I took his hand and said, "Luís, were you going to our meeting?"

"*Dios mio*," he said, "I have been so busy, it totally slipped my mind."

I felt sad. I had hoped that the traitor would not be a priest. But I still had to push further. I had to know. I had to confront him. "Luís," I said, looking at him carefully, "we have been betrayed."

"So, I have heard," he said. "What a shame."

It was difficult for me to go on. He had given me my answer. I knew who had betrayed us. But I had to continue. "We are being expelled from Guatemala," I said.

"Oh, really? That is unfortunate," he said.

I felt like hitting him. "Are you being kicked out also?" I asked.

"No, I am not," he said frowning and looking to the ground.

"Luís," I said, and waited until he glanced back at me; then looking him in the eye and biting out the words, I said, "We know that it is you who betrayed us."

When I had said those words to the others, each was amazed. When I said them to Marian, she was shocked. Tears came to her eyes as she demanded to know why we thought such a thing. I quickly answered her, "Forgive me, Marian. I know it is not you, but we all have to be confronted."

When I said the same accusing words to Luís, he showed no surprise or disturbance, but shifted nervously and answered, "Do not be silly. I would never do such a thing." I kept looking in his eyes without retracting my statement. He made no attempt to convince me otherwise but changed hurriedly to, "You will have to excuse me, Arturo. I need to have some work done on my car. I have to be going." I did not need to hear any more.

He had been at the meeting in Esquintla and yet was not required to leave the country. He knew of the betrayal, yet never contacted us or tried to help. The traitor did not know Cathy and Marian, and Luís did not know them. And now he was willing to depart without asking that I retract my charge.

But what could I do with a traitor or an infiltrator? I was not a fighter or a killer. Although Luís was weak I could not blame him for weakness or fear or even disagreement. I could not punish him, could not demand his allegiance. I knew from the beginning that as I chose the only way left to the people, the way would never be clear or easy. In other circumstances I might do what Luís had done.

But I felt sad and angry. Luís had promised security and secrecy. He had promised not to betray our confidence in him. Nor had he ever offered any argument against our involvement. Now he had taken on the responsibility of a traitor and the consequences of a traitorous act. That he was on the side of the system did not lessen the immorality of his act. He would have to live with it. I turned, spat on the ground, walked to my truck, and left Padre Luís standing in the dust.

I was a boiling-pot of emotions. I yelled and pounded the steering wheel and began driving recklessly, and then caught myself and took control. I drove into the city and to the store of a man who had once offered to help me and asked if he would buy my truck. He said no, but he would take it and sell it for me and hold the money until I next saw him. He could be trusted.

I felt strange to be in the city with nothing to do, no shopping, no offices to visit or people to see. I felt sad not to be at the Maryknoll Fathers' house with my friends and companions, and so different not to have a vehicle. Except for the money in my pocket, I felt like a Guatemalan. I saw the prostitutes on the corners. One tried to attract my attention; I was not interested. I killed time nervously, waiting to meet Tom and Marji. I felt fear. In fact, I began to feel as I had at the roadblocks: I thought people were looking for me and at times at me.

When I met with Tom and Marji, they seemed to be in good form. They were handling their situation much more easily than I. I told them about Padre Luís. It made sense to them, but they were undisturbed. They said they had gotten Mom on her flight. We went to a movie, but I could not enjoy it. At one point an usher came down the aisle and shone his flashlight in our row. I grabbed Tom's arm and whispered, "They're looking for us." Tom was to tease me many times about that.

The next morning Father John met us at the airport and gave us our tickets. He said, "You'll be met in New York." We went through immigration without any problem. John stood with us in silence. A man kept taking our pictures. He walked around us, taking them from all angles. Other than that, we just stood nervously until boarding time. John shook hands with each of us and said, "Good luck." I was leaving Guatemala a few days before Christmas, six years and four months after arriving.

In the air, as Tom examined his ticket, he saw we had a stopover in Miami. He pointed this out and said, "Why not get off there and head back to Mexico?" So in Miami we simply did that, walked off the plane and away. Tom said he and Marji wanted to stay in Miami for a while. I left them to what I considered their honeymoon and found a flight to San Antonio, Texas. I felt jealous of them but also wanted to get on with the work.

I had only the pair of shoes I was wearing, and what I needed was all-weather durable boots. So between flights I bought a good pair and left the shoes with a street person. I also got a Clairol hair-dye kit; blond hair calls too much attention to an American living underground in Mexico. Having blue eyes stands out enough, but it was something I thought I could manage.

I caught a flight to Mexico City and took a room in a cheap hotel by the airport. I read the directions on the box and applied the dye to my hair. I had started growing a mustache the day we left Guatemala, and it was coming slowly. The dye applied, I was taken aback: I looked so strange with black hair, eyebrows, and mustache.

The next day I went into the city and found a room in a sleazy boarding house. Although I had money I didn't know when I would next have an income and had to watch my cash flow. I also wanted to acquaint myself with the life of the underprivileged in Mexico City. My first experience came that night with a knock at the door. One of my neighbors was making herself available for a hundred *pesos*. I was so lonely I could have cuddled with a bear, but I refused.

We had arranged our first meeting for the day after Christmas at the Museum of Natural History. I spent my days walking around the city, reading newspapers, and waiting. On Christmas Eve I was still walking. The bells started ringing, people were merry, carols were being sung. My loneliness was intense. I walked into a church to get out of the cool, damp air and to listen to Christmas music on the organ. The smell of burning wax took me back to San Antonio. I wondered how the people there were celebrating. I wondered what Cathy and Marían were doing, how Límbano was, whether he had given the animals away.

These Mexican people were poorer than those in San Antonio. Although their income was higher, they grew none of their own food and had to pay high rents. Unemployment was rampant. I watched the people. They said their beads and mumbled to the statues and their candles. Two lines of elderly folk were making their way slowly into the two sides of the confessional. Devout, simple souls. I felt sorry for them. An overweight priest came out for midnight Mass. No one paid much attention to him. When he got into his sermon on the union of the Father and the Son, I left. I felt better walking in the crisp, damp air.

I was at the museum when it opened. After an hour of walking from room to room, I recognized a man leaning over a glass case of bones. I approached. "Chico?" I said. He stood for a moment before he recognized me, let out a shout that called too much attention, and gave me an *abrazo*. "I saw you earlier," he said. "I looked and thought how similar that man's features were to Arturo's."

He had arrived two days before and had also spent a lonely Christmas. He had a room with a large bed, so I moved in; it was such a relief to have company. We did a lot of reading and walking, went to the appointed meeting places, and waited out the unusually long week.

We had two meetings in southern Mexico coming up. The first was on New Year's Day at the zoo in the city of Oaxaca, near the monkey cage. The second meeting was on the following day in the town of Comitán near the Guatemalan border. The latter was the first meeting with the *campesinos*, so that one was particularly important: to miss it might mean losing contact with them.

Chico and I discussed the visits. I suggested we do them together. He said he did not want to risk going near the border. I had hoped he would have more of a commitment to the *campesinos*, but I also realized he had spent his life in the city and did not know them. That made me sad, but I was anxious to go and did not mind making the trip alone. I said I would make the Oaxaca appointment en route.

I took the long walk to the bus depot on the thirty-first. Having trekked so much in the mountains, I was now afraid of losing that exercise to the city buses. After an hour's wait at the terminal, I was about to board when out of an arriving bus stepped José and Roberto. I ran to them yelling as they looked at me quizically. When they recognized me, we practically danced with delight.

They told how they had received Tom's message at their jungle camp telling them to leave Guatemala and meet at a particular site in Mexico City. They had broken camp immediately and set out on foot for distant Belize, where they had some trouble with a border guard until five *quetzales* helped them through. In Belize they got the first of a series of buses that took them into Mexico and to Mexico City. Except for the message they received from the scout who found them, they knew nothing of the betrayal and what had ensued and had even forgotten the date and the place for meeting us. If we had not run into each other, they would have had trouble finding us.

I quickly filled them in on everything, from what happened with John Breen, my mother, and Padre Luís, to meeting Chico in the museum. They were really enjoying the story, but I had to cut it short. I told them I was headed for Oaxaca and Comitán, and I gave them Chico's address. I was sorry to leave them so quickly but said goodbye and jumped aboard my waiting bus, thanked the patient driver, and headed south. It was a fine bus, smooth, comfortable, and air-conditioned, and once out of the city it passed through endless beautiful scenery. The joy of seeing my two companions along with the magnificent view of valleys, plains, and mountains helped me forget worries and concerns.

New Year's eve in Oaxaca was another story. Again, seeing the merry couples and the gala celebration was difficult. I found it terrible to be alone during such festivity and suffered from intense loneliness. It had to be the worst New Year's Eve ever.

On New Year's day at ten in the morning I was at the monkey cage. No one was in sight, so I walked on, viewing the animals. I returned at ten thirty and was taken by surprise to see a student named Patricio, tall, well-built, always concerned about his appearance, quick to laugh but with suffering eyes. He had been in each study group I attended, had shown much interest in the literature discussed, and had spent several weekends at the parish. Patricio's presence in the movement had an unusual significance. His father was an Army colonel and assistant to the president.

He was sitting on the grass. I approached and said his name, only to go through the now-accustomed moment of non-recognition, followed by joy in finding another friend. We sat for several hours talking about the latest events and sharing hopes. The conversation finished, I was giving him Chico's address when I noticed he wasn't listening. While looking away from me, he reached over and touched my arm and said in a deep low tone, "We are being observed." I followed his eyes and felt fear as I saw a lone man leaning against the monkey cage. He looked as if he might be a policeman and seemed to have no purpose, occasionally letting his eyes scan across us. We waited. His pattern did not change. Patricio reached slowly into his belt saying, "You take my gun and let's go. If he hassles us, shoot him. I'll run into the street and commandeer a car. You come right after me."

I felt frightened, more of Patricio than of our observer. His monologue sounded as if it had come from a dime novel. Although it was possible we were being watched, it seemed as if Patricio needed to fill some fantasy action. Maybe his dad had been heroic in battle, and the son needed to show himself that he too could be valiant. I didn't like my assigned role of shooting someone. I didn't even want his gun. What I saw was Patricio getting us into a lot of trouble. It also sounded as if he didn't want us around very long. I hadn't known he was carrying a gun, but his way of letting me know did not impress me. And his willingness to have someone else use it scared me. Dealing with a policeman was one thing, escaping from one another, but showing a gun to a law enforcement officer was trouble, and shooting at one could spell death or a lifetime in prison. It was certainly not the way to build a fledgling underground organization. I didn't reach for the gun he slid across to me. "No, Patricio," I said, "stay calm." I remembered his intensity in several of our group discussions as he described the movie, *The Battle of Algiers*. Now he was acting as if he had a role in the sequel. I didn't want to be in that movie. I knew I didn't want to be captured and thought I would struggle not to be, but I wasn't ready to shoot someone.

Patricio relaxed, and we lay on the grass, again pretending to enjoy ourselves. The man remained and continued to glance at us. Finally I suggested that we walk to the street and that if he moved toward us we would run. We got up and nonchalantly walked to the curb—and then blew our plan. I don't know who made the first move, but neither of us ever looked back. We both bolted into the traffic, dashed between cars, ran down several streets, then stopped, huffing and puffing, never to see our "policeman" again.

Walking to the depot together, we talked about the need to make appropriate decisions in stressful circumstances, the responsibility of carrying a gun, and our objective for being in Mexico. "This was good practice for us," Patricio said. I agreed.

On the bus to Comitán I had more time to think. Clearly, we would be sought by the authorities. We were dangerous to them because the world might listen as we revealed the truth about Guatemala and the United States. And we were dangerous because we could give added impetus to the revolutionary movement. We had to be careful. We could be our own worst enemies.

Comitán was a place the Guatemalan authorities would look for us. I had to be alert and cautious.

The bus arrived in the early evening. I found space in an out-of-the-way place—really a section of a shack with a bed, but my section had a padlock. Living there wasn't much different from being in a village, except that the people in the shack could not be trusted, but it offered more cover than a hotel.

I had been in Comitán several times before. The last time, Límbano, Cathy, Marian, and I had ridden horses to the Mexican border and hitch-hiked into town. That time we had stayed at the only hotel and had a wonderful visit, doing some shopping and relaxing. This time I walked around town, to familiarize myself and select a place for a meeting. The next day I skirted the plaza, observing from a distance. I was thrilled when I saw someone I knew. I kept walking and saw another and another. I was excited as I counted five *campesinos* from San Antonio, all members of our group. I waited until ten o'clock to see if any arrived from Tom's parish. A few minutes after ten I walked up the steps to the plaza and sat on the bench beside one of my former parishioners, a man named Toribio.

As I sat down, he moved over a bit to make room, and in his normal friendly way said, *"Buenos días."* I responded the same. A barefoot shoeshine boy approached and stood before me, looking at my new boots. I said, "No, *gracias*, but perhaps this other gentleman."

Toribio laughed and quickly responded, *"Gracias*, no." The boy left.

While looking toward the youth walking away, I said, "Toribio." He heard his name and turned to me. I remained looking straight ahead. He said nothing, and turned away. Again without looking at him, I said, "Toribio."

He turned and asked, "Pardon me, *señor*, are you talking to me?"

"Toribio," I said, "I want you to look at me and tell me my name."

He looked at me for a moment and then exclaimed, *"Ave María purísima.* Is that you?"

I laughed with him as I had done so many times in the past,

and then, moving closer said, "Talk in a low voice, and remember not to call me *Padre*."

He got the message and went on with the conversation almost in a whisper. "I did not know it was you, Arturo. *Dios mio*, what have you done to yourself?" We laughed again, and I recalled some of the pleasant moments shared with this man.

"Other companions are here," he said. "We are five in all."

"How wonderful," I said. "Now let's see what you think about the place I have chosen for us to meet." I described the street that led to a chapel on the edge of town, and then asked, "Can you bring the others there in a half-hour?" He said there would be no problem. I left and went ahead to make sure the area was clear. The chapel had stained-glass windows and was clean and bright, obviously well cared for. No one was around, inside or out.

I sat on the ground in the shade of the church wall and shortly felt waves of joy running through my body as I saw the first two approaching, then behind them Toribio, then the other two a bit further off. As they got close they were shaking their heads, not believing I could have changed so much. The two pairs were talking softly and trying to control hilarious laughter. Toribio was doing well, keeping a straight face. As the first pair approached the chapel, I stood and walked to them. I wanted to run. We all gave the *abrazo* and *saludos* and then sat together. I felt good being in their company, such caring people, sincere, honest and loving. I looked around the circle and said, "Each of you, tell me your news. How are you? Your families? The crops? The co-ops? San Antonio? I want to hear it all."

A man named Santos spoke up, sadness in his voice, "First, we must tell you that the *Madres* have left San Antonio."

"What?" I said. "What happened?"

"Well," said Santos, "They spent Christmas with us, but it was very sad because they told us they were being sent to other countries. We are all very heartbroken at what is happening to our parish. It was bad when you left, but at least we thought we would have the *Madres*." He held out two envelopes saying, "They asked me to deliver these letters to you."

I took them and asked, "Will you all please excuse me for

a few minutes while I read what the *Madres* have written?" The letters were dated December 26. They both explained that, after we had left Guatemala, they were advised of an immediate reassignment out of the country because of their close association with the movement. They requested permission, however, to stay in San Antonio through Christmas and were permitted that. They would be leaving the same day that they were writing the letters. Marían was called back to the Motherhouse in New York, and Cathy was assigned to a convent of Maryknoll Sisters at a parish in Mérida, Yucatán, Mexico. Both felt sad at leaving San Antonio and the country. Neither had any idea of what the future held but said they were willing to see what unfolded before making their next decision. Father Denny had been assigned as new pastor of the parish.

"I am also sad that the *Madres* have left San Antonio," I said putting aside the letters. "So many changes are happening so quickly, it is difficult for all of us."

Toribio said, "*Padre* Denny made a public announcement that if you returned to San Antonio, he would join with those who would kill you. Many people are angry at him." The man who had once been my pastor and then followed me at La Libertad had now followed me to San Antonio. I knew there would be no more marimbas during Mass.

Santos said, "When the people did not respond to *Padre* Denny, he got angry and announced that he would not stay in San Antonio. He left the *pueblo* and moved to the *convento* in Santa Ana."

"A few days after you left," Toribio said, "a Jeep with four Spanish-speaking Americans arrived in the *pueblo*. They all wore pistols and had telephones like radios, and maps. The people say they were agents of the C.I.A. They took photos and asked many questions about you and the *Madres* and the people who visited you, and they wrote many things in their books. They wanted to know the places you went to, who were your friends, what you did, and what you talked about. When they questioned Límbano, he told them he had nothing to say. *Padre* Denny told Límbano he had to talk to the men, but Límbano told the *padre* he had nothing to say. They hired Máximo, and he talked to them much and led them to places we used to visit.

Santos said, "Límbano does not like being with *Padre* Denny. He told us he is going to leave soon. He said to give you *abrazos* and *saludos.*"

Toribio said, "People have been threatened. No one has been hurt. But the people fear a storm. *Quién sabe?*"

Santos said, "We are willing to be with you. But it is difficult for us to support ourselves. Perhaps we can get work on the farms here in Mexico for a while, but we must go back and forth for our families. If it gets dangerous, we must think of hiding, or bringing our families here to Mexico."

I said, "If you can find work here and remain in contact with us, or come back across the border for meetings, we will come from Mexico City to be in contact, to see how you are, and to find out what is happening in the *pueblos* and villages. We want to advise and consult with you on plans being made and eventually be together with you. I, or someone in my place, will be back in two weeks, on Tuesday, January 16th. If some of you could come with information on how you are and what is happening, we will let you know of any advances we are making. We want to know if you are in danger and if we can help."

They all agreed to try to stay in contact. Each then told of his family, crops, animals, problems, sicknesses, and his view on what was happening and what the future might hold. After two and a half hours we gave *abrazos* and parted. I was sad to leave them but so happy to have seen them.

Riding the bus north, I read Marían's letter again and Cathy's several times. My life had been taking strange twists and turns, and now theirs were doing the same on a path they had not chosen. I wondered where it would lead. I sat back and closed my eyes, mulling over the strange and complex web that kept us together.

Cathy, I mused, is here in the same country with me. Little did our superiors know that by reassigning her they were bringing us together. I wondered how we would get to see each other, if she would come to the capital, if I would be able to visit her. But why not visit her? I wondered. And why not now? I am rushing back to Mexico City, for what? The group would simply be adjusting to the new surroundings while waiting for others to arrive. I had given Chico no estimate of the time of my return. I went to the front of the bus to talk to the driver. He told me to get off at Tuxtla Gutierrez and get a bus to Villahermosa, where I could get my bus to Mérida. As I moved back to my seat, I was amazed at the way things changed. All of a sudden I was going to see a woman who was important to me.

I arrived the next afternoon. Mérida was baking in the sun. My clothes stuck to me. I walked around town, bought a grape ice bar from a vendor with a little white cart on bicycle wheels, then got a room in a small, two-story building. I talked to the proprietor. We chatted about the weather, a good place to get refried beans, and finally about a church with English-speaking priests and nuns. I got directions. As the sun sank, I started out for the church, about a mile's walk on streets still radiating heat. I entered and sat in the next-to-last pew. A few people came and went, stopping long enough to talk to a statue or clank a coin in the box and light a vigil lamp.

The bells started tolling. I waited. Fifteen minutes later they tolled again. Mass would start soon. An American woman entered with the black veil of a Maryknoll Sister. I was in luck. Two old women and a girl entered. An old man. Another nun. Each time one of them entered I thought it would be Cathy. Then no one else entered. Mass started and ended. I was alone again. I left and walked the neighboring streets. Then I saw the convent and watched it for a while from a distance. I thought of telephoning. But what would I say? If Cathy answered, it would be easy. I phoned, but someone else answered. I hung up. It was getting dark, and I went to my room. It was too hot to sleep, so I got up, went out, and walked around the plaza. I had a plate of rice, chicken, and refried beans. Back to the room. Awake. Thinking. Finally cool enough, I fell asleep.

The next day I bought another newspaper and walked by the *convento*. No sign of her. I stood on a corner reading the paper, hoping I would see her coming or going. Then I remembered: a young woman from Mérida had stayed briefly with the

Sisters in San Antonio, helping with the work. I knew that Dori Hidalgo could be trusted. I looked up her name in the phone book. There were many Hidalgos, none with Dori. I called the first. Wrong number! I called the second and she answered. I told her who was calling, that I was visiting Mérida, and asked if she would come to the plaza.

Dori and I sat in an outdoor café as I explained my change of appearance, what had happened, and why I was in Mérida. She responded as Mexicans generally do, with sympathy and generosity, particularly in the face of adversity. She went to a public phone and called the convent, then handed me the keys to her car. We parked a block from the convent. Dori went to the door and brought Cathy to the car. I watched in the rear-view mirror as they walked down the sidewalk. Cathy looked wonderful. When she was close and saw someone in the car, I heard her ask, "Who is your friend?" I looked out the window and said, "Hi, Cathy." She was speechless. "Get in," I said laughing. Dori slipped in back, and Cathy got up front. I leaned towards her and hugged her, almost speechless myself. "Where is your blond hair?" she asked, I turned on the engine and we started off, Cathy and I both talking at once. We drove around talking, but our conversation was suddenly cut short when Cathy said, "I'm sorry to ruin the party, but I said I wouldn't be gone long. I have to get back."

It came as a jolt. I had forgotten that she was still bound by the community. "Will you have any time tomorrow?"

"I'm still so new here that I'm afraid to push it. But wait," she said thinking, "I can take my day off tomorrow." I was delighted. "How about if we meet in the Cathedral around ten o'clock?" she asked. We parted with a hug. Dori and I drove to the plaza. I thanked her and hugged her goodbye, and she agreed not to tell anyone of my visit. I walked until the evening cooled a bit, then went to my room to read and write.

I was in the Cathedral as the nine o'clock Mass ended. Cathy arrived a few minutes after ten. She looked fresh and shining as she approached. I felt a shiver of joy. She smiled as she sat down beside me, and in the obscurity of a rear pew we talked quietly. She filled me in on everything from her reassignment to her arrival in Mérida. Marian had written her saying she would be in the States for a while.

I was delighted to hear that two other Maryknollers, men whom I respected highly, had also been expelled. As Cathy explained it, Father Breen had asked all priests and brothers to sign a promise that they would in no way assist us if we returned to Guatemala. Father Blase Bonpane and Brother John Hogan had refused to make the promise and were sent back to the United States. Blase was immediately reassigned to Maryknoll's mission in Hawaii. After being there for a few days, he decided he could not abandon his commitment to Guatemala. Refusing to be silenced, he returned to Washington, D.C., where he set up residence and was doing a great job making known the plight of the people of Guatemala and the effects of United States involvement.

Cathy wanted to know what was happening with the group.

"We're running on a lot of hope," I said. "Except for José, we are totally lacking in experience. If we can keep up the motivation and make the right steps and connections, we might be back in Guatemala in six months. If our attempts to organize take longer than that, we'll probably never get back." She was leaning against me. "But the *campesinos* are key," I said. "And we cannot invite them to participate unless we are prepared to move out. Continued communications with them are going to be difficult. Also, if the Army moves against them, there is no telling what will happen. It's really scary for me. All we can do is keep going, keep planning, make contacts, train, and discipline ourselves."

"Do you know if the authorities are looking for you?" she asked.

"I don't know," I answered. "But planning to subvert another government from Mexican territory is, of course, against Mexican law. So we have got to stay out of sight and keep our plans secret. If the Guatemalan Army finds out what we're doing, they could send out a team after us. And of course the C.I.A. has its people all through Mexico. We will be on the C.I.A.'s list. If they look for me, Mérida will be one of the places." I leaned close. She came toward me. I touched her hand.

She closed her fingers on mine. The door of the confessional squeaked open. We drew back quickly. Out of the corner of my eye I saw the black cassock pass. I could feel his frown.

"Let's go," she said, tilting her head towards the cassock walking down the center aisle. She took my hand and was almost skipping. "I have brought my chariot," she said, pushing through the swinging doors and pointing to a Volkswagen Bug at the corner. She gave me the keys, saying, "You drive. I want to look at you."

"Where to?" I asked pulling away from the curb.

"On a day like this," she said, "where else would we go, but the beach?" So we drove and laughed and were soon at the shore.

"We are going to let go of our troubles for a while," she said. "And for that purpose, this is what I brought." She lifted a multi-colored string hammock from the back seat. I laughed and felt like a kid. She took it and a straw bag, stepped from the car and stood with the sea in the background. As if she were a painting, I leaned on the roof of the car, looking at her. "What do you think?" she asked.

"I think you're gorgeous," I said.

"No, I mean the beach," she said laughing, the wind blowing her hair. There was no one else on the long white strip of sand. We shared the beach with a few gulls, dried seaweed, some driftwood, and a few palm trees.

"I feel as if I've gone to heaven," I said.

"Great," she said, "but this hammock is not for heaven. This is a matrimonial hammock," she laughed.

"Exactly what we need," I said, walking toward her.

"No, wait!" she screamed. "That simply means it holds two people. It does not mean that they act married." She pointed her index finger at me and laughed, saying, "No ideas, Arturo."

"Far be it from me to act as if I'm married," I said stepping beside her. "However, I might act as if I'm in love."

She kissed me on the cheek, and said, "No!" She meant it. I think I looked disappointed, but I knew I had to respect her. I was also afraid of compromising my commitment to the revolution. She turned away and said, "But let's get a move on." I

untied my boots and dropped them and my socks in the back
seat. Taking the bag of provisions, I put my other arm around
her slim waist, and we strolled down the sand. At a small grove
of palm trees we stopped and tied up the hammock. I rolled up
my pants and took off my shirt. We sat cross-legged in the sand
looking at each other. We talked. We held hands. She told me
about convent life. I touched her face. She stroked my hair,
asking when I would wash out the black color. The conversation
became serious. We talked about the possibility of death. We
talked about finishing our task and still having a life. I asked,
"If we both come out of this alive, will you live with me?" She
leaned forward and kissed me lightly. I put my hand behind her
neck and felt the silky hair.

"Want to try the hammock?" she said.

I took her hands and pulled her up. She started running to
the hammock. I ran after her and tackled her gently, and she
fell in the sand laughing and screaming. I wiped the sand from
her lips. She was breathing deeply. I wanted to kiss her and
knew she wanted to be kissed. I lowered my lips. I thought of
the times I had been unwilling to let her know my feelings.

"The hammock," she yelled, pushing me away and jumping
up. "There is a skill involved in two people getting into a hammock," she said, lifting one edge and pretending she was serious.
"Let me show you." We tried it and ended up on the ground
wrestling. The third time we succeeded, but I had laughed so
hard my throat felt sore. We lay in the hammock together, trying
to get comfortable, at times facing each other, at times side by
side. We kissed, and I felt excited. She smiled and said, "But
no more than that." We lay quietly together for some time.
"Hungry?" she asked.

I was relieved to say, "I'm starved." I climbed from the
hammock and held it while she rolled out. We hugged. She
hesitated, looked me in the eye, and then pulled back. I thought
we might never have an intimate relationship. "Do we Catholics
ever get over sexual hang-ups?" I asked.

"That's a good question," she said moving toward the straw
bag. "If we looked to our parents, I would say not," she laughed.

"And sexual preparedness certainly isn't part of the convent curriculum; and priests have so many hangups, I doubt that many can overcome their sexual ones."

"With sufficient practice, I bet some can," I laughed defensively.

"No," she said grinning, her hands on her hips. "Priests will always expect their women to be nuns, playing the subservient role, as they, the all-knowing ones, try to overcome their hangups."

I thought of the woman a few years earlier who would never have thought of saying anything like that. "Wow," I said. "That hurts. You've given that some thought." She nodded her head and smiled. I hesitated, then added, "I suppose if I were truthful, I might agree with you."

She continued to nod her head as she threw me the small green tablecloth. I recognized it as a Guatemalan weave. We sat on the beach and ate sandwiches and some crispy cut vegetables, drank soda, and talked. When a cool wind blew up, we climbed back into the hammock and hugged against the breeze until it got too chilly. She said she had to be getting back anyway. So we packed up and drove to town and parked on a side street of the cathedral. "Will you be coming back soon?" she asked.

"I have been asking myself that same question," I said. "I would love to, but we are short of money. I cannot continue to spend the amount it takes to come here and stay over. This may be my last visit for a while."

"I may be able to come to the capital some time," she said.

"I don't know how we would make contact," I said. "If the opportunity arises, I'll write you. It won't be possible for you to write me. And if we do get some income, I'll surprise you with a visit." We kissed goodbye. I had tears in my eyes as I watched her drive away. She waved out the window as she turned the corner.

I went to the depot and bought my ticket. A thousand miles to Mexico City. I must be in love, I thought. I suppressed my frustration and enjoyed the long ride to Veracruz. With almost an hour to wait for my connection, I bought a newspaper and found an empty bench in the park. I had read most of the major news when I suddenly sat up and stared. Not believing what I saw, I had to look several times. Pictures of Tom and me. Our ordination pictures. We looked like young, innocent kids, with close-cropped hair and big smiles. I had eyeglasses on, something I didn't need after the seminary. The report was issued from the Motherhouse in Ossining, New York: "Two Maryknoll priests, brothers Arthur and Thomas Melville, expelled from Guatemala along with a Maryknoll nun, Sister Marjory Bradford, for revolutionary activity, suspended as priests for disobedience, now believed to be in Mexico."

Suspended as priests. I expected to feel sad. I didn't. I read the words several times, then sat looking at the pictures. The words became almost physical as their meaning seemed to sink in deeper and deeper. Then something strange happened. It was as if a cool breeze began to blow over me, refreshing and nurturing. Not knowing what was going on, I put the newspaper in my lap and closed my eyes, and the wonderful experience intensified. I put my head back. A smile came across my face. My heart felt light and open. I knew what it was, but at first I didn't believe it.

I was free. I had arrived. The process of all those years had been one of personal liberation. I felt exhilarated. Everything made sense. In looking for the freedom of the Guatemalan people, I had liberated myself.

I smiled even more. I never felt a smile so meaningful or true. I never felt more healthy or happy. I had found what I had been searching for since childhood. I had found myself. Tears came to my eyes.

It was as if my life then made sense. It had been necessary for me to become completely involved in the Church and religion in order to be free of church and religion. I had to be willing to accept the Church's beliefs and teachings, then go beyond them to think for myself. Only by this route could I have learned to trust God and recognize my personal beliefs while not forcing them into someone else's mold. All I had been through was necessary in order to find myself and in order to have a relationship with God. I sat on the bench knowing that if I had remained on the periphery of life for the sake of religion, I would never have found God or myself. If suspension had not triggered the realization, something else would have done it. But as it was, Maryknoll's statement to the press moved me to my new awareness.

I knew my life would never be the same. Come what may in our revolutionary movement, my personal revolution had succeeded. The old structures had fallen. The old values held no weight. The old laws, judgements, condemnations, rewards and punishments did not matter. The hierarchy no longer held power over me. I was free.

20
COMPLETION

Having learned to suppress my feelings from an early age and having done so all my life, I generally tried to deny any emotional experience and to cover myself with my casually-unconcerned mask. Only belatedly did I learn how deeply I was feeling during those days in Mexico and how damaging was my emotional denial.

I felt anger at many people, but especially at the archbishop of Guatemala, who condemned my brother and me in order to draw attention from the issues we were confronting and he was avoiding. His action led to my anger at the Vatican for refusing to select as bishops anyone sympathetic to the problems of the poor. I was disturbed that the Church failed to trust bishops who did involve themselves at some level with the oppressed and considered them renegades. It hurt me deeply that a number of priests in Latin America, living amidst poverty and injustice, risking their lives to teach a theology of liberation and preach a gospel of social justice, received no support from the Church but instead were watched and controlled.

I was afraid of being assassinated by a highly effective, officially mandated terrorist group, the Mano Blanca, or White Hand, which had imposed a death sentence on Tom, Marji, and me. This organization of off-duty police officers and henchmen of the rich stood above the law and considered as an enemy anyone who actively took the side of the poor. Its members were at liberty to seize, torture, and assassinate even those suspected of opposing the oligarchy while remaining immune from investigation and prosecution. I had to live with the fear of knowing that I would be killed on sight. I was also afraid of my own tendency to violence, of deliberately doing harm to other human beings.

I was lonely. I missed Cathy and Marían. I had to put Cathy out of my mind and deny that I wanted to be with her. It was especially difficult when I saw Tom and Marji together, enjoying each other's support.

I had yet to learn to work with and complete these and many other suppressed and neglected feelings, responsibly experiencing them to their depths and expressing them appropriately in a process of healing and of further regaining my identity, a process that would lead me to assist others in healing their wounds and sicknesses caused and maintained by the suppression of emotions.

C HICO HAD MOVED out of the rooming house. The landlady handed me a note that read, "Stay here. We will pick you up." She showed me to the same room as before, saying, "The young man of the note came by yesterday and again today to see if you had arrived." I knew that would be José. I spent the day alone, probably for the first time in my life simply enjoying being myself, aware that I was still the same person but experiencing myself and everything else differently.

The next morning José stood at the door. "Welcome home," he said, pleased to say a few words in English. I picked up my satchel and we headed out, walking slowly, filling each other in on what had transpired since our conversation at the depot. I told about the meeting with the *campesinos* and their sad situation and my wonderful visit to Cathy. I told him I was falling in love with Cathy. He smiled his beautiful smile as he patted me on the back, always ready to enjoy anything that pleased me. José was always supportive.

He listened carefully, asking questions, and then filled me in. He had the good fortune of making contact with the Mexican underground, whose members were willing to act as a conduit of information for us. He said that Tom and Marji had arrived and that besides the students I had already seen, six more had come, five men and one woman. They were all known to me from the study group and their visits to San Antonio. "One other thing," he said. "About Padre Luís. . . ." He hesitated. I looked at him. He had his head down. "I was too eager and made a big mistake. I'm sorry."

It was the first time I ever heard him speak humbly. I nodded and said, "After the betrayal I never really had time to be angry at you. I too am sorry about what happened. I wish it could have been different, but I do hope that we can make good come of it."

We continued walking and talking, and when we seemed to have caught each other up on the news, I asked, "Did you see yesterday's paper?"

"*Sí!*" he shouted, raising his hands with enthusiasm, as if he had meant to bring up the subject. "You people are grabbing the news. You are famous renegades now."

We both laughed. I was closer to José than anyone else in the group. I enjoyed being with him, trusted him, and was eager to share with him what had happened when I read the article. "I have something unusual to tell you about that article," I said, putting my hand on his arm. "Let's sit down." He nodded, and in silence we went to a cement bench on the edge of a small park. He pulled a few leaves from a tree and brushed off the bird droppings.

I gathered my thoughts and began. "Well, José, this is strange for me to say, but as a result of reading that article in the newspaper, I am feeling like a different person." He looked at me carefully as he nodded his head. "Inside I am a different person," I said, extending my hands, as if the gesture summed it all up. "I feel free for the first time in my life. I never knew I could feel this way until yesterday, when I read in the paper that I was suspended."

He turned away for a moment. Then with a look of confusion, turned back and said, "*Perdóname*, Arturo, but this suspended thing, is that like excommunication, or do they really want to hang you?" We both laughed.

"It is a crazy word," I said, "but being suspended means that I am no longer permitted to perform priestly functions."

"*Dios mio*, you cannot hear my confessions any more," he said, putting his hands to his head.

I nodded, laughing, and went on, "Well, as I read of my suspension, I felt a conviction that I had to let go of all connection with the Church, that my future growth was dependent on that. So I did, immediately and clearly." He was smiling. "It was a very simple conclusion, a decision made in an instant, but one that I know now I had been preparing to make for many years. The impact was immediate, powerful, and enduring. I still feel it." He was listening carefully.

"I never suspected how much weight I had been carrying until the moment the burden lifted. I didn't know to what depth the Church had taken over my life. It was done so gradually, from such an early age, in a manner so subtle, so absolute and complete, that a big part of me had not been alive and I didn't know it." He was nodding agreement. I went on, "Although I always felt as if I were missing a part of life and had even entered the priesthood looking for that something, I never realized that I had given over, or even lost, that part of me to the Church." I felt the same chill of the day before as I added, "And then, in the moment that I decided to let go of the Church, a cool breeze blew over me, and everything changed." Still amazed at what had happened, I extended my arms and said, "Look at me, José, I am alive."

He clapped his hands until he stopped laughing, then put a hand on my arm and with his big smile said, "I understand. I know what you are saying. And I am very happy for you."

But I wondered if he could hear any more than my words. I knew there would be very few people to whom I could explain myself, and even then I didn't know to what extent I was capable of doing it. I wanted to go further. "Wait, José," I said. "I am not sure you understand. You, who have never given your soul to a religious structure, have always been free of the chains and the weight and so do not know what I, who am feeling freedom for only one day, am possibly experiencing. Somehow I have to be able to explain my experience more fully."

He looked at me, probably a little hurt, and said, "Arturo, I have never experienced blindness; but when the blind person sees for the first time and wants to communicate the joy and excitement of vision, I, who have always had sight, can share in the experience and grasp with joy what is being said."

I nodded, realizing that it was I who had not understood him. He went on, "I have never seen you so happy. I know what you are talking about. And even more, without your realizing it, I know that this is the quality of happiness that you wanted to bring to the people of San Antonio."

We were walking again. We had a strong connection. Neither spoke. Finally I broke the silence, saying, "*Bien*, now that I have that off my chest, at least for the moment, let us get on with business. What is next?"

"Where you are going to live," he said. "Tom and Marji have decided to live alone and are writing a book. The rest of us are together in a one-bedroom apartment. We are cramped but would be glad to have you with us." So I moved in with eight young people. It was like a college dorm, with arguing, crying, joking, and teasing. They had all seen the news article of the day before and talked about it excitedly.

Roberto was eager to show a clipping from the front page of *El Imparcial*, a Guatemalan paper. He took it out of a notebook and held it before me, running his finger down the lines as I read aloud. It told of our expulsion and of an interview that the reporter had with His Excellency, the Archbishop of Guatemala, Mario Casariego, in which the archbishop called Tom and me communists and the anti-Christ.

"Now that is dealing with some pretty powerful shit," Roberto said. The others laughed. I smiled, but I felt deeply angered that the head of the Church in Guatemala could be so ignorant, and I felt hurt that I had left the country I loved on such an ignominious note.

"The words of the archbishop," said Teresa, a student of psychology, "indicate that we are doing well. Those who might be acknowledged by the archbishop or accepted in association with him have clearly betrayed our people. These charges he makes translate into the highest of compliments." Everyone listened when she spoke and nodded support of her statement.

"Also, look here, *padrecito*," Pepe said. Pepe, whose father was a lawyer and adviser to the president, had never even called me *padre* before but facetiously started calling me *padrecito* from the time of my announced suspension. He held out another sheet of paper, a throwaway or flyer.

I looked at it and was aghast. With the logo of the cross-hairs of a gunsight, it was a bulletin from the *Mano Blanca* or White Hand, a Guatemalan right-wing terrorist group. There again were the same two ordination pictures of Tom and me and a picture of Marji in her habit. "Look," Pepe said pointing down the page, "you are enemies of the Republic and are to be killed on sight."

Immediately, my body shivered and my stomach tightened. I tried to hide my fear as the talk continued, but my gut stayed tight. Everyone knew that the people of the *Mano Blanca* were dead serious in their statements and carried official sanction. "This kind of notoriety I do not need," I said.

"Although this is frightening," Teresa said, "it is again clear that we are acting appropriately. To be condemned by the *Mano* means being effective among the poor."

I liked all the students, but my being ten to fifteen years older and accustomed to living alone made it at times difficult for me. They often discussed things of little or no interest to me, and they argued and disagreed on issues unimportant to me. They were, however, respectful of each other and of me. There was never any violence or picking on one another. Some did act jealous, usually regarding the one woman in the group. At times I wondered about their motivation, but they were willing to risk a lot and to live in difficult conditions. They had no income, ate poorly, and got no acknowledgement. They were committed. They knew they could end up like many students who had preceded them in the movement, "disappeared" into the Pacific or in ditches hacked to pieces and riddled with bullets.

The fifteenth of January found me on the bus to Comitán. I had looked forward to this solitary time. I read, wrote, meditated, and slept. At times I talked to passengers and never tired of the seven hundred miles of panoramic scenery. Arriving in Comitán late that night, I walked around the back streets until I found a room. I slept well on a crude bed and at an early hour entered the hustle and bustle of the street.

I checked out several possible meeting places, including the chapel, and decided to use that again. The *campesinos* started showing up at nine—at least, that was when I saw two of them. By ten I had seen five, all looking inconspicuous, each one separated from the rest. Three of them had been present at the last visit. Apparently, none had seen me. At ten o'clock I walked up the stairs to the plaza and approached Toribio on a bench. He pushed back his dirty white plastic cowboy hat when he saw me coming but sat still, smiling only slightly, as if we did this each day. Santos was sitting on a bench nearby. He nodded slightly. I felt my heart pick up beats of excitement. I sat beside Toribio. We did not shake hands. "We are five again," he said as if talking to himself.

"*Bien*," I said, without looking at him. "How do you feel about meeting at the same place?"

"I see no problem with the chapel," he said.

A barefoot, middle-aged woman with an infant on her back approached and asked for *unos centavos* to feed her baby. I put a quarter *peso* in her hand. She folded her hands in front of her and bowed. I stood and said, "How is ten-thirty?" He nodded.

I felt my armpits perspiring as I awaited them in the shade. They arrived as before in two pairs and a single, all of them slightly over five feet tall and wearing shirts that buttoned down the front, various colors of jeans, different styles of sandals, and cowboy hats. They looked as if they could not contain their big smiles. Giving *abrazos*, we were like children. One would think we hadn't seen each other in years. As they shared *saludos* from various intimates, I felt sad that I had left so many wonderful friends.

Sitting together under a tree, I looked around at them and said, "I could not be happier than I am at seeing all of you." I was smiling. But they now looked serious. "I want to thank each of you for coming here and for being in my life." They nodded their heads. There was so much I wanted to say to them. I tried to sum it up. "You have taught me to appreciate life, and I hope only that I can make an equal contribution to you." They looked at me curiously. "I know it is difficult, and even dangerous, for you to come here," I said. "I wish we could somehow facilitate your travel. Right now we cannot." Several shrugged their shoulders as if that did not matter. "But now I want to hear about you, how you are, what is happening in your lives, and your thoughts on the struggle."

They seemed to smile for a moment, and then as if by agreement the smiles disappeared. There was silence. They all looked to Evaristo, a popular man in the co-op, forty-one years old, a good husband, a hard-working father of three boys, frequently a spokesperson. And still there was silence. Clearly something was wrong. "Well, Evaristo," I said. He lowered his eyes and said nothing. One by one, as I looked at them, they cast their eyes to the ground. Then Evaristo seemed to find whatever courage was needed, raised his eyes and looked at me.

"Límbano is dead," he said.

Silence. No one spoke. I could not speak. I could not believe it. I could hear my heart pounding. I could feel pressure on my temples. Tears came to my eyes. "How?" I managed to ask.

Evaristo looked to his companions. Santos motioned with his hand for Evaristo to proceed. "He started to get sick not long after you left," Evaristo said. "At first no one thought it was serious. Then he got real weak. So they took him to the hospital in Jacaltenango. He died there. The *Madre Doctora* said he had dysentery. A large procession of people went to the hospital to bring his body back. They gave him a big funeral."

My tears flowed even as I tried to hold them back. Some of the others were sobbing. Límbano's words of our last night together came through clearly, "My job here is done." I saw him in my mind. He looked strong and healthy. He was smiling. "No more rivers," he said. I could not speak for a few minutes. When I did, I said, "*Gracias*, Límbano." The men looked at me. Again there was silence. After a moment, I spoke. "I am sad that I was not there for him when he was sick, when he was dying, at his death, for his funeral and burial. What would I have said? What do I want to say now?"

I paused, wiped away my tears with the back of my hand, and after another moment of silence, said, "No one I have ever known has lived closer to the life of Jesus than Límbano." They nodded their heads in agreement. "He knew what he was doing," I said. "He was truthful. He was guided, and he was a good guide. I am privileged to have spent so much time close to him. I will not forget the things he said and all that we did together. His work is done."

"No more rivers," I said out loud, and looked around at those looking at me. I still had tears in my eyes but also felt a sense of happiness. I thought it was the joy of knowing that Límbano had completed his task. I also felt that my new-found sense of myself was connected with him. "*Bien*," I said to the group. "You have been kind to be with me in my sadness. I will save the rest of my tears for later. Now I want to hear about you."

They talked of the military vehicles in the area, the helicopters flying overhead and landing in villages, and the soldiers mistreating people indiscriminately. They talked of the fear people felt and the sense of impending trouble. "There are many threats," Toribio said, "and we are unprepared if they should be carried out. We have no way of defending ourselves. There is much talk of communism, and everyone knows that such talk always precedes official violence. But we are willing to go on."

"I only wish we could do something for you now," I said. "I am frustrated that we cannot. We are having trouble organizing ourselves. We are amateurs at making revolution. It would have made an incredible difference if we had been able to make it into the wilderness undetected, to establish our base and form our front by force of circumstance. For some reason that I cannot figure out, we must do it this way. I do not know when I will be able to tell you that we are prepared to merge with those of you who are ready. We have no income. We cannot offer you financial help now. But we must find financial support and arms and soon move into training."

Toribio said, "We agree that only by fighting for our rights will we ever have them. When you are ready, we will be also."

I asked about their personal lives. The talk sounded very familiar. They told about their families, their sicknesses, their crops, their growing fear of working with the co-ops. There were no more meetings. The fear was that if they continued to organize themselves, the shooting would begin. We agreed to meet in two weeks, on Tuesday, January thirtieth.

I stood in the shade of the chapel and watched as they left. I had seen that walk so often. They were not talking. Heads down, single file, slowly as if without a goal. I wondered if I should feel guilty that it was they who had permitted me to liberate myself.

The ride back to Mexico City was mechanical, lacking the excitement of searching for Cathy or of seeing new country. I did not talk with passengers. I felt sad for the *campesinos*. I wondered if we could ever help them. I was sad for Límbano. I used a discarded bus schedule to write my thoughts. As I wrote about Límbano, I mourned him. I thought I was hiding my face, but an elderly lady tried to comfort me. A middle-aged man asked if he could help. I thanked them and said I was fine. I wished I were alone. Writing helped me to think and to impress on my memory details that otherwise may have been lost. About Límbano, I wrote:

> I think he is still nearby. I think he is still guiding
> me. I feel what seems like his presence. It comes as a
> refreshing breeze. Last night on the bus I dreamed about
> him. He was alive. Even now, I think I hear him. It
> makes sense that people should be guided or protected
> by a departed soul. I think if I had gone first, I would
> have wanted to continue to participate in Límbano's life.
> I would certainly use whatever energy or intelligence I
> had to assist and protect him.

I am willing to accept any help Límbano wants to give me. I am willing to receive any communication he might have for me. We have a connection. As long as I am willing to open my heart and my mind, he will be with me. Maybe such a relationship has something to do with the belief in Guardian Angels. Anita had told me to begin understanding her people by understanding death.

21

AWAKENING

I found the day-to-day existence of clandestine life somewhat monastic, a way of hiding from the world and taking the opportunity for reflection. As I considered the tradition from which my former way of life had sprung, I saw that those contributing to my unconventional awakening continued to be the most unlikely: first peasants, then women, and now students were my peers and educators. It seemed that I was unlearning what I had been taught by established male educators and learning from those long considered unprepared to teach.

My sequestered environment became a regular source of discussion and inspiration. Even if I hadn't wanted introspection, the continuing individual conversations with the students would have challenged and provoked me. With their perpetual vitality, philosophical curiosity, variety of opinions, and zest for the present moment, they stimulated me to further examine the values and beliefs I had accepted and defended as truth and to take further responsibility for their impact on me.

I found it fascinating in the midst of our anxiety and tension to have the time and motivation to deliberate on life in the Church and to lay bare the effects of giving over mind, soul, emotions, and sexuality to an institution. I perceived ever more clearly how officially-imposed dogma had distanced me from a relationship with God and myself; how the Church, despite pro-

testations to the contrary, had replaced God in my life; and how supposedly-divine injunctions had distanced me from intimacy, love, sexuality, and self-knowledge. Working through long-held and powerfully-implanted teachings led me to the further awareness that if I continued I could open a vast and exciting future of spiritual exploration. I became excited about the process and the possibilities and as a result never wanted so much to live. While I was in the Church, dying was of primary importance; living served so that I could die and get to the real life. Martyrdom made sense: get this life over in the process of defending beliefs that hold more import than the human beings defending them. That view devalued my life.

Now I was approaching life as something important in itself, exciting and meaningful in simply being lived. I now wanted to live and live fully. I believed in and was willing to die for the revolution; but as I freed myself from religious confinement, the life-and-death question took on new meaning. I wanted truly to be alive in the revolution and in the continuous discovery of what life held.

Starting with the lessons of my first earth teachers, the peasants of Guatemala, my life today continues to open up to such unexpected realizations as these: the Christ energy is available to me at any time and comes in the most unexpected of forms; I can be guided if I am willing to listen with my heart; emotions are life, springing from the soul; I am responsible for all I experience; the probable attainment of an objective is not the deciding factor in finding purpose; the intent to grow, the commitment to truth, and the process of growth itself give the desired and allusive meaning or purpose to life. I have also learned that profound joys are always accessible in their essential simplicity, such joys as knowing a woman as a human being, learning from an animal, listening to a plant.

Awakening to the fact that I had spent my years deeply imbedded in a structure and system whose intent was to overtly convert and covertly control in the name of Christ, I felt gratified to conclude and acknowledge that no system or structure can represent God, Who is honored only by truth, free will, and responsible choice; that no church can bring us God, Whom we already have; that no religion can offer salvation, for we were never lost; and that the Roman Catholic Church's unfortunate collaboration with the Guatemalan State will never end unless the people take their freedom. Probably my saddest and most surprising recognition was that my own country and government, despite all appearances to the contrary, has never intended to assist the poor of Guatemala or of any other nation of Latin America.

I WAS BACK IN Mexico City only a few days when the underground tipped off José that the police were closing in on us. With the Olympics a few months off, the Mexican government, very concerned about its image, was stepping up efforts to deal with undesirables. Although we were prepared to get away at a moment's notice, it still came as a surprise when at nine-thirty P.M. José came running into the apartment ordering us to move out. His contact had given him the addresses of a number of safe houses. We grabbed our few belongings and moved fast. He gave me a key and a slip of paper with an address on it. "Get going. I will come by for you as soon as I can," he said.

Satchel in hand, I ran into the street and grabbed the first taxi, then took a bus and then walked. Arriving at the address at 11:30 P.M., I knocked at the door. No answer. I knocked louder. I waited. I walked around the block. I knocked again. No answer. A little after midnight, I tried the key. It worked. I stepped in and closed the door. I hesitantly said, *"Buenas noches."* No sound. *"Hola,* is there anybody home?" No answer. I found a switch on the wall. It turned on a dim light. I was standing in a narrow hallway where several coats hung on hooks. I walked down the hallway to the living room, turned on a light, and put down my satchel. I checked the bedroom and found a mattress on the floor, bedcovers in a heap. The bathroom had an old tub with a hand-held shower. The toilet articles were those of a man. I walked freely through the apartment and saw only a stuffed chair and a couch. I sat in the chair and waited but woke up at two A.M. feeling chilly and with a sore neck. Buttoning my jacket, I lay on the couch, awakening at seven when I heard nothing but traffic outside, and again checked the apartment but was still alone. At a corner store I bought fruit, bread, cheese, and jam, avoiding conversation. I found tea bags in the cupboard and made breakfast. Not wanting to leave the apartment unnecessarily, I spent the day reading a book on Mexican history.

That night I slept soundly. I woke up in the early hours feeling aroused. I unzipped my pants to relieve the pressure, then for the first time in my life began massaging myself. It felt pleasurable. Chills ran through my body. The feeling grew and intensified and then opened up into a new world. I was shocked: For the first time in my thirty-five years, I had masturbated.

It took some moments to recover. I got up and cleaned myself, and then went back to the couch to consider the experience. I felt no guilt but rather wonder at how I had come so far in life without realizing the gratification of this act. How had it been kept from me? How could I have remained so ignorant? I needed little thought to find the answer: I had given my sexuality over to religion. The injunctions against sex that were taught to me as a child had been so powerful that I had never allowed myself to give serious consideration to masturbation. But I now knew that I had taken another step in discovering and freeing more of myself.

In the afternoon of the second day, my host returned while I sat in the chair reading a book, and I jumped when I heard the door open. I sat tensely as footsteps came down the hall, all kinds of fearful thoughts running through my mind. A man came into the living room, smiled, put out his hand, and said his name was Agustín. I introduced myself as Bruno, my underground name. He said he knew I was an American involved with the movement in Guatemala. He knew nothing more, asked nothing more, and I told him nothing more. He said to make myself at home and that I could stay as long as I wanted. I saw very little of him.

Three days later José came by. I had been lonely and anxious for the others, so I was delighted to see him. "All is well," he said. "We are getting the dorm back together." I left a note of thanks to Agustín. We went to our new two-bedroom apartment, but we were to live chaotically, moving often.

My desire to obtain information about the *campesinos* was continuous. I looked forward to the next scheduled meeting. On the twenty-ninth I arrived in Comitán. Although a day early, I hoped to meet one of them. On the thirtieth I began observing the plaza from a distance at eight in the morning but saw no one. At ten, the appointed time, I walked up the cement steps to the plaza. I sat on a bench but, feeling nervous, went back to the streets at ten-thirty. I viewed the plaza every half hour until siesta and once an hour for the afternoon. Nobody came. I spent the evening in my little room and tried to write but couldn't. I had no idea what had happened to them. I slept sporadically.

On the thirty- first I was up at dawn. I checked the streets, was at the plaza at seven, and continued to make checks at intervals during the day. I took my meals in different areas so as not to call attention to myself. I wondered what to do. I decided to stay another day: possibly one of them could make it. Unable to sleep, I rose early but stayed in my room. At ten I checked the plaza. No one. At eleven, the same. Worn out and depressed, I took the next bus back to Mexico City. I worried; I blamed myself; I made up reasons for their non-appearance, including the reason that they saw no action on our part. I could not sleep.

Back in the capital, I found that none of the group seemed particularly concerned about the possible loss of contact with the *campesinos*. José said, "Do not worry yourself. It will be worked out." But I worried about our possible loss and was afraid for what might be happening in San Antonio.

I continued with the schedule and went back on to Comitán the thirteenth of February, staying two days. Walking a number of times through the streets and the market, I began to feel desperate and started looking for anyone from San Antonio or Santa Ana, even if they were not part of the movement. I just wanted to make a connection and get any news. But I saw no one and felt that I could not risk staying longer.

When I arrived again in the capital, José showed me a typewritten note that had come through the underground. It was directed to *Los* Melville from *Comandante* Marc Antonio Yon Sosa of the revolutionary group MR-13. Yon Sosa, like the deceased F.A.R. *Comandante* Luís Turcios Lima, was a former Guatemalan Army officer trained by United States Forces in counter-insurgency warfare, a soldier turned fierce and clever guerrilla leader. In his letter he acknowledged our efforts, said he wanted to collaborate in any way possible, and offered to meet with us through his emissary.

This communication represented a break we needed, something that could get us off the ground. Four of us began meeting in student-frequented bars with an MR-13 representative, a tall, slim, tousle-haired, tough, twenty-five-year-old man dressed in a red plaid shirt and blue jeans. He was slick and acted as if he knew a lot about us as he filled us in on how to negotiate the purchase of automatic weapons. But we lacked what they were hoping we would have: money.

In the ensuing days, as we thought about how to get money, I felt a strong urge, something I was soon to recognize as guidance. I went to a pay phone and called information in Washington, D.C. After enduring a long period of static and clicking sounds, I reached an operator and asked for the number of Blase Bonpane. I could have jumped up and down when she simply gave me a number. I jotted it down, immediately put in my coins, and called. More clicking, static, and strange voices, then a final click, and I was beside myself with joy as I heard Blase's deep raspy "hello." He was equally excited when he heard who was calling.

"I want to know all about what is going on with you guys, and to tell you what I am doing here," he said. "But, unfortunately, my phone is tapped. It's a damn inconvenience that I've been living with for a while, but I've learned to handle it." He then asked for the number of my phone booth and five minutes later he was at a pay phone calling me back. We talked for fifteen minutes.

He said he was convinced his work was in the States, not in Mexico or Guatemala. He said he was doing everything he could to make the plight of Guatemala known and to expose the role of the United States in suppressing its people. "I'm bargaining with a publisher for the sale of a book on my Guatemalan experience," he said. "So if you keep in contact with me, I'll send you a big part of the expected advance as soon as I get it."

I yelled, "Allelluia!"

He laughed and then said seriously, "Art, in case any of you ever gets in trouble, I want to give you the name of a lawyer in Washington, D.C. who is willing to help." I jotted down the lawyer's name, address, and phone number, and I asked Blase to let the lawyer know that if I contacted him I would use the name Bruno. As I walked back to the apartment, I committed the phone number to memory, feeling much comfort in knowing what Blase was doing.

At the end of March we moved into a low-rent but rather elegant house with three bedrooms. We were now together with Tom and Marji, who took one of the bedrooms. The underground passed on the word that violence had occurred in San Antonio. I again expressed to the group the need to make contact with the *campesinos*, but no one seemed to share my concern. I said that it was my responsibility to make the contact and that I would make another trip in the next few days. José said, "I think, Arturo, you have been seen too much in Comitán. Someone else must go." He looked at the group. "Would you be willing to go, Tomás?" he asked my brother. Tom, who, with Marji, had already made a trip to the United States to be interviewed by a reporter and to another town on the Guatemalan border, nodded and said he would. José said, "Bien, but I think it would be better if you, Tomás, did not go as far as Comitán. You are easily recognized as an American, and Comitán is our hottest spot. I think it would work if you went with Chico only as far as Tuxtla, got a room, and stayed there. Chico can go on to Comitán to look for the *campesinos* and, if he finds any, bring them back to Tuxtla for you to interview." Chico looked pale, but agreed.

I later spoke to José. "Look," I said, "This is not going to work. Chico is hesitant to go anywhere alone, and he has been afraid to go near the border from the start. What's more, I do not think he will recognize the *campesinos*, and even if he could, they may not be able or willing to take the bus north with him."

"I understand," he said, "but let's give it a try."

"I think it is futile," I said. "More important than who is at risk is finding the *campesinos*."

"Let us give it a try," he said.

Tom and Chico returned on the third day. Chico had found no *campesinos* from San Antonio. In a conversation I asked which streets around the plaza he had taken. From his answers, I doubted that he had ever gone there. I said nothing more. A few days later, Chico and his belongings disappeared.

The following week I said to the group, "I am going to make another trip to Comitán." No one objected. "It may be that some people have fled San Antonio and are working on farms near the border. If I find no *campesinos* in the *pueblo*, I'll visit some farms and talk with workers. We just have to figure out a way to do that."

Roberto's idea started the ball rolling. "Why not go as a sociologist, studying the migration of the Mayas?"

After a brief discussion, José said, "The underground can probably draw up letters and documents on university stationary making you official."

Remembering the effectiveness of the underground in such work, I said, "I don't want to lose much time. Months have passed since we were in contact with these people." José talked to underground members. They were in favor of my trip. They would get the stationary and also invite a woman graduate student from the university to participate in "the study." She would add much credibility. I met with the woman, a confident person apparently capable of handling the task. We ironed out a plan. We would leave in three days. She would have the paperwork. We would be prepared to rough it, take a bus to Comitán, continue on foot from there. We would take bedrolls for sleeping. I would bring cash.

Roberto and Patricio were leaving for San Cristóbal de Las Casas, a city some fifty miles north of Comitán, to meet some Guatemalan students. I told them I would like to meet the students and would try to stop to see them en route. They agreed to check the plaza each day at one and five o'clock if I would just sit on a bench at the northeast corner at one of those times.

On the day of my departure word arrived that my woman companion could not leave, asking me to wait a day or two. I was disappointed and frustrated, knowing how long one can wait for the underground. I gave José a note to send back: "I will go to Comitán and stay there looking for the people. Come as soon as possible. I will be unable to go into the countryside without documents. I will check the bus from Mexico City each day for your arrival."

I was ready to go but scared, having no document to cover me. Tom said, "Take your own passport. You'll never get caught." I disliked the idea but had no option. I put on my slacks and sport jacket. Borrowing a blanket from the house, I wrapped into it two pairs of underpants, two pairs of socks, a small hand towel, a razor, a toothbrush, and my passport. I walked to the depot and boarded the bus South. The trip was uneventful, and as I watched the scenery go by and mulled over what our group was doing, I felt distressed. It seemed that we were losing valuable time and not accomplishing much more than being in exile. "A revolutionary makes revolution," we were accustomed to say. But we were just talking revolution and not getting close to making anything.

My bus arrived at my first stop, San Cristóbal de Las Casas, in mid-afternoon. As agreed, at five o'clock I would go to the plaza to look for Roberto and Patricio. San Cristóbal being one of my favorite towns, I did not mind having the extra time to walk around and look at the shops. At five I went to the plaza. In a few minutes Roberto approached, but he looked downcast and said they had not met the students. Patricio had gone back to Mexico City that day. We sat in his room commiserating, went out for a snack, and then to bed. I had to get up at four for my bus.

Roberto got up with me. He sat on the edge of the bed rubbing his eyes and asking again, "Are you sure you don't want me to go with you, Arturo? I could stay until the woman arrives."

"Thanks, Roberto," I said. "I would love to have your company, but there is nothing you can do. And there is no sense in risking two of us getting caught."

He put on his clothes and walked me to the depot. It was dark out, and the fog was heavy. Along the way he took his pistol from his belt and held it close to my bedroll, under his hand. "Take this with you, Arturo." I didn't reach for it. He looked at me. "You will need it more than I," he said.

"Thanks, Roberto," I said, "but those things really scare me. And if I had one I might be tempted to use it. It will not make me safe."

After a moment of silence, he asked "How about my watch? A sociologist needs a watch. Would you like to borrow it?" I thanked him and put the watch on my wrist. I bought my ticket, shook hands with him, and boarded. He stood by until the bus pulled out. He waved. He couldn't see me in the dark bus, but I waved anyway.

22

GUIDANCE

I felt ambivalent about my spiritual development. At times I believed myself on the path to further growth but then would not trust sufficiently, thinking myself unworthy, surmising that I needed to give up more control in my life while being unwilling to do so. I thought I needed a more loving approach to life but knew of no tools for attaining it. I thought I would have to base my approach on more integrity than the life of a subversive permits, but I made the social end justify the dishonest and manipulative means. As I was to learn, we humans don't get to choose when we are going to be guided; we don't get to determine how we will be guided; we may not even know when we are being guided. There are no rules in the matter of guidance.

It was only in retrospect that I knew: somehow and for some reason, I was guided to do things I had not previously considered, to say words that I had not thought of before, and to encounter people who would unexpectedly help me on my journey.

I know I would never have had these privileged experiences had I not spent time with my earth teachers, the Guatemalan peasants. Living in their simple environment somehow opened me to channels that otherwise would have been closed. Letting the peasants influence me somehow got enough of my intellectual "stuckness" out of the way. Building a relationship with Lím-

bano, a person obviously close to nature and to truth, made it possible for me to remain in contact with him after his death.

Kind people entered my life at unexpected times and in unforeseen places. People trained not to support were supportive. People considered bad were good. People normally expected to disappoint came through. People considered good served me.

What was at that time strange to me has now become fairly commonplace, and now I frequently perceive people I work with being guided along their life paths and feel myself guided in assisting them in their healing.

THE BUS PULLED INTO Comitán shortly after six in the morning. My trip had been uneventful, but I was feeling unusually tense without knowing why. Then, as the bus came to a stop, I saw the border policeman. I froze in my seat and watched as passengers began stepping down from the bus. The officer stood in front of the door so that they had to sidestep him. He looked into the face of each and said nothing. He was about five foot eight, good-looking, well-built, wearing a neat brown uniform. He stood with his feet slightly apart and his hands behind his back. The passengers nodded to him. He did not respond. He did not smile.

I did not want to be the last one to leave. My breathing quickened as I got up from my seat and stepped into the aisle. I took my bedroll from the overhead rack. My palms were wet. I started down the aisle. A drop of perspiration rolled from my armpit. I had to slow my mind in order to think about my exit. I told myself I would nod casually to him as the others were doing and would appear confident and businesslike. I would not hesitate. At the front of the bus, I tucked the bedroll under my arm, thanked the driver, did not use the stainless-steel handrails as I stepped down the first step. I nodded to the officer, stepping to the ground. My body shivered as he put up his hand and stepped in front of me.

"Damn," I thought to myself, "It's my blue eyes. I should never have looked at him."

"*Perdóneme, señor,*" he said. "Your identification, *por favor.*"

"Certainly," I said as I began searching my pockets. Then, trying to look confused, I smiled and said, "Oh, I am sorry, *señor,*" while still feeling my pockets, "I don't think I brought my identification with me."

"What is your destination?"

"Here, Comitán," I said frowning.

"For what purpose do you come?"

"I am a sociologist," I said smiling. "I am doing a study of the indigenous people of the area."

He looked me up and down, ending with my eyes. "Are you a Melville?"

I shook my head and asked, "What is a Melville?"

I looked at the forty-five on his waist. I thought of Roberto offering me his gun and knew I could never use one. He reached inside his jacket and removed a small manilla envelope. He withdrew three photos, looking at the first and then at me. I stretched my neck slightly forward and saw my ordination picture. My knees were wobbly. He went to the next picture: Marji in her habit. The next: Tom's ordination picture. His eyes went back and forth from Tom's picture to me. He hadn't recognized my picture. The mustache and black hair did it. I was beginning to think that I had a chance.

Then another officer stepped to my side from behind. "What do you say?" he asked his companion.

"I do not know," answered the first.

"Better not to take a chance," said the second.

"*Bien,*" said the first. Putting his hand on my arm, he said, "Come!" The other walked to my left as we went to their open Jeep. They directed me to the back seat, with the second sitting beside me. The first drove slowly around the plaza. I looked up the steps to see if any of the *campesinos* had arrived. I saw none and was thankful for that.

I began to feel stronger. There is something about being apprehended that gives one more courage, probably because there is not much more to lose. We stopped in front of the *municipalidad.* The first officer took my arm as I stepped down.

The other put his hand on my other arm. We walked through the door marked *Policía*.

The second stayed with me in the anteroom where several dishevelled *Policía Nacional* stood around in khaki uniforms and one sat behind a small, heavily-scratched desk. The first disappeared, returning in a moment with the *jefe* of the National Police. The disheveled ones came to attention. The border guards hesitated a moment and then left, as if in a hurry.

"So," said the *jefe*, looking me up and down, "put your blanket on the desk while we talk." I did so. "Now tell me," he said, "how does it happen that you travel without identification?"

"I usually do not," I said. "However, I have unfortunately come on this trip forgetting my papers."

"Yes, that happens," he said. "And for what purpose have you come to our *pueblo*?" He was looking at the bedroll. He did not wait for my answer. "We had better have a look in there," he said, pointing to the blanket. As the young officer opened the blanket and the underpants were unfolded, there lay my blue American passport. "Well, what do you know!" said the *jefe* as he stepped to the desk and picked it up. "From the United States," he said looking up at me. "Let me see here: your name is Melville Arthur." He took a step towards me, looked me in the eye and asked, "Are you a priest?"

"No," I smiled. "I am a sociologist."

He looked around at the others as if for some approval and then said, "Well, I am putting you in jail."

He looked at me, trying to appear sympathetic, as he said, "You had better leave your wristwatch here for security."

"No," I said. "I will keep my watch."

He shrugged. "Do you have money with you?"

"Yes, I have a little."

"You would do well to leave your watch and money in our custody."

"I would prefer to keep them."

"You do not know what it is like in our jails. You may lose your valuables in there."

"I will take that chance."

He squinted his eyes and nodded. "Lock him up."

A man with a wrinkled uniform and floppy cap stepped to the heavy wood-and-iron grate and selected a large key from the ring on his belt. He had to pull up his pants to insert the key and turn it several times. The mammoth old door opened. He and I stepped into a small hall. He locked the door behind us and then unlocked the door on the other end of the hall, opened it, and I stepped through. *"Buena suerte,"* he said. I turned and looked at him. He smiled and nodded his head.

"Gracias," I said, knowing Mexicans to be for the underdog and the oppressed. Mexicans do not like government. They love people.

I was standing in an outdoor cement quadrangle about forty by forty feet in size enclosed by a concrete wall some twenty feet high. The prisoners, about thirty of them, all male, stood or sat against the wall, looking at me casually. The sun was already warm. No one spoke. Except for a water-drain in the center of the pavement, and the prisoners, the quadrangle was empty. To the right beyond the wall was a room with a doorway but no door and just an opening for a window.

I walked about ten feet to my left, where there were no prisoners, and sat on the ground against the wall, resting my elbows on my knees and my face on my hands. I was angry at myself for getting caught. I suppressed my fear completely. Although I felt hot I kept my jacket on, thinking I might lose it. For about ten minutes the men moved very little. Suddenly one of the them started running around screaming. No one paid much attention, and he kept his distance from everyone. I pretended not to notice him, although watching him was an eerie experience. When he was covered with sweat, he ran through the doorway without a door. I heard someone on the inside shout, "Shut up!" His screaming stopped. After a few minutes he came out and began pacing the quadrangle, talking to himself.

The yard contained no benches or chairs or facilities for exercise or recreation. Some of the men started milling about. One, a man of about twenty years of age, came and sat beside me. He wore a green tee shirt, jeans with the left knee missing, and yellow plastic shower thongs. I looked at him and nodded. After a few minutes he asked, "What are you in for?"

"They did not tell me."

"You running drugs?" he asked.

"No," I said shaking my head.

After a moment of silence, I asked, "What are you in for?"

He raised his hands in frustration and said, "I hit the *patrón*, the owner of the land we live on."

"What did you hit him with?" I asked.

He shrugged and said, "My new hoe."

"Did you kill him?" I asked.

"No, my brothers stopped me. But the bastard does not deserve to live."

"How long are you in for?" I asked.

"It now makes two months that I have been here. My case, I do not know if the judge is going to hear it. My family cannot pay the bribe, and the *patrón* is a friend of the judge. How long I am in for, I do not know." I nodded.

"What do you call yourself?" he asked.

"Bruno," I said, "and you?"

"Lugo," he said. I nodded again.

We sat quietly. I took out a cigarette and offered Lugo one. A barefoot boy came out the doorway and crossed the yard. I kept my eyes down and watched his feet. He stopped before me, but I did not look up. He kept standing there so I looked up. "The *jefe* wants to see you," he said smiling.

I knew that Mexican jails had an infra-structure run by the inmates. *"Donde está?"* I asked.

"He is in the room," the boy said.

I stood up and walked to the doorway, the boy at my side. I knew that the next few moments were going to decide my place among the prisoners. I entered. The human stench was strong. A half-dozen men sat against a wall. No one spoke. I looked around: the room was about fifteen feet by thirty, with two doors at the far end. I figured those were toilets. The room was bare of furniture except for a low three-legged stool set to one side, with a man sitting on it, his legs stretched out in front of him. *"Aqui!"* the man called to me.

I walked to him. He looked up at me. I looked down at him. Silence. He was about twenty-five, dark and stocky, his black hair semi-long—about like mine. His shirt was stained, his pants rolled up above his ankles; he wore no socks, and the soles of his scuffed shoes were worn through. "What are you in for?" he asked.

"No one has told me," I said. He looked at me questioningly, and then laughed.

"I am in for murder," he said. I nodded my head.

"I am the *jefe* of the *cárcel*," he said. I looked at him. "I run things in here. Everybody who comes in gets fined according to what they are in for." He raised his hands as if to say it all made sense, and added, "The fines pay for cigarettes and things for the boys. We take care of each other." I looked at him. "So how much do you think I should fine you?" he asked.

"I do not think I should pay a fine," I answered without changing my expression.

He put his hand to the stubble on his chin as if thinking. "Then, for the time being, I am fining you ten pesos."

I waited. I had to play it right. He looked at me. "I will pay the ten *pesos* when I leave," I said. He did not answer. I continued to look at him. "*Bien*," he said. I turned and walked to the two doors and saw a toilet behind each. They obviously did not flush. The flies were thick, the stench horrendous. I stepped into the one with the shallowest puddle. The door would not close, and there was no paper. I urinated.

I went back to the yard, walked around, and nodded to anyone who nodded to me. No one acted tough or offensive. A few said, "*Qué tal?*" I answered, "*Qué tal?*"

It was about noon. I was walking in a big circle with one of the men. As we passed near the grated door, a guard said, "Hey, this is for you," sliding a tray through the slot. I looked at the guard, then at my companion. My companion said, "He has some food for you." I stepped to the grate and took the tray. It had a dish with rice and beans and a few chunks of meat with a sauce, a glass with some kind of punch, a fork on a folded cloth napkin. I stood with the tray, not knowing what to do. "It is from *Doña* . . ." the guard said. I couldn't get the name.

"Who is she?" I asked.

"She is a woman in the *pueblo*. She said to give it to the priest." He smiled.

"Tell her *mil gracias*," I said.

I turned with the tray in my hands. Everyone was looking at me. I felt funny, standing with a tray of food. No one else had eaten. I was probably hungry, but I couldn't feel it, and even if I were hungry I would not eat alone in front of the others. I walked across the yard to Lugo. "Want some food?" I asked.

He looked at the plate. He was hungry. He shook his head. "I ate yesterday," he said. "*El Loco* has not eaten in days. Why not let him have it?" I nodded my head. "Hey, *Loco*," he called out. The man who had run around screaming was sitting in the corner. He looked up. "Some food for you," Lugo said. The man looked at me. I held the tray out toward him. He looked around at the others. No one said anything. He got up and came slowly, eyeing me suspiciously. I handed him the tray, and he took it back to the corner.

I turned to Lugo. "When do you eat?" I asked.

"When my family can bring food," he said.

"Does the family live close?"

"About two hours from here."

"And if the family does not come?"

He shrugged his shoulders, "Then I do not eat."

I milled around with the others for a while and then sat down. I wondered to whom the border patrol and the police reported. My biggest fear was that they might turn me over to Guatemalans. I tried to block out the thought. If that happened, I would simply disappear. Everything was quiet. None of the prisoners was talking, as if it were siesta.

About one o'clock everyone looked up as the grated door swung open. A priest dressed in black cassock with a white stole around his neck stepped in hurriedly. "*Buenas tardes, buenas tardes*," he said in several directions, walking to the wall and standing with his back to it. I was sitting with Lugo. "What in the hell is that?" I asked, thinking it was some kind of a set-up.

"That is the priest," Lugo answered. "He comes in every week or so, does a sermon and confessions. He is harmless. I usually go to confession. Something to do. It cannot hurt."

As the priest began to speak, most of the men approached and stood in a semi-circle in front of him. He explained the ten commandments, spending a couple of minutes on each, telling the ways one could sin against that commandment. The sun was hot. Lugo and I sat and listened.

Well, I don't know if Lugo listened. I didn't. I kept wondering about this priest, who seemed to be unaware of what went on in the lives of these men. For some strange reason I felt very drawn to him. He was young, good looking, and a bit heavy-set. He finished his sermon and raised his hand in a blessing, then walked toward the doorway without a door, turning his reversible stole from white to purple. He entered the room. Some of the men lined up outside the doorway. One by one they entered.

Lugo got up to get in line. I stood up with him and without understanding why, knew I had to encounter the priest. When it came my turn, I entered. His eyes met mine. He did not look away. He was sitting on the low, three-legged stool. I knelt beside him. He raised his hand in a blessing, mumbling a few words. I looked in his eyes. They were black. Our faces were close. I had no plan. I wondered what I was doing. I had to do something. Knowing I would never confess again, I began, as if to confess. *"Bendígame, Padre. . . ."* I did not want to say the next words, which would declare that I was a sinner. I stopped and words came out that I had given no thought to. I heard myself say, "I need your help."

He looked at me, waiting for me to go on. "I am a priest," I said. He did not take his eyes from mine. "I have been working in Guatemala. I joined the revolution." He nodded his head. "We were betrayed by a priest." His eyes opened wide. "I was expelled. I came to Mexico. I was arrested here this morning." He never blinked. "I need your help."

"What do you need my help for?"

I didn't know what to say. But the words flowed out, "I am afraid they will turn me over to the Guatemalans. If that happens, I will disappear."

He nodded his head. "What do you want me to do?"

The words came unbidden. "I have to get a message to the United States. I have to get word out that I have been arrested."

He looked at me. "How would one do that?" he asked.

I did not know. And then it came to me suddenly. "Would you be willing to call a lawyer in Washington, D.C.?" I asked, amazed at the way this was happening.

"By telephone?" he asked.

"*Sí*," I said, "by telephone."

He raised his eyebrows and shrugged. He was not refusing, but he knew that such a call was difficult. I went on. "I would want you to say that Bruno has been arrested, that he is in jail in Comitán, and that no one should follow." He was nodding his head. "Can you speak English?" I asked.

"Yes . . . ," he said sheepishly in English, finding his first word a bit difficult. "I speak it little. Studied in school."

"*Bien*," I said. "I will give you a lawyer's name and number. Will you write it down?" He took out a package of matches and on the cover wrote the name and phone number of the lawyer Blase had given me. I repeated the message again, took two one-hundred peso bills from my pocket, and gave them to him. Then I said, "You will, of course, treat this as a secret under the seal of confession."

"No," he said, a bit taken aback. "You have not confessed a sin, and I have not given you absolution."

I could not believe it. "I have had impure thoughts," I said.

"*Tres Ave Marías*," he said, and raised his hand in absolution.

I said, "*Gracias, Padre*," stood up and left the room. I joined Lugo against the wall. A short time later the priest left as he had come, in a hurry.

It was about two-thirty. I was passing the grated door. "Hey," the guard said. I walked over. It was the same one who had ushered me in that morning. He came close to the screen and whispered, "A group of people has gathered outside the jail to see you."

I scratched my head. "How will anyone be able to see me?"

"Oh, you will be leaving. They are coming for you."

"Who is coming for me?"

He looked around. "The army. We just got word. They will be here late this afternoon."

"Where are they taking me?"

"We do not know, but they are coming from the base in Tuxtla Gutiérrez." He paused. "Be careful," he said, turning away.

I went back to the wall and sat alone. I had to think, but I did not know what to think. My forehead and neck were wet with sweat, and my back was sore. What would the army do with me?

Lugo came and sat at my side. "*Qué pasa?*" he asked.

"I do not know," I said.

"What did he want?" he insisted.

I shook my head, almost not believing my own words, and said, "He wanted to tell me that the army is coming to get me late this afternoon."

"For Christ's sake, *hermano*, what in the hell have you done?"

"Look, Lugo, you have been a friend. I do not know if we will ever meet again. But if we do, I will then tell you everything."

"Shit, man, and I thought *I* was in trouble," he said.

The grated door swung open. I jumped. We both looked up. It was the priest carrying the ciborium of communion hosts. Lugo laughed and slapped me on the shoulder. I tried to laugh with him as I said, "I thought it was the damn army."

The men started gathering before the priest. "Time to eat," Lugo said as he got up. "Why not try a wafer? It might bring you luck." I was surprised to realize that I had not thought of the priest coming back with communion. I watched the men step up one by one to the priest. I wondered if he had made the phone call; I thought not. You were lucky to get through to Mexico City from Comitán, never mind to Washington, D.C. I figured that if I asked, he would tell me he was going to do it later.

I got in line and watched the guys ahead of me, as if I had never been to communion before. Each stood before the priest.

He raised the host and said, "*El cuerpo de Cristo.*" They answered, "*Amén,*" put their heads back, and opened their mouths. The priest put the host on their tongues.

I stood before him. He raised the host and said, "I made the call."

I felt my body lurch. I looked into his eyes. They were kind eyes, gentle eyes, black Mexican eyes. He was waiting with the host raised. I wanted to say something. He smiled. I said, "*Amén.*" He put the host on my tongue.

Lugo and I sat against the wall. The sun was still hot, but sitting there felt better than being in the smelly room. I closed my eyes and tried to relax. We had a smoke.

About four-thirty the door opened. We all looked up. Two men were pushed in. Both were fairly drunk, and one had a bloody nose. They moved in different directions and sat alone against the wall.

It was shortly after five when the door opened again. We all looked up. The guard glanced around, then pointed to me. "*Vamos,*" he said. I stood. Lugo stood up beside me. A few of the others stood. The *jefe* looked on from the doorway of the room; our eyes met. I put out my hand to Lugo. We shook. "*Cuídate, hermano,*" he said. As I walked to the grated door, I saw the barefoot boy coming across the quadrangle from the room. I waited for him, took a one-hundred-peso bill from my pocket, and handed it to him. He looked at it with big eyes. As I turned to the guard I heard the boy say, "*Cuídate!*"

I stepped through the grated door into the hall. The guard locked it. "They are here," he said. He opened the other door. I stepped through. Standing stiffly on the other side was a handful of soldiers in battle gear with automatic weapons, a lieutenant and captain in formal uniform, and a general. I looked at them and felt oddly important. No one spoke. Two of the soldiers pointed their automatic rifles at me. The guard stepped away cautiously.

I watched the general as he looked me over from head to foot through squinting eyes. He stood with his hands on his hips, appearing more than six feet tall, about fifty years old, with short grey hair and a powerful build that had turned to fat now pulled in tightly by a wide belt. He wore battle fatigues, his shirt front unbuttoned at the top showing a hairy chest, a maroon beret tilted on his head, and high combat boots. He sneered as he said, "Get into this room," indicating which room with a flip of his head.

The captain stepped in ahead of me. The two soldiers tried to jam through the door at the same time as I went in. The general came behind. The room had only a desk and a chair. The general told me to step to the front of the desk. On the desk were some typed sheets. The general handed me a ballpoint pen. "Start signing," he said. I looked at him, then leaned over the desk and began to read the single-spaced, poorly-typed first page. It had to do with some violation I had committed. I had read only a few lines when the general hit me on the upper arm and said loudly, "Sign it."

I pulled back when he hit me. The soldiers jumped and shoved their rifles towards me. "I have not read it yet," I said angrily.

"I do not have time for your games," he said. "Sign the goddamn papers." I stared at him. I wondered if this was the beginning of a railroad. He pointed an index finger at me and in a low controlled voice, enunciating each word, said, "Now! I tell you, sign, now!" I leaned over the paper and signed my name. It was my normal signature, which looked scribbled. He thought it was not my signature. "Oh," he bellowed. "I know how to take care of this kind." He flipped open the ink pad on the desk, grabbed my right hand, isolated my thumb, pushed the thumb brusquely onto the pad, pulled it to the page, and pushed it down with such weight and force that I thought he was trying to break it. He was cursing as he flipped to the second page and repeated my thumb imprint. I caught a few words on the page " . . . being transferred to the custody of the Army. . . ." I didn't resist, but by the time he had finished five or six pages he was very upset and breathing heavily.

"Put this son of a bitch in cuffs," he barked. The captain

signalled to the doorway. The lieutenant came in and pulled my hands in front of me, slipped on the cuffs, putting his finger between my wrist and the metal to make sure they were not too tight. "Get him in the car," the general said, raising his hands as if shooing me away.

The captain indicated for me to follow. I stepped behind him, trying to massage my sore thumb, the soldiers taking up position on each side and pointing their rifles close to me. As we stepped out the side door of the old building, four other soldiers stood in the middle of the street, automatic rifles ready. I should have felt fear. I didn't. I was not letting myself feel anything. I had to control my emotions in order to handle the situation. For the first time I realized that they were taking caution against a possible rescue attempt. I felt acknowledged by the army and disheartened that our group could not dream of such an action.

I wondered how many plainclothesmen were there. A group of people stood watching. As I was marched across the street, I made eye contact with an old man and saw what I thought was an approving smile. A child pointed and said *"padre."* One woman with a handkerchief to her face may have been crying. I thought it was probably she who sent the meal. I wondered if she got her tray back.

Three Chevrolet sedans were parked across the street, the center one black and the others cream-colored. Several men seated in the front and back cars watched intently. As I was ushered into the back seat of the middle car, the lieutenant put my bedroll in the trunk. A soldier jumped in on each side of me. In the front a soldier in formal uniform got behind the wheel, the captain sitting on the right, and in the middle sat a man dressed in civilian clothes, whom I soon recognized as the arresting Border Patrol officer.

We drove quickly out of town. The soldiers at my side were squaring off against me, trying to point their rifles in my direction. The situation seemed very dangerous. I wondered whether they had ever done anything like this before. One of them banged me with his elbow several times and looked angry. No one spoke.

After about fifteen minutes the front car picked up speed, opening up the distance between us. The captain said, "There they go." I turned my head slightly and saw the rear car dropping back at the same time. We never saw them again. Everyone seemed to relax, and occasional talking began.

We arrived late at the base in Tuxtla Gutiérrez, passing through the checkpoints and going directly to the empty dining hall. We waited a few moments until an elderly officer entered; he smiled at me and spoke in a gentle voice. I didn't know his rank, but he was in charge. He told the captain to let me sit at a table alone. The others sat nearby. I was served bread and milk and a hot meal. Although I was still not feeling hungry, I ate, manipulating the utensils with my hands chained together.

Finished, I sat waiting. They all seemed relaxed until the captain told the soldiers that there was no time to be wasted and that they were to bring me outside immediately. The same group, each sitting in the same place as before, set out in the same car and drove through the night.

The following morning we arrived in Mexico City and drove to a large old building of grey stone. As we drove through the gate I saw the brass plaque on the post that read *Gobernación*. The lieutenant got my blanket roll out of the trunk, and the Border Patrol officer went into a first-floor office. My military escort ushered me up the wide, well-worn wooden stairs to the third floor, where a group of four plainclothesmen stood, awaiting us. The captain stepped aside and talked to one of them, then returned to remove the handcuffs. The lieutenant passed the bedroll to one of the plainclothesmen, and without another word the military went back down the stairs, not to be seen again.

The four plainclothesmen moved quickly, one taking me by the arm and rushing me, as if expecting me to resist. They hurried me into a large room with many desks. The room was abandoned except for one man who sat at a desk in the middle of the room. I wondered why there were not more people; I thought maybe it was Sunday. I was brought to the man, a balding, bespectacled little man. He drew papers from a folder, indicating where I was to sign. I signed. I knew I would be signing no matter what the papers declared, and I was too tired to want to read them. Flashbulbs went off. The balding man then fingerprinted me. He was gentle. As he was finishing, he leaned close to my ear and said, "Be careful. These types are bad. You may be in danger."

23

GRATITUDE

If we choose to return to the values of the earth, the natural workings of the human spirit will replace mechanical living. If we return to God, the wisdom of the human spirit will replace mechanical religion. The ability to heal and grow through responsible choice will displace automated salvation. A morality based on truth, love, and freedom and a liturgy that calls on the creative cooperation of the community will rise above automated sacraments and prayers. A person's value will not be a number or a dollar sign. Religion will not be bought and sold. God will not be subject to a system.

If Church and State stopped imposing mechanized techniques, we would be able to accept and cooperate with the poor and indigenous peoples of Guatemala and Latin America as earth teachers. But it is not yet that time. Instead we appear to be entering still another stage in the conquest of these people. The United States intends to be the principal mover in a long-range plan to develop Latin America for business. Americans have nearly completed the primary stage of this plan: maximizing profits by supplying military training and armaments to repress a restive populace of potential producers and consumers.

Bloodied fields, soon to be prepared for high-tech planting, have been taken from their earth guardians. The time has come for big business. Both State and Church are readying to sow and reap the fruits of business exploitation. As the United States tightens its noose, drawing the Latin community into the empire of major corporations, seducing and insulting earth people displaced by war with the carrot of employment on superfarms and mechanized factories, the Church is adjusting economic salvation and financial redemption to again align with the elite, supporting destructive corporate enterprises that will co-manage the lives of the faithful of God. Afraid of losing numbers in the upheaval in which business replaces the military, the Church broadens its support of the new power brokers as it steps up its campaign of fear and intimidation to keep displaced souls within the confines of Vatican rule.

To know these displaced souls who continue to suffer under our protracted political and religious blunders is to know a simpler, more generous, more godlike way of life. In my naivete I went to Latin America to teach and to save souls; I left a changed person, rewarded with the privilege of knowing those who could lead us back from five hundred years of destructive dominance to an era of spirituality, cooperation, and sanity.

THE FOUR AGENTS rushed me out of the office. Two stayed out in front; the third, an older man, probably in his early sixties but very agile, nearly pushed me down the steep stairs as he ran at my side; the fourth was close behind. On the ground level they hurried me out a back door to a blue Chevrolet station wagon. The older one pushed me into the back seat and got in on my left. A darker middle-aged man jumped in on my right. The other two got in front, and we took off immediately. They acted nervous and drove quickly, going down several alleys and making many turns. I gathered that they, too, thought a rescue could be attempted.

The driver, whom they referred to as *jefe*, was short, well-built, about my age, with rimless glasses, wearing grey slacks and a dark blue sport jacket. After about five minutes on the road he broke the silence by snapping his fingers and asking,

"Who brought the blanket?" The other three looked dumbfounded. "Jesus Christ . . . ," the *jefe* said, pounding the steering wheel. He turned to the youngest of the four, a well-built man in a blue suit, about twenty-two years of age sitting in the passenger seat, and said, "You are in charge of the goddamned blanket. You are not to leave that damn thing anywhere." He did not use the man's name.

The *jefe* swung the vehicle around in a fast U-turn and sped back to *Gobernación*. The young fellow dashed into the building and came right back with my bedroll. He jumped in, breathing heavily, and passed it back to the one on my right, who put it on the rear shelf. Off we went again, making turns and darting down alleys and finally taking a direction out of the city. After a half hour, by then traveling in an area free of traffic and buildings, the *jefe* pulled to the edge of a road with high grass growing on both sides and stopped. The man in the passenger seat and the man on my right stepped out. The *jefe* told me to get out with them and watched until I did. Then he and the older man came around the front and rear of the car, and the *jefe* started joking with me, as if we were friends. He said he needed some photographs of me, took a Polaroid out of the glove compartment and snapped me from different angles. For some he tried to make me smile, making a comment like, "My priest is so fat he has to be celibate." I didn't smile. He snapped away, putting the prints in his pocket. The others laughed and talked to me as they moved around so that I would turn to them. The *jefe* asked me to lean on the open door and then to sit on the back seat with my feet in the street. I noticed that, even though the men got close, he never included any of them in the pictures.

The roll of film finished, the older man slid into the back seat, the *jefe* telling me to get in beside him. The *jefe* then got in the front passenger seat and turned around to face me. "Have you heard that they assassinated Martin Luther King?" he asked.

"My God, no!" I said in amazement. "When did that happen?"

"I think it was yesterday," he said nonchalantly.

"Who did it?" I asked.

"*Quién sabe?*" he said, "Probably an agent of the F.B.I."

I sat staring out the window, thinking about the apostle of non-violence, when the *jefe* interrupted with, "Now I am going to show you some photos of interesting people. If there is anyone you recognize, you may want to tell me. It will be to your advantage." He then reached in the glove compartment and took out a pile of twenty or thirty pictures. They were all black and white, like mug-shots without names or numbers. He started, holding them up one at a time, while he and the older one watched me, as if looking for any tell-tale change of expression on my face. With each picture I would say no or shake my head, and he would go to the next. Most were men, tough-looking gangster types. I knew none of them.

Finished, he said, "How unfortunate that you do not recognize any of them. That would have been to your advantage." He then began talking about people, places, and happenings in Guatemala, showing that he knew a good deal more about the organized movements there than I, and leading me to suspect that he and his associates were C.I.A. or Interpol.

I tried to show no interest. He dropped that approach, smiled and said, "Now I have some questions." He looked at me again as if he cared, saying, "I do not want anything to happen to you. But what does happen depends on how you answer the questions and cooperate." I felt my heartbeat pick up and a lump form in my throat. This was the first time anyone had implied that something might happen to me. I knew it was not to my benefit to show any emotion, particularly any demonstration of fear. I tried to look cool as I felt my finger nails dig into my palms. "Take your time," he said. "And if you cooperate, I will do all I can to help you."

He looked at me for a moment, then took a tape recorder from under his seat, turned it on, adjusted it, stated the date and time, and said "Let us begin." I looked at him. "Are you ready?" he asked. I shrugged my shoulders as if it did not matter. He took a small notebook from his pocket from which he read some questions.

"*Bien.* How well did you know Luís Turcios Lima?"

"I did not know him," I said. "What I know about him is

from what I have read in the newspapers." He looked at me and then made some mark in his notebook.

"Do you know Camilo Sánchez?"

I shook my head. "No, I do not. Although I read something about him also."

"Do you know Marc Antonio Yon Sosa?"

"I have only heard and read of him."

He paused before he asked, "How do you contact the Mexican underground?"

I smiled and shrugged my shoulders as if it was a ridiculous question. "I know nothing about a Mexican underground." He raised his eyes as if in disbelief.

"How do you purchase or negotiate for weapons?"

"I have no idea."

"What were you doing in Comitán?"

"I have been visiting Comitán for many years. I am accustomed to go there periodically for a rest."

Emphasizing each word he asked, "Do you know José Alfaro?"

I wondered if José knew I had been arrested. "*Sí*," I said, "he is a friend of mine."

"I need to know about this Alfaro," he said sternly. "Is he in Mexico?" He was getting angry and trying not to show it.

"I do not know. I have not seen him since leaving Guatemala."

It was clear that he did not believe me. "Was José Alfaro a member of the *Fuerzas Armadas Rebeldes*?"

"*Sí.*"

"Were you associated with the F.A.R.?"

"No."

"But you did associate with José Alfaro in Guatemala?"

"*Sí*. But only as a friend. He had left the F.A.R."

He leaned towards me. "We know you have been with him in Mexico. Where the hell is he?"

I raised my hands as if in frustration and said, "I do not know. I have not seen him."

"You are not cooperating," he said clenching his fist.

"I am telling you what I know," I said in as stern a tone as his. "More than that, you cannot expect."

He took a deep breath and tried to smile. "*Bien*, let us ask some easier questions." He looked at the notebook and then paused before asking, "Where are the students from Guatemala?"

"I do not know."

"Where were they when you last saw them?"

"I have not seen any students since leaving Guatemala." He studied my face, his brow creased heavily.

"Where is your brother and the nun?"

"I have not been with them and have not seen them. We have been independent of each other since leaving Guatemala."

Again he paused, then shut off the tape recorder. "This stupid priest, he is not cooperating," he said to the old one.

"I agree," the old one said. "I think he has made his choice." My teeth wanted to chatter. I closed them tight. I was petrified.

"Do priests screw nuns?" the *jefe* asked with a straight face. The others laughed.

"Do Mexicans sell out to the C.I.A.?" I asked. The old one snickered and then caught himself.

The *jefe* frowned. "You are humorous," he said. He looked at each of the others. They showed no expression. He looked at me. "Do you think our people would go over to those criminals?" he asked. I did not answer, just looked at him, trying to show no expression. "Of course not," he answered for himself, forcing a smile. "They do not pay enough." The others laughed.

"Do priests jack off?" he asked after a pause. The old one laughed.

"Do secret agents take kickbacks?" I asked. He smiled, but it was not a real smile.

"We have a bad priest on our hands, *Jefe*," the old one said. "They are the worst of sinners. We perhaps need to teach this bad person about repentance and bring him back to God." The *jefe* nodded without taking his eyes off me. I looked back at him.

The *jefe* moved over to the driver's seat. "Get in," he said to the other two. "Put the cuffs on him," he said to the older one gruffly.

"Gladly," the old one said, reaching in his pocket and taking out a set of handcuffs. He and the man on my right each grabbed a wrist and pushed them together in front of me. The old one slapped a cuff on my left wrist, then let go of it and did the same on the right. The *jefe* began driving more slowly; where, I don't know. We were not on main roads and went through no towns. They simply seemed to be using up time. I did not understand, and I was becoming more afraid. We drove to a restaurant and entered. No one else was there. We sat at a table. The *jefe* got up and made a phone call. I asked to go to the bathroom. The young one stood outside the stall. I sat on the toilet and made grunting sounds as I went through my pockets and removed all papers, dropping them in the toilet. I pulled some toilet paper from the roll, found it would be impossible to wipe myself even if I had to, and flushed the toilet. The young one led me back to the table. The others were serving themselves from bowls. They offered me nothing, and I asked for nothing. I thought I might get sick if I ate. Finished, they sat at the table making small talk. None of them had a drink or a cigarette.

Back in the car, the *jefe* drove in a leisurely way. He asked if I wanted to reconsider any of his questions. I did not answer. We stopped for gas, and he made another phone call. Getting back in the car, he said, "It's settled." I felt afraid, although I had no idea what was settled. The moon came up. The four seemed to be looking about casually. Finally the young one pointed and said, "There's a good spot." I looked to where he pointed. My body tensed. It was all woods. The *jefe* shook his head.

My mind started racing. I had my first indication that they were going to kill me. I tried to quiet my mind. I told myself that I was getting paranoid, that they had no reason to do any such thing, that they were trying only to scare me into giving information. But what if they did intend to kill me? I asked myself. Are you just going to let it happen? Although I knew that I could do little against the four of them, I also knew that if I could come up with a plan, no matter how far-fetched, it would be better to make every attempt rather than simply submit to their devious plan.

"How about there?" the young one said pointing into the woods. The *jefe* looked around and again shook his head. They were going to take me to the woods. They were going to try to get information. But whether they got it or not, all would be over. I made my plan. The road was elevated on both sides. If I could get my hands on the steering wheel, I could possibly force the car over the embankment and into a roll. I would be the only one prepared. In the ensuing confusion I would try to open a door and escape into the woods.

But what if they don't intend to kill you? my mind screamed. What if you are making this up? What if you get killed in the crash? I slowed down my mind and thought everything through carefully again. I assured myself that they could be intending nothing else. They had forewarned me clearly. Although my plan was almost futile, if I waited too long I would have no chance to do anything. I looked at the speedometer. We were doing eighty kilometers. The four men were concerned about looking for a place. I called on all the strength I had, leaped across the back of the front seat, grabbed the steering wheel with both hands and jerked it to the right. The car swerved. The *jefe* struggled. The young one pulled on my right arm, and the two in the rear pulled on my clothing. I put every ounce of strength into turning the wheel. There was much screaming. The *jefe* was strong, and I had no leverage. I could hear the brakes screeching. The car lurched to a stop. I could smell burning rubber as I was dragged to the back seat. With both hands I reached across the old one for the door handle, grabbed it, turned and pushed the door open. I had a chance and knew if I didn't use it I was dead. Like a wild beast I kicked the man behind me with all my strength and driving my elbow into the old one as I climbed across him.

Out of nowhere the *jefe's* fist caught me in the face, sending me onto the lap of the old one. He and the one on my right pulled me onto the seat, each clinging to an arm. The young one, kneeling on the front seat, punched me in the face and chest.

Suddenly my head jerked back. The *jefe* had climbed onto the rear shelf of the station wagon and pulled my head by the hair until my neck was stretched across the back of the seat.

Then it seemed as if there was no movement and total quiet until I felt the cold metal against my right temple, and the *jefe* yelled, "I am going to do it right here. This son of a bitch is dead." The men on each side of me, as if in slow motion, moved away, holding me at arm's length. I thought of Jackie Kennedy with her husband's brain splattered over her. I was numb as I waited for the end. There was a pause. The *jefe* withdrew the gun—why, I will never know. Still shouting and cursing, he put the gun away and clapped his hands on my ears several times. He pulled out a cord, put it around my neck and tightened it until I could not breathe. A fist punched deep into my stomach, and I passed out.

As I regained consciousness, the men on both sides were shaking me and yelling. The cord was still around my neck, but it was loose now. The *jefe* tightened it again, and I lurched with the punches. It felt so good to drift into unconsciousness. Again they revived me, tightened the cord, and hit me, and again I drifted into a beautiful space. I did not know if I was dying, but it was so pleasant that I did not care.

When I regained consciousness again, it took a few moments to realize what was happening. I lay on the floor face down with my hands tied behind my back. The two men on the rear seat had their feet on me. As they felt me stir, they stamped their feet on me and cursed. I heard the *jefe* speaking. His voice seemed distant. Then he laughed, and I heard him say clearly, "Since you only get buried once, we thought it a good idea to let you be awake to appreciate it." I felt terror. Would they really bury me alive? My teeth chattered and my body shivered. The cord was so tight on my hands that I thought if I lived through this, I would lose my hands. I realized that they had taken the cuffs off so that the old one would not lose them if they buried me alive; the old one did not want to lose his cuffs.

Although it seemed pointless, I felt a deep need to talk. I turned my face towards the front. "*Jefe*," I said. He did not answer. "Loosen the cords on my hands, *por favor*," I pleaded.

"No," he said. "You won't need hands any more."

Then I heard a voice telling me that I had to talk to him. It was strange. It sounded like Límbano's voice. I wanted to speak but didn't know what to say. "Talk to him," the voice insisted.

"*Jefe*," I said hoarsely.

"Drop dead," he said. I felt heels of shoes twisting the skin and flesh on my back and legs.

"Talk to him," the voice demanded.

"*Jefe*, it is important that I speak to you," I said. There was silence, just a shoe digging into my back.

"You must talk to him now," it said firmly.

"*Jefe*, you have to listen," I screamed.

"What the hell do you have to say, you lousy excuse for a priest?" he shouted back.

"They know," I said, and then was amazed. The words had just come out, as if on their own. I didn't know I was saying them or where they came from or what they meant. I hadn't planned them. But I had said them, and the *jefe* was listening.

"What the hell are you talking about?" he asked. "Who knows what?" There was concern in his voice.

Then it became clear. I knew what to say. I knew the answer to his question. It just came to me. I took a deep breath that burned in my throat and blurted out, "They know in the United States. They know I have been arrested." There was silence.

"Sit the son of a bitch up on the seat," the *jefe* said. I had no strength. The two men jerked me up onto the seat, my numb hands crushed behind me. The *jefe* pulled the car to the side of the road and stopped. He turned to me, and I saw the face of a killer, as he said, "This may be the last time you speak to me, so make it good. How the fuck would they know?"

"They know in Washington, D.C."

"What the hell are you talking about?" he shouted.

I thought of the priest at the jail. The voice said, "He can take care of himself. They will not hurt him. Now speak!" I hesitated. "Speak now!" it insisted.

"A priest came into the jail in Comitán. I went to confession to him." My throat was hurting. I had to force the words out. "I asked him to help me. I asked him to call a lawyer in Washington, D.C. He wrote down the phone number and name of the lawyer. I gave him some money and asked him to call and say that I had been arrested in Comitán. Later, when he came back to the jail with communion, he told me he had made the call."

The *jefe* looked at me for a long time. No one spoke. He turned to the front and started the car, saying, "We have to get to a damn phone."

After driving in silence for about ten minutes, I said, "*Jefe*, will you please loosen the cords."

"Loosen the cords and tie his hands in front," he said.

I leaned forward, and the man on my right roughly untied the cord. My arms were limp. I could not move them. Each of the two men grabbed an arm and pulled it in front of me. The old one held my hands together and the one on the right started tying them tightly again. I pushed my elbows against my hips and used what little strength I had to try to keep my wrists from coming together. He knew what I was doing and dug his elbow in my ribs. Almost blacking out, I said, "*Jefe*, tell him he has to tie them loose."

"Loose," the *jefe* said. "For now." The one on the right eased up, and I managed to hold my wrists slightly apart.

In about a half hour the *jefe* pulled up to a phone booth. It seemed to be in the middle of nowhere. It had a light over it, so we had to be close to a town. The *jefe* got out and slammed the door. I could see him in the booth talking but could not hear him. He started shouting and pounding on the booth. He slammed the phone down and made another call. It was similar to the first. After slamming the phone down again, he waited. Those in the car said nothing. After five minutes the phone rang. He answered it and then listened. He said very little. He hung up and came back to the car. He sat on the seat with the door open, his feet on the outside. His face in his hands. No one spoke. It seemed like a long time before the phone rang. "About time," he said as he went to the booth again. He listened. He yelled. He listened. He hung up and came to the car. Getting in he said, "We are taking him to the Texas border at Nuevo Laredo."

Even with that incredible news, my body never stopped trembling. I had no control over it. The one on my right jabbed his elbow into me and said to the others, "He is trembling like

a chicken." The young one snorted a laugh. The one on the right
went on, "I knew priests had no guts. You know, I think we
ought to cut off his balls." The old one laughed. "Priests do not
need balls," he continued. "They do not know how to make them
work. Maybe if we cut them off, he would be a better priest."
Except for the *jefe*, all the others were snickering. The one on
my right reached down somewhere and took out a small knife.
He held it in his right hand and with the other reached between
my legs and grabbed me. He brought the knife close. I was
afraid to move. I closed my eyes. He was squeezing my testicles.
I gasped, beginning to get faint.

"*Bien*, Eduardo," the *jefe* said. "Let him have his balls."
The one on the right pulled back as soon as his name was mentioned.

"Eduardo," I mumbled. He jumped at hearing his name,
put the knife to my throat and said, "If you say that once more,
you will never speak again."

"Enough," the *jefe* said. "We have to deliver him."

We drove all night. At some point Eduardo found my loose
shoe. From time to time he would pound my right thigh with
it. Under normal circumstances it would have hurt a lot. I felt
little pain but jumped from fear each time he hit me. It rained
for a while. Only once did I know where we were. Then I saw
the headlights shine on a sign, "San Luís Potosí."

The old one felt something under his foot, reached to the
floor, and picked up my wallet. He opened it and said, "The
padre ran off with the collection." He started counting, saying,
"And a damn good one it was. I bet the poor bastards in his
parish did not know he had this much or they would have killed
him." The *jefe* laughed and reached his hand back. The old one
put the money, several hundred dollars' worth, into the *jefe's*
hand. The *jefe* put it inside his coat. The old one put the empty
wallet in his pocket.

I fell asleep several times, only to be awakened by a jab in
the ribs or a shoe pounding on the thigh. As we neared the
border, Eduardo asked, "Have you ever walked across the International Bridge?" I shook my head. "Well," he said, "we are
going to assign the *guardia* to accompany you across the Río

Grande, and halfway along they are going to throw you off the bridge." The others laughed. I had no way to know if he was telling the truth. His threat added to my fear.

We pulled up in front of the small building. The sign said *Migración*. We all got out. Eduardo threw my shoe on the ground. I nearly fell over trying to get it on my foot. My body was so sore I could hardly walk. The old one grabbed my arm and tried to rush me. I pulled my arm away from him. As we entered, a fat immigration officer took one look at me and laughed. "So this is the priest," he said, trying to be arrogant. Then as if to impress the agents, he pointed his finger and said, "You just go stand in the corner there and keep your mouth shut."

"Go to hell!" I said, as I slowly lowered myself into a chair. He was taken aback, looked to the others for support, but they acted as if they had heard nothing. I looked down and for the first time saw that my pants were torn open from the waist half way to the knee. I wondered how the rest of me looked.

"Does he have a passport?" the officer asked, clearing his throat.

The *jefe* looked around and then said to the young one, "For Christ's sake, are you in charge of the blanket?" The young one rushed to the car, came back with the bedroll, opened it, and took out the passport.

The officer stamped it and said, "That's it. These two boys will walk him across the bridge." He pointed to two young officers.

"*Bien*," the *jefe* said to him. "*Vamos compañeros*," he said to the other three. They all shook hands with the officer and started to leave.

"*Jefe*," I said. He stopped in the doorway, turned and looked at me with a contemptuous smile. "I have no money," I said. He did not answer, but only looked at me, not changing his expression. "Could I have a little?" I asked.

With that he laughed, spat out the door, and said, "Take up another collection, *Padrecito*." They left.

One of the young officers wrapped my passport in the blanket and asked, "Do you want me to carry this?"

"*Por favor*," I said. We started out. The fat one said, "*Adiós, Padre.*" I did not answer.

Part way across the bridge I began to tremble badly. "What is wrong?" one of the officers asked.

I stopped and said, "One of those plainclothesmen said you were going to throw me off the bridge."

They looked at each other, and one said, "They are bad men. And they lied to you. We will walk you to the other side." He offered a cigarette. I felt my lips tremble as he lit it for me.

At the door of the white building on the other side of the border, I thanked the guards and said goodbye. I was in Laredo, Texas. I felt relieved to be in the United States. I stepped into the Office of Immigration and was greeted by a fat, blond, balding man. "So you have arrived," he said in a high sing-songy voice. "Sit down and tell me about your trip."

"No, thanks," I said, shaking my head and sitting down. I unwrapped the blanket and took out the passport.

"Okay," he said opening it to a blank page. "We been hearing 'bout you on the radio. Sounded kinda interesting." He stamped my passport, looked through my bedroll, and said, "You're free to go." I was amazed. It was 6:30 in the morning and already hot as I walked into Laredo. I tried to ignore the pain and just walked slowly, needing to put some distance between me and the border. I had to go to the bathroom. I was exhausted and had to get some rest. And I couldn't do anything without money.

An elderly woman, her head down, was walking towards me. As we got close I said, "*Perdóneme, señora.*" She looked up and said, "I don't *hablo* Spanish." I asked her in English, "Can you please tell me where the Catholic Church is?"

"It is right ahead of you," she said, and then stepped towards me. "You can almost see it from here. If you hurry, you can catch Mass."

I stood in front of the old, cold red brick church with the newer, cold red brick rectory to my left. A sign in front of me stated the various services. I walked to the rectory, went up the few steps one at a time, and rang the bell. I waited. No answer. I rang it again. Another long wait, then footsteps and the door opened. A young priest, probably fresh out of the seminary, neatly dressed in a white-collared sport shirt, black slacks, and black shoes, stared at me. I thought youth would be in my favor as I said in my hoarse voice, "Excuse me, Father, but I am a priest. I have been working in Guatemala, but while in Mexico, I got robbed and beaten. I wonder if you could help me."

"I am not the pastor," he said. "You will have to talk to the pastor." He started to close the door.

I was amazed. "May I please use your bathroom?" I quickly asked.

"I am not the pastor. You will have to talk to him."

"May I speak to him then?"

"He is celebrating Mass," he said, as he closed the door.

My body pain was intensifying. My arms, legs, every part of me seemed to ache. I felt like an old man going down the steps. I walked to the church and stepped in. It was dark in the church but lit brightly at the altar. I made my way to the front. Mass was half-finished. Five people were present. I sat in the second pew. The priest at the altar, facing into the body of the church, kept his eyes on me as he said the memorized words. He was of medium height, about fifty-five, balding, stern-looking. As he performed his routine, he kept glancing at me. I hoped the presence of a stranger was not threatening to him. It seemed as if it took him hours to finish. He finally retired to the sacristy.

I left the church, made my way around to the outside entrance of the sacristy, and went in. He was unvesting, pulling the alb over his head. He turned as I entered and looked at me. "Pardon me, Father," I said. But he turned away quickly and faced the vesting case, saying nothing. "Pardon me, Father, but I am a priest," I said. He turned to me and let out a sigh, as if exasperated. I went on. "I have been working in Guatemala for six years. While in Mexico, I was robbed and beaten up. I have no money."

"Why did you get mixed up with those communists?" he asked angrily. I was dumbfounded. "I know what you were involved in," he said pointing a finger at me. "I have been working on the border here for thirty years and have never had a problem." He turned away, saying "No, I cannot help you."

"Father, if you can lend me the money to fly to New Orleans, I have friends there," I pleaded. "I will wire back your money immediately."

Facing the vesting case and removing his vestments, he said, "I repeat. I cannot help you. Go to the Saint Vincent de Paul Society. They help people who are down and out."

I waited. He turned to me again. Looking into his eyes, I asked, "Can I please use your bathroom for a moment."

"I told you I cannot help," he said sharply.

"Can you tell me where I can find the St. Vincent de Paul Society?" I asked, feeling frustrated and foolish.

"The president lives at. . . ." He gave me the address.

I walked out and asked the first person I met for directions to the address. Following the directions, I passed beautiful old homes with neat shrubs and lawns. It was a short walk, but it took me about twenty minutes to reach the well-kept house of white wood with a large porch on the front and side. I went up the steps, and as I reached the porch the front door opened. A man put the latch on the screen door and said, "Yes?"

"Pardon me, but are you the president of the St. Vincent de Paul Society?" I asked.

"That I am," he said.

"Well . . , I am a priest, and I have a problem. I was in Mexico, where I got beaten up and robbed of all my money. I wonder if you could help me."

"If you are a priest," he said, "go to the priests for help. The St. Vincent de Paul Society helps the laity." He closed the door. I stood for a confused moment, then slowly went down the steps and made my way toward the center of town. I passed a taxi stand, where three men were leaning against an old taxi speaking Spanish. I stopped and went back to them and asked, "*Perdónenme señores*, but would any of you be interested in buying a blanket?"

They looked at me, then one of them smiled and said, "For what would we need a blanket in Laredo?"

I turned and walked on. One of them called, "Wait." I stopped. As he approached he asked, "What is the problem, *hermano*?"

I needed to talk to someone. I needed to let out what was happening. I looked into his black shining eyes and decided that I was going to talk. "I am a priest," I said. He pouted his lips and shrugged his shoulders. "For six years I have been working in Guatemala. There is a revolution going on there. I joined the revolution." He smiled. "I got kicked out of Guatemala and went to Mexico. I got arrested, beaten, and robbed."

"The police beat you and robbed you?"

"*Sí*. They left me without a cent."

"That fits," he said.

"And now I need some money to get me out of here."

"Well, why do you not go to the priests, *hermano*?"

"I did. They refused to help."

"The devils. That fits." We stood looking at each other.

"Well, let us see," he said as he took his wallet from his pocket. "I do not have much." His black eyes were smiling. "But what I have I will share with you." I could see two one-dollar bills. He withdrew one and held it out to me. Everything from my past said I was not to take money from this man. I looked into his eyes, reached out, and took the dollar. "Maybe we should get you something to eat," he said. I nodded. As we walked, he said, "I call myself Carlos," and put out his hand.

I took his hand and said, "*Gracias*, Carlos. I call myself Arturo." There was a small taco stand around the corner. We entered. He sat on one of the two stools and pointed to the other for me. I eased myself onto it.

"What will it be, *amigos*?" the man behind the counter asked. I shrugged my shoulders.

"Well, how about some toast with butter and a cold Pepsi for my friend?" Carlos said.

I nodded and after a moment said, "*Perdóname*, Carlos, but I have to piss real bad."

"Oh, sure," he said, "Go right around back." I left the blanket on the stool and walked behind the shed into the high weeds. When I was back with Carlos again, he told me that he was a day laborer and that he hoped he would be working that day. The food came. The toast smelled good. Carlos pulled out his other dollar. "No, Carlos," I said. "Here, take it from this," I said to the man behind the counter as I pushed my dollar forward. He took it and gave me my change.

I took a swig of the Pepsi. It was cold and refreshing to my mouth. I swallowed, or tried to swallow, but it wouldn't go down. I could not swallow. My throat hurt. I went outside and spat in the gutter. When I came back, Carlos looked amazed. "They choked me, Carlos. With a cord. I cannot swallow. You eat the food." It took Carlos about thirty seconds to finish it off.

As we left Carlos asked what time it was. I told him it was seven-forty. He stopped walking, touched my arm, and said, "Look, why not pawn your watch?" I hesitated; it wasn't my watch. "Pawn shop opens at eight," he said. "You will have some money, and with a little luck you can come back and get the watch."

We were looking in the window of the pawn shop when the clerk unlocked the front door. I had never been in one before. There were cases of watches, jewelry, guns, and tools. Racks of clothes. "What will it be, gentlemen?" The clerk asked.

"My friend wants to pawn his watch," Carlos said in heavily-accented English. I handed Roberto's watch to the man.

He looked at it, then at me, and said, "Sorry partner, can't give you more than ten bucks."

He tore a ticket in half, tied one part to the watch and put it in the case, and gave me the other part and a ten-dollar bill.

Outside, Carlos stopped, smiled his black eyes, put out his hand and said, "I have to get going, *hermano. Cuídate.*"

I took his hand. "I do not know how to thank you, Carlos. I will never forget you." His incredible eyes glistened.

I walked to the drugstore and asked the pharmacist what he had for pain. He said, "Without a prescription, Anacin." I had forgotten that prescriptions were needed. I bought a bottle of Anacin and asked where the Western Union office was. When I got there I sent a telegram to my parents in Newton, Massachusetts: "I am back in the U.S. but broke. If you will send two hundred dollars, I will fly home."

I had passed a house with a sign hanging out front that said "Rooms." I walked back to it and paid two-fifty for one night. The room had a bed and bureau; a common bathroom was down the hall. In the bath I looked in the mirror. My face was cut, my eyes were swollen and dark, my upper lip was broken, a front tooth was chipped, there were blotches of scalp showing where hair had been pulled out. I went back to the room and took off my clothes. Scratches and black-and-blue marks covered my body, and several swellings disfigured my arms and legs, particularly my right thigh. I put an Anacin tablet in my mouth and forced it down my throat with my finger, gagging myself in so doing. I continued to do the same until I had taken eight tablets. My back hurt. I could not bend it. I lowered myself, naked, onto the bed. I finally fell asleep, only to wake in a few hours. I took more Anacin and continued the process through the night.

In the morning my body did not want to bend, but I knew I had to get going. I dressed, washed my face, took my blanket, and went to the street, standing outside a barbershop until it opened at seven. The barber, a small, late-middle-aged Mexican man, took the blanket and placed it on a shelf. He then lowered my jacket from my shoulders and hung it on a hook. I sat in a chair identical to my old dental chair and asked for a haircut and shave, saying that the mustache was to go. He moved gently about my scalp, careful to avoid the lumps and bruises. His fingers messaged gently. His English was perfect. He never asked a question. At one point he said, "They really did a job on you." He applied salve to the cuts.

I told him I had been a missionary in Guatemala. He said his father had been a pastor but that he himself had left religion because he found it unGodlike. Several times he held up a mirror for me. I noticed his hands. They were gentle, with a large ring on one finger. They drew my attention each time he held up the mirror. Finished, he took my jacket from the hook and brushed it off, then held it out for me. When I couldn't raise my arms, he lowered the jacket and guided me. He gave me a safety pin saying, "This will pull your trousers together a bit." As I took the money from my pocket, he shook his head and said, "There is no charge for this." He held the door for me and handed me the blanket as I left.

I walked to the Western Union office, where the moneygram was waiting. I sighed with relief and called the airport. I could get a flight that morning. I went by the pawn shop. The man took the ticket and said, "Twelve bucks." I put Roberto's watch on my swollen wrist, but it hurt, so I put it in my pocket. I was ready to leave Laredo.

I wanted to see Carlos once more and went to the taxi stand. The driver was shining the hood of the old car. He looked up as I approached. "Where is Carlos?" I asked.

"Found work today." He smiled. "You are the priest."

I nodded my head. "I came by to thank him."

"*Bien.* I can tell him."

"*Gracias.*" I looked at the old car and wondered. "You know, I have to get to the airport. Do you go there?"

"I go anywhere."

I stretched out on the back seat, put the bedroll under my head, and closed my eyes. I saw images of the barber. I saw his hands, hands that truly ministered. I saw his ring, like that of a bishop. These people are the priests, I thought. Benito, Límbano, Carlos, so many of the people of Guatemala and Mexico, the barber. They need no institution, structure, dogma, or doctrine to attain spirituality. I began to doze, and I smiled as I felt a breeze move across me. I had a sense of gratitude for the opportunity to have been witness to the goodness of such people.

EPILOGUE

The lives of all the characters involved in this real-life drama were deeply changed by their experiences in Guatemala. For my part, after a rest at my parents' home I went to Washington, D.C., still burning after Martin Luther King's assassination, where Blase Bonpane was publicly addressing the situation in Guatemala and John Hogan was living in a community devoted to anti-war activity. I joined this community, as did Tom and Marji, who returned to the United States several weeks later. Subsequently, I began traveling the country giving talks, lectures, and interviews, addressing the problematic effects of United States foreign policy on Third World countries and the destructive influence of the Church in Latin America. When Cathy returned four months later, we married and together continued the lecture circuit for two years. After four years we divorced, Cathy eventually going on for her Master's degree in English and I for a Ph.D. in psychology. Marsha Utain and I met and married in 1978.

Tom and Marji each earned a Ph.D. in anthropology and have published several books. Marian continues her mission among the poor, now in Nicaragua. Padre Luis is also in Nicaragua, working among Guatemalan refugees. Camilo Sánchez was assassinated in Guatemala. Marco Antonio Yon Sosa was

killed by a Mexican Army detachment in a skirmish along the
Mexican border. The students I knew returned to Guatemala,
and there my contact with them ended. I received several letters
from people in San Antonio, but it was too dangerous to continue
corresponding. The co-ops were wiped out. I do not know how
many of those I worked with have been killed.

In the decade of the seventies, the guerilla movement
gained in strength. In the eighties the government launched
massive attacks on the areas of guerrilla penetration, with the
added and special purpose of destroying the indigenous population and its ancient society—the very hope of Guatemala and
possibly of the hemisphere. The army's indiscriminate massacre
of human life and destruction of property still goes on today,
under the present civilian puppet government, forcing more than
a million indigenous people to flee their ancient habitat to the
slums of Guatemala City or migrate to the expanding farms of
the wealthy, some now owned by the new military elite. Another
half-million are in exile in Mexico, Nicaragua, and the the United
States, and more than eighty thousand have been killed. The
human rights abuses in Guatemala are worse than in any other
country of the hemisphere.

While those who have prospered from such injustice celebrate five hundred years of dominance over the indigenous people of the hemisphere, an intolerable history is perpetuated, with
the United States government supporting the latter-day conquistadores and the media disregarding their horrible perpetra-
tions. Not only is the existence of the indigenous population at
stake, the very soul of the United States is in jeopardy.

When will we start profiting from our mistakes? Surely it
is time to realize and accept the truth that the indigenous people
of Guatemala and of the hemisphere must have their land, their
heritage, and their culture returned to them, and that the
church-state power structure must begin to respect, listen to,
and learn from these strong, wise, and ancient people.

To open ourselves to this changed approach, we must start
a gentle and loving awakening process within ourselves. We
have to learn to listen to our own inner voice. We need to learn

to deal truthfully with our own emotions, communications, and beliefs. We desperately need to learn to confront our dependence on irresponsible and controlling structures. And, finally, we must learn to honor equally men and women, to respect people of all races and cultures, and to revere all life forms, accepting the responsibility to esteem and preserve all of nature.

Photographs are often better than words to tell about people and their relationships. In conclusion to this book, I would like to share a few pictures of the people and the land of Guatemala.

Many simple people graciously shared their lives with me. Some of them have been obliged to die in the silence of history, with few to witness or testify as to how or why. I will always love the Earth people and hold dear my many memories of them and of their beautiful but ravished nation.

—Arthur Melville

If you would like to get in touch
with the author, write:

Dr. Arthur Melville
P.O. Box 3343
Long Beach, California 90803

PUBLISHER'S NOTE

This logo represents Stillpoint's commitment to publishing books and other products that promote an enlightened value system. We seek to change human values to encourage people to live and act in accordance with a greater and more meaningful spiritual purpose and a true intent for the sanctity of all life.